Award-winning journalist Andrew Jennings contributes to publications world-wide on many topics including sports politics and international organised crime. He worked for many years as an investigative reporter for the BBC and then Granada Television's *World In Action* programme and is a Faculty Fellow at the University of Brighton.

*Also by Andrew Jennings*

*Scotland Yard's Cocaine Connection* by Andrew Jennings, Paul Lashmar & Vyv Simson, Jonathan Cape, 1990.

*The Lords of the rings*, by Vyv Simson & Andrew Jennings, Simon & Schuster, 1992.

# The *New* Lords of the Rings

## *Olympic Corruption and How to Buy Gold Medals*

### Andrew Jennings

POCKET
BOOKS

LONDON · SYDNEY · NEW YORK · TOKYO · SINGAPORE · TORONTO

First published in Great Britain by Pocket Books, 1996
An imprint of Simon & Schuster Ltd
A Viacom Company

Simon & Schuster
West Garden Place
Kendal Street
London W2 2AQ

Simon & Schuster of Australia Pty Ltd
Sydney

A CIP catalogue record for this book is available from
the British Library

0-671-85571-9

Printed and bound in Great Britain by
Caledonian International Book Manufacturing, Glasgow

This book is dedicated to Dimitri Krikoriants, journalist and hero, gunned down at the front door of his mother's apartment in Grozny, Chechnia, in April 1993. Dimitri knew the risks of helping us investigate the mafia. He did his job as a reporter – and lost his life. Dimitri was poor and his killers were rich but Dimitri enjoyed more happiness in his thirty-three years than they will ever know. We remember your huge smile, and still gulp.

# Contents

Introduction: Save the Olympics, Before It's
Too Late 1

1  Our Games, Oh Really? 3

2  Norway Says No to Fascism, Greed and
Fancy Coats 17

3  Looking After Old Friends and Good Nazis 28

4  Sex, Death and Horst Pulls It Off 39

5  Roll Up, Roll Up, Ideals for Sale 47

6  It's a Tough Life 55

7  Spies, Lies and How They Nobbled a Princess 64

8  If You Know the Right People, You Can Buy
a Gold Medal 79

9  Spooky Mickey Kim, Chief Guardian-In-
Waiting 93

10  Black Belts and Dirty Money 105

11  No Lady, No Vote: Rubbing Up and Shaking
Down On the Bid Circuit 115

12  Move Over Reverend King, Billy's Had a
New Dream 133

13  The World's Richest Man Wins Olympic Gold 150

14  An Old Blueshirt Comes Home 170

15  Serial Freeloaders Stop Off In Berlin 183

16  On Your Marks, Get Set, Lunch! 199

17  Knickers Off Girls, the Olympians Are Coming 214

| | | |
|---|---|---|
| 18 | Too Few Tears For the Disabled | 223 |
| 19 | Keep Taking the Medicine, But Don't Let Us Catch You | 232 |
| 20 | Gunning For the Peace Prize | 250 |
| 21 | Death In Paris | 264 |
| 22 | Keep Taking the Monkey Glands | 281 |
| 23 | Buy a Coke, Pay By Visa, Fund the Great Doping Cover-up | 289 |
| 24 | We Win the Samaranch Prize for Literature | 300 |
| | Appendix A List of IOC members with ages and occupations | 305 |
| | Appendix B Key members of the Olympic Family | 317 |
| | Appendix C The Olympic Games | 319 |
| | Notes | 321 |
| | Acknowledgements | 350 |
| | Index | 353 |

# INTRODUCTION

## *Save the Olympics,*
## *Before It's Too Late*

It's Olympic year – and here we go again! A warm
welcome to new readers – hold tight, you may find some
of the revelations make for a rocky ride. Hello again to
old friends; I don't think you'll be disappointed. And to
the judge in Switzerland who jailed me for the previous
edition of *The Lords of the Rings* – take a sedative and lie
down in a darkened room before reading any more.

The last edition was translated into a dozen languages
and the TV documentary we made, based on the
book, was screened in around thirty countries. The
response was astonishing. Back from sports officials
and fans around the world came amazing new information and disclosures about the Olympic money-making
machine.

Allegations that bribes have been paid to win gold
medals, sex scandals and positive dope tests covered
up and Olympic funds diverted to a campaign for the
Nobel Peace Prize all pointed back to the secretive
leadership of the IOC – the International Olympic
Committee – who own and control the Games. They
bank substantial profits and live like royalty while
young athletes sweat and make sacrifices just to qualify
for their heats.

Massive media attention is lavished on the sport and

its stars, but the IOC remains a mystery. We're told little about the motives behind its arbitrary decisions affecting the Olympics, an event most of us naively assume belongs to all of us. If they are to survive as a great international multi-sports festival based on fair play and decency, the cartel behind them needs exposing to a summer of bright sunlight, shining into every corner of the organisation.

The health of the Olympics could dramatically improve if journalists asked more questions and fans and athletes spoke up for sport not clouded by doping scandals and the sell-out to sponsors. The centennial Games in Atlanta are likely to reflect all that's gone wrong with the Olympic movement and in the conclusions to this book I've tried to suggest some remedies.

Andrew Jennings
London, January 1996

# CHAPTER 1

# *Our Games, Oh Really?*

For a man in his eighth decade the Chief Guardian of All Things Moral looks well. The humid Atlanta night and the hot lights don't fatigue him as he waits on the rostrum. He smiles, as much as a person with lips so thin can smile. A short, slim, taut man, he rarely unbends. He won't unbutton his conservative suit, doesn't find it easy to reach out and pump hands, can't quite let himself go even on this wildest, loosest of nights, the opening ceremony of the Olympic Games.

Momentarily, his outsized domed head fills a billion television screens, as if Earth has been invaded by the Mekons. His eyes flicker across the arena. Is everything in place? Is the flag ready? Pray God they fly it the right way up. Has the band rehearsed the anthem again? Let every note sound true. Will the flaming torch arrive on time? Please don't let the last runner trip. Nothing must go wrong for these are the centennial Games, the most important anniversary in the history of world sport. The Guardian has fought off every challenge to be in control tonight and Christmas could bring him the gift he's striven for, the greatest humanitarian award in the world. Then he may retire, the Olympic movement changed forever and his life's work vindicated.

He's manoeuvred through bloody civil war, cruel

dictatorship, democracy, rejection and then exile to claw his way back triumphantly to lead the Olympic movement. What lessons on life he might give us! But he can't. He can't talk about his past because it conflicts with every idealistic value, every moral virtue being claimed here tonight. So for now the Guardian ducks back into the security of the shadows as the television pictures broaden out for the formal ceremony and the exuberant festival to come.

The very best seats were reserved years ago, long before the stadium was built, for the Olympic high-muck-a-mucks and their VIP playmates: heads of state, European royals, diplomats flown down from Washington and high government functionaries. These eminences may find unsophisticated, testosterone-soaked sport a little wearying but tonight the place to be seen is here, they have to be here, taking part in the opening of the Atlanta Games.

Joining them in the free seats are other friends, the captains of international business whose hundreds of millions of dollars in sponsorship have bought the Games, lock, stock and logo. Tonight's paid-for seats – the embarrassed organisers won't say how few were left after the locusts took their bite – fetched up to $600 each, if you could get one. Georgia's elected officials had to pay – but were encouraged to jump the queue. After all, they did vote around $200 million in taxes to the event.

Beyond the wasteland of carparks and Interstates 75 and 85, Mechanicsville neighbourhood people hear the revelry, but the only seats they can afford tonight are in front of the TV. These folks were promised dividends from the richest games in history; the new jobs and neighbourhood sports facilities are a social contract yet to be honoured.

Dusk has fallen for the last time on a provincial, non-descript southern town. By sun-rise tomorrow Atlanta will have been reborn. It's joining a larger world order, say the local Olympic spin doctors. Here in the floodlit new $200 million stadium we're promised hours of television spectacular. The menu is still secret but we've been told to expect a rich mix of *Gone with the Wind*, themes of global brotherhood, and perhaps the civil rights struggle of the sixties choreographed by one of Hollywood's most decorated emperors of entertainment. It'll be tight and pacy, the sequences timed to fit between the commercials.

These Games are the culmination of a century of dreams and disappointments, golden glory or defeat for the athletes. Atlanta must deliver something special and the organisers' Mission Statement promises their Olympics will 'leave a positive physical and spiritual legacy'.

Ahead lie sixteen days of gold medal sport, although the stadium will be empty for the next eight days. Then the lucky ticket holders come back for a final week of track events, climaxing with the marathon and another message-laden closing ceremony. The memories may live on. The track won't. As soon as the sport ends it will be removed and the oval arena sliced in half to make a new professional baseball stadium. So much for 'positive physical legacies'.

Up to the rostrum steps America's President, clutching a fifteen-word formal declaration opening the Games. It's been written for him by a mysterious club of old men holed up in Atlanta's best hotel, the men who run our Games. Olympic protocol says this is the head of state's duty; he's been summoned in his own country. He has to do as he's told; stand up, speak up, sit down, be quiet. That's the Olympic rules.

But who makes these rules? A Greek God wreathed in olive twigs atop Mount Olympus? Or the consortium of multi-national sponsors who now rent the Five Rings? The answer lies midway. Meet the Lords of the Rings, the International Olympic Committee, the IOC. Ninety-nine ingrainedly conservative elderly men and seven token women (two of them European princesses), hand-picked by their leader. The IOC occupies the Stand of Honour, claims to be the Guardian of Olympic Morality, and has gleefully banked a substantial profit in their Swiss accounts.

The US President's advisors will know this and more about his hosts. But it's election year, Americans are enthralled by the Olympics and he'd be crazy not to go with the flow. So an elected, constitutional leader must this day defer to the IOC, a secretive, unelected, unaccountable élite.

*

Now an athlete steps up to make a solemn pledge. 'In the name of all the competitors I promise that we shall take part in these Olympic Games, respecting and abiding by the rules which govern them, in the true spirit of sportsmanship, for the glory of sport and the honour of our teams.' There's an appreciative murmur; the athlete is one of America's finest, personifying the idealism they say sets the next two weeks apart from all other sporting contests. We've just heard a warranty to the world: trust us, we will not cheat. Not one of the 10,000 athletes flees the arena. Can this be the first dope-free Olympics?

The Olympic committee takes a tough public stance on drugs in sport. It's 'the evil of evils', but they claim victory is near after a thirty year 'war' on doping. Leading their crusade all that time has been a personable Belgian with no medical qualifications but a rather grand title, Monseigneur the Prince de Merode. He is one of the most senior members of the committee and is here in the Stand of Honour in Atlanta. Surely, we can trust a prince?

Well . . . not entirely. When the Games were last in America a dozen years ago the Olympic committee hid the true number of dopers they caught. It's difficult not to believe that profit lay at the root of the deception. Commercialisation at the Los Angeles Games reached a new crescendo. It was hard to find the Olympic five rings away from the stadium – unless attached to sponsors' merchandise. There was a time when the committee earned little from the Games. Then they discovered the Olympic dream could be a product. It could be sold; it could be turned into mounds of dollars on long-term deposit; but only for as long as that dream could be brought clean, fresh – and drug-free – to the market place.

A dozen athletes were exposed as dopers in Los Angeles. The committee and its confidential bank accounts could take that level of damage. But no more. The news that other athletes also tested positive for banned drugs was suppressed until an investigation by British television ten years later revealed the truth.

But nothing changes. The Olympic motto, *citius, altius, fortius* – faster, higher, stronger – reflects their ever rising credit rating and bank balances; but the money mountain grows only if the big lie is repeated remorselessly. Six weeks after the Prince de Merode was forced to admit that positive results in Los Angeles had been destroyed, his boss blundered anew; sport in China, he pronounced, was 'very clean'.

Oh dear. Nobody warned the Chief Guardian that at that very moment the dope cops in white coats were grinning maniacally over their bubbling gas chromatographs, their capillary columns and their diode-array detectors. Seven swimmers, a hurdler, a cyclist and two canoeists were caught cheating; Beijing's world-class athletes train on a diet of steroid flavoured noodles. There were no resignations from the committee; the Guardians have no shame.

If they make a clean breast about the doping epidemic, the grapes will wither on the sponsors' vines and the value of television rights plummet. Consumer product peddlers will flinch from associating their brands with health-threatening, doped sport. It's the Olympic copywriters' nightmare slogan: buy a Coke, pay by Visa, fund the dopers.

Even the athletes don't trust the Olympic committee. Some élite competitors claim the officials are out to get them and that other, golden, stars have official protection. Mention one particular champion of the Barcelona Games and they will tell you, not for publication of course, 'Oh, him, he always tests positive.' The athletes know something the public don't; whatever the labs discover it's the old men at the top of the committee who decide whether sports fans should be told that some of their heroes are cheats. Look across to the Stand of Honour and wonder, how candid will the Guardians be this year?

Seated next to them are the sports barons, the presidents and general secretaries of the twenty-six international summer Olympic sports federations who govern the athletes and supply the judges in the events that lie ahead. In their own territories, over their championships, their cups, their grand prix, they have absolute control; here at the Olympics they pay public fealty to the Guardians and plot rebellion in private. Like the committee, the barons speak of Olympism; a mix, they say solemnly, of sport, culture and humanism wrapped in 'universal fundamental principles'. They don't acknowledge greed as one of those fundamental principles. But it's pretty clear to the rest of us. Billy Payne, president of Atlanta's organising committee, had to fight off demands from the barons to hijack one per cent of all the Olympic tickets.

Another oath at the rostrum: 'In the name of the judges and the officials, I promise that we shall officiate in these Olympic Games with complete impartiality, respecting and abiding by the rules which govern them, in the true spirit of sportsmanship.'

The crowd applauds, none more enthusiastically than one grey-haired, well-built man, sitting in the reserved seats with a claque of elderly sports barons, some with the misshapen faces of old pugilists. He is comrade Karl-Heinz Wehr, sixty-six this year, general secretary of the International Amateur Boxing Federation for ten years and a lifetime Soviet bloc *apparatchik*. Wehr is desperate to nurture confidence in the Olympic judges and their decisions.

Wehr knows about the graft paid at the Seoul Olympics eight years ago to steal gold medals from American boxers. He knows who paid the dollars, the middlemen who skimmed the cream, the names of the crooked ringside judges and how much they pocketed. He may even recall the names of the boxers who were cheated. In those days Wehr was unmoved by the protests of Olympic officials from capitalist America as they saw their athletes robbed and their country forced below the Soviet Union and East Germany in the medals table. Some of the bribe givers and takers are seated around him, all graced with free limousines and drivers and the best hotels in Atlanta, all paid for by their unwitting American hosts.

Wehr enjoys another, potent secret; he knows who on the Olympic committee approved the cover-up, stitched together a year later. That was his job, to know these things and conceal them. For thirty years Wehr was a secret policeman, a member of the East German Stasi, under orders to penetrate sport's ruling councils. In 1989 he wrote down the whole murky saga and his reports were filed in one of the most secure places in the world, the Stasi archives in Berlin.

When his communist bosses read Wehr's reports, disclosing bribery, cheating, election rigging and the take-over of Olympic policy by commercial interests, they knew these must be buried. The movement which garlanded their regime with gold could be destroyed if the truth leaked.

East Germany died; Karl-Heinz Wehr and the Olympics thrived. Once again, this time in Atlanta, the health, safety and Olympic dreams of young boxers are in his hands.

So many of the Olympians here tonight have other lives, secret lives they can't disclose. Take the Number Two Guardian, seated close to his Leader: South Korea's Dr Kim Un Yong. Short and stocky, often surrounded by his ominous black belt entourage, Kim has dominated world taekwondo for more than twenty years without the hindrance of elections. He's also first vice-president of the committee in this Olympic year and tipped as its future leader.

He's a great Olympian; it says so in the Olympic committee's paper mountain of brochures, briefings and press releases and in selective histories by onside academics. Not one of them knows his real story. That comes later – but here's a taste. In the 1970s the US Congress investigated a cluster of conspiracies linking the Korean embassy in Washington, the Korean CIA and the Moonie cult. Headline writers dubbed it 'KoreaGate'.

The rubber-heels identified Dr Kim as an embassy

intelligence officer known on the streets as 'Mickey' Kim. It was alleged he solicited election campaign funds from an American arms manufacturer. Copies of cheques Kim received from other sources were published in Congressional reports.

It's odd that Kim, a man who less than two decades ago was doing his professional, spooky best to undermine America's system of government now heads the Olympic committee that organises the television coverage of the Games and is courted by the moguls of America's networks. For Kim Un Yong, this is also a glorious night.

The rank and file members of the Olympic committee in the Stand of Honour are a motley crew. In pages to come we'll meet arms dealers cheek by jowl with aristocrats, politicians and businessmen, multi-millionaires, a rain forest logger, former KGB-endorsed officials, sex criminals, Boris Yeltsin's tennis coach, a judge from the International Court of Justice, an NBC vice-president, opportunists and others on the sponsors' payroll.

Some conduct themselves with integrity. Many don't. Some care about sport and its values. Others are more concerned about their wallets. Unfortunately, sports fans know little about them. Individual committee members stay out of the stadium floodlights and conspire to have their disagreements in private. That's because of another Olympic oath, an astonishing one, that they take when they are appointed.

After solemnly pledging not to fall prey to political or commercial influences they swear, 'I undertake to serve the Olympic Movement to the very best of my ability, to respect and ensure the respect of all the provisions of the Olympic Charter *and the decisions of the IOC, which I consider as not subject to appeal on my part.'*

It's the first part of the promise – the stuff about

working hard for sport – that some find hard to keep. But no-one objects to a gagging order that outlaws healthy public debate. The incentive to accept such restraint (it's moolah of course) is plain to see in the document that governs the Olympics. They like to make out that the Olympic Charter was drafted by poets, philosophers and altruists. In fact it was hammered out by a bunch of lawyers.

There's a page or three of grandiose slogans about sport and human dignity and then another hundred pages that show whose interest the Olympic committee really serves. Take Rule Eleven. It's an awfully long way from Mount Olympus: 'The Olympic Games are the exclusive property of the IOC which owns all rights relating thereto, in particular, and without limitation, the rights relating to their organisation, exploitation, broadcasting and reproduction by any means whatsoever.'

So you thought the Olympics belonged to the world? Wrong. The Olympic Games are *their* exclusive property. If the committee hadn't got the rights to this multi-billion dollar exercise in global marketing locked up and ring-fenced by sabre-toothed attorneys, they could kiss good-bye to their first class flights, five-star hotels, police-escorted limos and fawning hostesses. No more mountains of Beluga caviare, creative expenses claims or free seats at the front row everywhere from Wimbledon to the Olympics. Fans may be surprised to know that many of them prefer Wimbledon.

At the last Games, in Lillehammer, a rabble of Guardians turned up, collected their guaranteed cash allowances and sponsors' gifts and went home. They didn't bother to stay for the sport. But there's no need for the public to know that. Just to be sure, they employ armed guards to keep nosy journalists out of their hotel.

*        *        *

Up in Stand E – Olympic protocol is very precise – are the reporters and commentators. Tonight is the beginning of days of scurrying, tracking down medallists for interview and scribbling to beat deadlines and competitors. The public demands exhaustive sports coverage, leaving little time to scrutinise the Guardians.

The Olympics is a tough beat for reporters who care. The Summer Games take place only every four years and there's not much interest in the minutiae of the movement between times. The committee is headquartered far away in a small town in Switzerland and its members are scattered world-wide. Helpfully, the committee faxes out thousands of press releases asserting its successes; these find their way, without much editing, into the news.

Other analysis is provided by a few deferential European reporters in the grander broadsheets plus a handful of journalists at the international news agencies. Some have tight bonds to their subject. One Associated Press hack sat on the editorial board of an Olympic committee magazine produced for its sumptuous congress in Paris in 1994. Other reporters from AP and Reuter are on the committee's news gatekeeper, its comically titled Press Commission. It's all very cosy.

There's much more to worry about in the unregulated world of Olympic reporting. The committee rewards other journalists when they contribute helpful (never controversial) articles to its publications. Just a little extra to top up the wages you understand. Others earn extra money writing uncritical blurbs in paid-for magazine supplements, praising the committee and its sponsors. Their employers see no ethical dilemma. Their readers aren't told.

Then there are the well-lubricated trips; the most trusted messenger boys are flown free to Olympic functions where they're treated like honoured guests. Their often admiring, reassuring reports appear in the press and no-one admits who paid the bill.

Just occasionally journalists outside this loop dish the Olympic dirt. Pandemonium! Then denials and evasions get the headlines, the unpleasant truths minimised and marginalised. The committee says there are only fifteen journalists in the world capable of reporting on it. What a relief and a compliment for the rest of us.

For many thousands of reporters in Atlanta, this will be their first encounter with the Olympians. They'll discover that press conferences are blatantly stage-managed. Questions unhelpful to the greater glory of the committee or the Games are simply not taken; 'constructive' enquiries from their friends are answered at length and their kindly articles distributed next day in the press centre, to reinforce the right kind of reporting.

The media is expected to deliver a certain line here in Atlanta and many of them will. By the time the Olympic flag is hauled down and handed over to Sydney for the next Games, the committee wants us to think of it as a force for world peace. Don't laugh. The Chief Guardian is after the Nobel Peace Prize. Atlanta is the hundredth birthday of the first modern Games in Athens and the centenary has become the target date for the Nobel. Expect preposterous claims during these Games about the Olympic movement's contribution to world harmony.

In fact, there is no evidence that the Olympic committee has contributed anything to world peace. The meeting of young men and women in Olympic arenas for a fortnight has never stopped their countries' politicians unleashing the artillery. It hasn't stopped most of the athletes enlisting. Any connection between the

Olympics and peace is only in our heads, in our dreams for a better world.

A more formidable obstacle is the political record of the Chief Guardian, President Juan Antonio Samaranch, carefully censored out of every IOC publication. All you learn from his official biography is that he is a banker, was active in local government in Barcelona and became Spain's National Delegate for Physical Education and Sport. All you see is a smallish man in his mid-seventies with a large head and an imperious manner.

But check the dates of his achievements and you'll see that they came during the fascist dictatorship of General Francisco Franco, ally of Hitler and Mussolini and tyrant over Spain until his death in 1975. Samaranch was an enthusiastic servant of the Franco regime for nearly forty years, wore fascist uniform and gave the straight-arm salute until the very end. He revelled in his duty to control and deliver sport to the greater glory of the fascist regime.

Breathtakingly, when pressed, Samaranch still defends Franco. At this Olympic opening ceremony he wants the world to see him as the Guardian of Olympic Idealism. More telling images exist in the newsreel archives of Madrid: Samaranch, in fascist uniform, salutes the dictator.

The Olympic movement needs inquiry and reform urgently but is unlikely to get it on the world's television screens this summer. In America, the NBC network has paid nearly half a billion dollars for the US rights and won't want to undermine that investment. Rivals CBS and ABC still bid for Olympic rights and so does the Murdoch empire. Foreign broadcasters will mostly be as supine. They've all paid big bucks and don't want to damage the Olympic cash cow. America will be a no-go area for Olympic truth in 1996.

It wasn't like that in Lillehammer. The Norwegian media did its job properly. The Lords of the Rings were probed, questioned, their peace campaigns found to be empty, their arrogance insufferable. Eventually the country turned its back on them and enjoyed the sport. The Guardians of Olympic morality took their profits and left, vowing never to return.

# CHAPTER 2

## *Norway Says No to Fascism, Greed and Fancy Coats*

You couldn't miss the guardians of the flame in Lillehammer. They were the most expensively dressed tourists, flaunting white or dark blue knee-length padded greatcoats with the Olympic rings on one breast – and the name of Descente, the Japanese manufacturer on the other. They were walking billboards, the only advertising allowed inside the Games venues.

Spying these coats displayed prominently in the window of a temporary store rented by the company on Storgata, Lillehammer's busy pedestrian shopping street, I went in and asked to buy one.

'I'm sorry sir,' said the personable young American salesman. 'They're not for sale, we make them only for IOC Members.'

I persisted: 'What's the price?'

'They cost nearly $1,500 to make but they would be a little cheaper if we mass produced them,' he said.

'And you've given one to each IOC member this year?'

'Yes, sir.'

'And didn't you give them one each in Albertville two years ago?'

'Oh yes sir,' he beamed, 'and we did the same in

Calgary. We may have done it before but I didn't work for the company then.'

Let's say that's three $1,500 coats for each of the then ninety guardians – worth around $400,000! That's four times as much money as the committee gave the disabled sport movement in the 1980s. Lucky chaps!

It was no way to welcome the Chief Guardian. Waiting for him when he landed at Oslo's airport a little over a week before the opening ceremony was *VG*, Norway's biggest selling paper. 'Juan Antonio Samaranch arrives in Norway today,' reported its front page. 'He will be met by an opinion poll which is a complete disaster for him and the IOC.' Only one per cent of Norwegians had a very positive view of Samaranch, six per cent had a fairly positive feeling and fifty-eight per cent were negative. 'The IOC is seen as a careerist organisation which feels most at home with red carpets and champagne,' *VG* concluded.

Even Lillehammer Olympic bossman Gerhard Heiberg, who had ambitions to join the guardians, joined the onslaught. 'The lack of democracy and the way people are elected [to the IOC] is unworthy,' he said. As the flak flew prime minister Mrs Gro Brundtland begged for restraint, 'We are used to egalitarian thinking,' she cautioned. 'But we have to remember that everybody doesn't have the same background.'

The attacks continued across the media and even God had his say. 'The majority of the Norwegian people are very much aware that the international Olympic organisation is governed by a self-recruiting flock of old men with an old Spanish fascist as their leader,' wrote Pastor Oyvind Segedel, from the little church close to the Hafjell alpine ski runs, in his parish magazine. 'The people have by no means missed the fact that this leader wishes to use the Olympic organisation to decorate himself with the Nobel Peace Prize.'

The guardians' new spokesman Andrew Napier, who served his apprenticeship at the Philip Morris tobacco company and Ford Motors, retorted that the coverage was 'quite unlike anything that the IOC has seen in any country to which it has awarded the Olympic Games'. Napier claimed the *VG* poll was 'unrepresentative' and suggested that many of those who responded probably 'don't know the IOC or President Samaranch'. Asked whether Samaranch was upset at the newspaper coverage Napier said grimly, 'The President's priority is the Olympic Games.'

Even the athletes were against Samaranch. Five days after he arrived, Norway's TV-2 channel interviewed Vegard Ulvang, the world's leading cross-country skier and Norway's favourite athlete. Ulvang had won three gold medals and a silver two years earlier at the Albertville Games; he was about to swear the Olympic oath at the opening ceremony on behalf of all the competitors. Public feeling towards him was particularly strong just then. The nation knew that he was grief-stricken; his brother Ketil had disappeared in the northern Finnmark snows only three months earlier.

'How do you feel about the leader of the International Olympic Committee being a former fascist?' enquired the interviewer. Ulvang echoed most Norwegian opinion: 'I think it is bad, and maybe not worthy of sport as a movement . . . Norwegian sports leaders ought to try more to do something about it, and not all the time defend him and the Olympic Movement, because not all they are doing is worthy of sport.'

The guardians were aghast. They had professionalised the Olympics and now athletes could get rich. Had they no gratitude? François Carrard, the IOC's director general, a well-fed Swiss lawyer, haughtily told reporters, 'Nobody is compelled to participate in the Olympic

Games. We note he is still quite eager and happy to participate.' Carrard should have stopped himself there, but he stumbled on, outraging many Norwegians, 'He owes his international and world celebrity status to a certain degree to the Olympic Games, to the Games of the IOC.'

It would have been wiser to abandon the issue after Carrard's misplaced remarks but one of Norway's two guardians, Olaf Poulsen, foolishly demanded that Ulvang be banned from the opening ceremony. This was raw meat to the tabloids. The second biggest selling paper, *Dagbladet*, urged readers to call in with their views. Ten thousand did and ninety-five per cent of them supported Ulvang.

His remarks had gone around the world and something had to be done to limit the damage, quickly. Ulvang was persuaded to talk with Samaranch and Gerhard Heiberg in private. After that meeting the gentlemen of the press were told, confusingly, that Ulvang had apologised to Samaranch 'but stuck to his criticism of the IOC as undemocratic'.

The same day the press disclosed that some of the guardians had threatened to go home, before the Games began. 'They had begun to ask themselves if they were unwelcome in Norway,' Heiberg said. Later, a committee mouthpiece confirmed that several Olympians had departed; it seems they had little interest in Olympic winter sports.

Samaranch was so offended by the attacks, so chilly towards the Norwegian organisers that King Harald stepped in and suggested an intimate dinner party of just himself and Queen Sonja, Gerhard Heiberg and his wife and the Samaranchs to smooth things over.

Never have the guardians so misunderstood an Olympic host. Norwegians believe in social democracy, accountability and openness – and they're proud of it. In

Lillehammer I asked Jorunn Veiteberg, then head of arts at the state television channel, why had Norway campaigned so hard for the Games? 'We wanted to show the world that a little country could deliver a good Olympics,' she explained, 'but more importantly, we want to communicate Norwegian values to the world.' Such idealism makes the guardians uneasy. They prefer what they understand, the locusts and the percentagemen, ambitious politicians, boosters and on occasion, the plain crooks who find refuge in the Olympic cathedral.

Five years of brutal Nazi occupation during World War Two scarred Norway, but also brought out the heroism of that tiny nation. They fought back against the invaders; many partisans were veterans of the fight against fascism in Spain's civil war. When it sank in that hosting the Olympics meant breaking bread with an IOC president who had supported the fascist victory in that war, taking tea with people who disdained democracy, the Norwegians' blood was up. There was no way the 1994 Olympics could pass off without confrontation.

'The Norwegian people are very concerned about social justice, equality, decent standards of living and democratic ideals,' says Inge Eidsvag, a leading Olympic scholar and rector of the humanitarian Nansen Institute in Lillehammer. 'The IOC represents a culture that is strange and in opposition to core Norwegian values.'

Did the guardians understand this? Had they any idea why they grated on Norwegians? The state radio channel invited me to find out. Off I went to the Lillehammer Hotel, high up on the hill above the town, the temporary home of the committee and a privileged pair from the international press corps. It was a blue-sky, sunny afternoon and I didn't expect to find anyone indoors while outside the best skiers of their generation were showing their skill and courage on the slopes.

On a settee in the foyer were two dormant guardians. One was Augustin Carlos Arroyo, a dapper retired diplomat. In reply to a question I had not asked, he volunteered that his father had twice been president of Ecuador and a cousin, only once. Next to him was Kevin O'Flanagan from Ireland, aged seventy-five and with eighteen years among the Olympians. O'Flanagan had a newspaper on his knee and as soon as I introduced myself he pulled it tight against his face, like an adulterer caught with his secretary.

Leaning over the top of the pages, I asked him how he reacted to complaints in Norway about his IOC. 'I won't discuss anything with you,' said O'Flanagan, curtly. 'I've found the Norwegian people absolutely fantastic and I think it's all overdone, it's only a small minority.' And he subsided back behind his paper.

I turned to Arroyo. Did he think the IOC was democratic? 'I believe it is,' he enthused, 'and it is getting more and more democratic all the time.' Were Norwegians asking too much of them? Arroyo seemed to think so. 'You know you cannot give everything to everybody. You take General Motors. They don't give their cars away to everybody and say they're not democratic because they don't let all the population of the United States . . .' This was so eccentric that I asked, 'Is that your definition of democracy? Giving motor cars to everybody?' But Arroyo was long gone. 'That's what you say. That's exactly what you have said. That things should be given to everybody. That's exactly what you have said.'

I wanted to ask the seventy-one-year-old whether he thought his mental faculties would be up to the task of ruling world sport until he was seventy-five – his scheduled retirement date – but it seemed rude to mock the afflicted.

Thank goodness Mr Arroyo, Dr O'Flanagan and the

rest of their Olympic committee did not cross skis with Big Otto Jespersen. Dressed in what looked like a dead sheep and wearing shades and a trucker's cap, comedian Big Otto popped up every night on television, doing spoof interviews and fooling around in front of the camera. Norwegians loved it but what they hooted at most was Otto's badge. At the time of the Games there was a campaign against school bullying and pupils were encouraged to wear a badge with the slogan 'Don't bully my pal.'

Big Otto sported the same slogan on a badge bigger than a dinner plate and wore it on television every night of the Games. In the middle was a picture of President Juan Antonio Samaranch.

All modern sports events have mascots, a device dreamed up by marketing men to empty our wallets in exchange for trivial memorabilia. The Norwegians chose blonde, blue-eyed tots Haakon and Kristin – and what a costly exercise they were. In 1984, during Lillehammer's first, unsuccessful bid to win the Games Pedro Ramirez Vazquez, a senior and influential Guardian, visited Norway with his son Javier, said to be a designer. Foolishly, the bid organisers fell over themselves to please and asked young Javier to create their mascot.

When the Norwegians finally saw his twee Haakon there was uproar. Historians groaned that he was decked out as a Viking warrior – the real Prince Haakon had lived a couple of centuries later. One designer scoffed at 'a Peter Pan with a Viking helmet', another thought he should be 'less like Mickey Mouse and more like a Norwegian'. A rescue mission had to be launched and according to the Lillehammer organisers, Vazquez junior was paid $5,500 and it cost another $250,000 to complete it.

The Olympic committee's rules insist on a cultural festival alongside the Games. It helps round out their image

– but it's not supposed to reflect on them. The original producer Bente Erichsen planned a worthy seminar on how ancient Nordic symbols had been hijacked by the Nazis during the occupation and the problems of using them again after the war. She recalls a meeting with Gerhard Heiberg who told her, 'We have had a board meeting. The seminar on Nazism is out of the culture programme.' Erichsen said she did not understand.

'It has to go,' he repeated.

'I am not used to taking orders,' she replied.

'The Germans do not want the seminar on Nazism,' Heiberg said, ending the discussion. He has since been elevated to the ranks of the Guardians. Erichsen later resigned.

The Games were an outstanding commercial success, assured the IOC's Richard Pound, as he briefed the press that Lillehammer had generated record revenues. 'It's clear now you don't have to be one of the giant countries,' he assured us, 'to host a financially success-ful Games.' He didn't mention that enduring Olympic sport, soaking the local taxpayers so the committee can pocket a profit. Norwegian taxpayers picked up a bill for about half a billion dollars – but the guardians pocketed forty per cent of the cash from television companies and a further chunk from selling Olympic endorsements.

The committee's spivvy friends didn't only grab their rake-off from the Games; they did their best to ruin the Norwegian landscape with high-profile advertising. Lillehammer was defiled with eyesores like 'The Olympic Games prefer Visa.' That was more than a slogan; it was a statement of legal fact and a nightmare for foreign media. Reporters from television companies without Visa, that preferred piece of plastic, carried bags of cash to pay for satelliting their tapes home.

When American Express, who had declined to sponsor the Games, ran a cheeky television ad pointing out 'If you're travelling to Norway you'll need a passport but not a Visa,' Pound, going always for gold, attacked them as 'parasites'.

Half-way along Storgata, looking out over Lake Mjøsa, was a sculptured block of ice, surrounded by flickering candles, that reminded us daily of the children deprived of sufficient calories to enjoy sport. It was the beacon of Lillehammer Olympic Aid set up to raise cash for Sarajevo, Olympic hosts in 1984. Later the aid was extended to include Eritrea, Beirut, Guatemala and Afghanistan.

The guardians had also sent aid to Bosnia and Samaranch constantly exploited the tragedy of his 'beloved' Sarajevo where he'd presided over his first Winter Games. As the public debate about the IOC's aversion to democracy died down, Juan and the boys swaggered into another diplomatic mess.

Norwegian skater Johann Olav Koss had won gold in Albertville in the 1,500 metres and silver in the 10,000. Now the medical student was racing the world again in the Viking ice hall in Hamar, at the other end of Lake Mjosa. His first race was the 5,000 metres; the result was a world record and Norway cheered their first gold. Then he did it again in the 1,500 metres. Could he go for the skating grand slam? Koss swept through the 10,000 metres and this, his third world record in these Games, was a phenomenal thirteen seconds ahead of his previous best.

Koss donated his prize money, put up for Norwegian medallists by their government, to Lillehammer Olympic Aid. The guardians announced grandly that they would match athletes' donations. It sounded good. Then the public read the small print and discovered that the

IOC would match *only* the fifth share that went to Bosnia. To hell with Eritrea and the rest.

Stein Wellumstad, head of the church-based Emergency Aid Kirkens Nødhjelp, suggested the IOC chose to give to Sarajevo 'because you can see graveyards with crosses. But in Africa nobody sees the graves.'

In the weeks before the Games Samaranch had announced an Olympic Truce, based on a wilful misunderstanding of the traditional cease-fire during the Games in ancient Greece. Peace-loving Radovan Karadzic of the Bosnian Serbs leapt to support the cause. 'We have agreed with Samaranch to an Olympic truce which may be the introduction to a long-lasting peace,' said the UN-indicted war criminal, whose gunners celebrated by lobbing a mortar shell into Sarajevo's central market, killing sixty-eight people. A brief cease-fire was conceded, but only under threat of Nato air strikes.

Midway through the first week of the Games Samaranch and a small party descended on Sarajevo. They must have informed every television cameraman in the world about their private visit to support the besieged; they arrived late on the Wednesday morning, posed outside the wrecked Olympic stadium, and left sharply in the afternoon. 'We did not go there to make headlines,' insisted IOC director general Carrard. It's difficult to think of any other reason. Only the sponsors benefited. Samaranch showed off his gift coat with its conspicuous label to the cameras and Descente won gold for compassion. If the party had wanted to make a useful gesture, they could have donated their $1,500 greatcoats to the freezing Bosnians.

The Norwegian media hadn't been fooled. 'Some call his little "package tour" a PR gimmick,' commented *Dagbladet*. 'We regret the IOC has chosen to direct its modest contribution where it is most visible.'

The daily *Arbeiderbladet* ran a cartoon showing Samaranch with an Olympic torch running towards an already burning Sarajevo. The foreign press joined in. 'Carrard said that the IOC delegation were moved by the gesture made by the Bosnians to knit sweaters for the party,' said the London *Daily Telegraph*. 'But in a city where poverty is rife, the notion of wasting much needed materials on the most pampered sports officials in world sport surely defeats the object of the exercise.'

Unable to comprehend that his every utterance affronted Norway, Samaranch persisted. At the closing ceremony he proclaimed: 'Let us hope that this truce – to which in our own very limited way we may have contributed – will turn into lasting peace.' Anyone with the least knowledge about Sarajevo could see this was blatant exploitation. Samaranch couldn't even see that the Nobel had slipped forever from his grasp.

*

Lillehammer in 1994 was a revelation: the Norwegians proved it was possible to stage a great Games without the guardians. The success of the Games – and they were a success – was achieved by the athletes, the Norwegian organisers and most of all the Norwegian people who were themselves truly Olympian. They volunteered for unglamorous tasks, cheered their rivals in the most sporting way and generously contributed aid to less fortunate nations.

Yet their efforts were all betrayed. Norway's own Olympic guardians went off to the IOC's centennial congress in Paris later in the year and were silent as Samaranch forbade debate about democratic reform. All the protests, all the exposés were forgotten. The guardians had their eyes firmly set on Atlanta, where they hoped to be spared the irritation of media scrutiny.

# CHAPTER 3

# *Looking After Old Friends and Good Nazis*

His ageing Excellency the Marqués de Samaranch (the title is a recent windfall from his one-time comrade King Juan Carlos) is a lonely man. Most of his old *Franquista* friends are gone. They shared his secrets and backed his ambition but only a few lived to see him elevated to Chief Guardian of the Five Rings, a great comfort in their discredited old age. It hadn't been easy. One day they were running a country and almost the next they were being cast out for the old Nazis they were. Honest elections had been kept at bay for forty years and then in one deluge of voting slips the comrades were sacked, retired, or in Samaranch's case, exiled.

They were comrades you could really trust. They had fought for their beliefs on the battlefield and when democracy had been defeated, Spain was theirs. Not that it wasn't achieved without a little help from their friends in Berlin and Rome. Hitler's Games, the 1936 Olympics, inspired a generation of fascist youth as they trained for war. Hitler and Mussolini's pilots bombed Barcelona until the city, crushed and broken by 1939, surrendered to the rebel army of Generalissimo Francisco Franco.

The teenage Samaranch did his best to help; active

in the youth fascists, a deserter from the government army, he was ready and eager to welcome those goose-stepping heroes. What would they do? Nobody had ever seen a fascist army storm a nation. The executioners headed straight for Barcelona Football Club, a symbol of national pride for six million Catalans – and of their rivalry with the Spaniards from Madrid and their club Real. Barcelona FC was purged of dissidents.

The future guardian of world sport registered as a supporter of the city's rival soccer club Espagnol. Its very name was a bugle call to the camp-followers of the Madrid regime. Samaranch was showing he was made of the right stuff – but how could he catch the attention of the senior Blueshirts, those neatly turned-out commissars of the fascist Falange, the single party now with all the power?

Samaranch spotted a corner where he could shine. By 1951 he'd acquired enough wealth from his father's textile business to throw himself into sports administration. He staged the roller hockey world championships in Barcelona and at the end of the tournament Spain emerged victors. This has since caused some mirth among the disrespectful in Olympic circles – it's hardly a world-wide sport – but was heady stuff then in a country still ostracised for its recent allegiance to the defeated Nazis.

Success at roller hockey may have been good politics for the guardian-in-waiting but it didn't alleviate the dire poverty suffered by the masses under the Franco dictatorship. Troops suppressed a popular uprising in Barcelona in 1951 and Samaranch achieved his first mention in the files of the secret police for his enthusiastic strike-breaking.

He hoped this would be enough for the Blueshirts to appoint him to the city council (elections were not permitted) but the rubber-heels had reservations. They were upset about his 'many and changing girlfriends.' Samaranch was not deterred. Rolling up his blue shirt-sleeves, he organised a Mediterranean sports festival in Barcelona. It worked. This time, the sleuths conceded. 'This man enjoys great prestige in sport.'

The Blueshirts went into conclave and Samaranch, now in his mid-thirties, emerged as a city councillor with special responsibilities for sport. He goose-stepped his way up the regional Falange ladder and was soon reporting to the Blueshirts in Madrid, signing his letters like a good fascist: 'I salute you with my arm raised.'

For ten years Samaranch pumped his arm in the direction of Madrid and at the end of 1966 he was ordered to take control of the nation's sport and bring greater glory to the regime; at last, he was a junior Führer.

It was fun on the sports fields of Spain under their new management. The dictator Franco claimed he was fighting a crusade against communism. One prodigious victory was changing the shirts of the national soccer team from red to government regulation blue. There was free entertainment for the fans; before each game the players paraded, their right arms raised in the fascist salute, as the whole stadium chanted the fascist anthem 'Cara al Sol' – 'Face the Sun' – ending in a chorus of 'Viva Franco!' The presence of uniformed and secret policemen on the terraces ensured compliance.

The Blueshirts decreed there would be no criticisms of their brothers who ran sport: Samaranch got a good press. The masses got more soccer; Spanish television had more of it than anywhere else in Europe and on May Day, most likely time for agitation, Brazilian soccer was broadcast around the clock to sedate the workers.

The Blueshirts also controlled the Spanish Olympic committee and in 1968 Samaranch led their team to Mexico. His official exhortation to them was pure

Nuremburg; the athletes must show the world 'we Spaniards are becoming a more virile and potent race.' Virile they may have been, medal winners they were not. It was a barren games for Spain. A few months after Mexico he told the captive reporters, 'We are on the right road.'

But he wasn't. After four years the regime sacked him and it was back to full-time politics in Franco's rubber-stamp parliament and presiding over Catalonia's unelected, regional government. Up until the dictator's death in 1975 Samaranch was still proclaiming himself 'one hundred per cent Francoist'.

For all its avowed commitment to sport and affection for fit young male bodies, fascism achieved nothing for sport in Spain. The Blueshirts ruled through six Olympiads; Spaniards won one gold, two silvers and a bronze, mostly for sports practised by the army or the rich. Smaller nations like Finland, New Zealand or Ireland achieved more.

As soon as Samaranch and his crew were sent packing Spain's dismal Olympic record improved. From the next five Summer Games they bought home sixteen gold medals, fifteen silver and eight bronze. Franco's sports officials had failed to create a nation of sportsmen, construct much needed sports facilities or win the respect of press and competitors. This was the school report on the man who would take over world sport.

Samaranch schemed for years to be appointed to the Olympic committee, sending unsolicited letters to its president, Avery Brundage, eulogising in one of them the American's 'intelligence, laboriousness and love for [the] Olympic idea' and in another promising 'I will entirely devote myself to go with your personality and prominent work.'

Samaranch and his socialite wife Bibis entertained

Mrs Brundage at their summer home on the coast, and comradeship between the two men grew, bolstered by the American's own alarmingly right-wing views. In 1965 the IOC took its annual convention to Madrid, where General Franco obliged at the opening. The guardians of sport seemed happy to shake the hand of a man who signed opponents' death warrants, by the score, over breakfast.

Nor was Brundage concerned by a tip-off that his young Falangist friend was rumoured to be part of a conspiracy to launder $100 million to offshore accounts, breaching Spain's currency laws. In 1966 Samaranch was appointed to the committee.

Unlike many of his old fascist friends, Samaranch was politically astute enough to know that the days of Franco's police state were numbered. Apart from neighbouring Portugal, Spain was the only nation in Western Europe without free elections, a free press or free sport. It was a throwback to the age of the dictators that had been purged in 1945, a political anomaly that must disintegrate when the old Generalissimo died. It was time to jump ship. Where could he find another vessel for his out-moded authoritarian views?

Brundage dominated the Olympic committee; he selected new members, arbitrarily took the big decisions and devolved little power. Samaranch felt entirely comfortable as he moved effortlessly from Franco's fossilised Spain to the unchanging world of the IOC. His political background may have swung his selection. Two years before he was admitted the last of a succession of old Nazis and fascists, appointed to the committee in the 1930s, had died.

Three decades of devotion to fascism had taught Samaranch a peculiar language. All the institutions in Spain – the monarchy, politics, the church, industry and its workers – were forced into slavish obedience; the dictator and his mouthpieces called it 'sacred unity'.

This has been one of Samaranch's contributions to Olympic jargon. He calls frequently for the 'unity' of the Olympic movement and hails the 'sacred unity' of the committee, the international sports barons and the national Olympic committees around the world; all of course under his leadership. For a decade and a half now the world of sport has unquestioningly accepted Samaranch's 'sacred unity', unaware it derives from the coded language of the totalitarian state he served so loyally.

Samaranch found the oaths of loyalty on the Olympic committee were little different from those at home; the ritual of hailing Franco for his inspired and benign leadership was echoed in the glorification of the founder of the modern Olympics, the French aristocrat, Baron Pierre de Coubertin. Indeed it was easier. The Baron was long dead. Few read his collected works and (like the Bible and Karl Marx) he could be interpreted to suit any occasion, a point which would be a blessing when the spivs took over the Olympics.

Coubertin was born into troubled times. In 1870, when he was seven years old, France rashly declared war on Germany, discovering too late their undernourished infantry were no match for the enemy. Military humiliation led to a brief occupation. A year later the nation was traumatised by revolution. Radicals, socialists and the dispossessed seized Paris and were dislodged with the loss of 25,000 lives. For the first time, the complacent ruling classes of Europe were confronted by class war.

Coubertin was a small sparky man, an intellectual fascinated by education and sport. Behind his glittering eyes and magnificent moustache was a brain that wrestled with these new dilemmas of political progress and stability. He wasn't a reactionary but he had the values of an aristocrat with a private income and family estates.

He travelled to Britain and America, studying sport in schools and colleges for the élite. Concluding that sport was a positive force which could bring reconciliation between the hostile classes, he resolved to create a great international festival. There was a model, mouldering fifteen centuries back in the basement of history, that could be dusted down, polished up and projected as a new philosophy of fair competition and sportsmanship. Coubertin would serve as midwife at the birth of the modern Olympics.

It was delivered at a glittering gathering of the élite at the Sorbonne in the summer of 1894. Coubertin called for a 'universal' movement, yet the only common people in sight that day were the waiters, the doormen and ostlers looking after the horses and carriages. His descendant, Geoffroy de Navacelle, writes of Coubertin roaming his Normandy estate and sharing 'the meals of peasants in their cottages. He appreciated their simplicity and common-sense.' Maybe so, but he didn't invite them to join his International Olympic Committee.

Among the first fifteen members were five European nobles and two generals; the rest were wealthy bourgeois. Between 1894 and the turn of the century Coubertin added ten more princes, counts and barons. From then until 1914 thirty-five more toffs graciously accepted invitations to run the people's Games. Among them was Coubertin's successor as president of the committee, the Belgian Henri de Baillet-Latour – a Count, of course.

The Olympic boosters in Atlanta will hark back to Coubertin's first Games in Athens and even further, to the Games of antiquity – and parallels may be sought. Let's hope not. The ancient Olympics were for their ruling classes practising for war. The work was done by slaves, women were excluded and athletes sometimes fought to the death.

The Greek Games were all about men: big beefy men, pretty men, heroic men; Coubertin picked up the message and fought to bar women from his new Olympics. His call to the youth of the world was intended for male ears only.

All this ideology reached its peak in the 1930s, as Hitler's panzer factories went on to night shifts to meet demand. Fun times loomed for big muscular boys with a taste for martial music and foreign travel. World war was three years away but for the Olympic committee it was a great time to be in Berlin, fêted and loaded with gifts – as long as you weren't Jewish.

Before taking power Hitler denounced the Games as 'an invention of Jews and Freemasons'. He may have been close to the truth about Freemasonry. Avery Brundage was a high-ranking Mason; who knows how many fellow Masons he recruited to the committee. Perhaps the guardians have formed their own sports lodge, affiliated to the international brotherhood!

The Führer mellowed when he saw the propaganda value of the Games. Coubertin was no Nazi but their movements shared common ground: both glorified the physically perfect, lily-white male. Hitler's reaching out to the IOC should have alarmed them; instead, the love affair flourished. The committee spoke up for their host and looked the other way as the Nazis ejected Jewish athletes first from sports clubs, then from the German Olympic team.

'The Committee were seriously alarmed at the ill-treatment of the Jews,' said Lord Aberdare, one of three British IOC toffs, 'but decided that they could not be drawn into political and other controversies.'

This, the authentic voice of the committee, would be heard again years later when they handed over the games to repressive regimes in Mexico, Russia and Korea. Thirty years later, in the early 1960s, Aberdare was delighted to pose with two elderly Nazis and one of Mussolini's former ministers, still in the bosom of the committee.

Apologists for the Olympic committee put their best gloss on the relationship between Nazism and the Games, citing the friendship between the African-American multiple gold medallist Jesse Owens and the blond German long jumper Lutz Long. 'Olympic reality defeats totalitarian ideology,' claims one reporter as if the two philosophies were poles apart, rather than worryingly similar. Ironically, it's more likely that Lutz Long, even under the Nazis, had the vote than did Owens, the son of sharecroppers.

Nobody was alarmed when the Germans, asked to suggest their own exhibition sport for the 1936 Games, slyly chose gliding, soon to play an important role in German invasions. Gliders in the Olympics! Paratroops dropping silently to conquer countries three years later! The committee happily turned their Games over to the Nazi war machine, even licensing the five rings to the German navy. The guardians all got heavy gold chains, and hunter-killer submarine crews recruited that Olympic year decorated their conning towers with the symbol of the interlocked rings. This may have confused Allied sailors, torpedoed into the sea, as they watched the five rings of their assassins emerge from beneath the waves.

At the end Avery Brundage, who had fought brave opposition from what he dismissed as 'the Jewish lobby' to take an American team to Berlin, wrote that the Games had contributed to 'international peace and harmony'. The committee gave the next Games of 1940 to Tokyo, soon to join the Nazis in the Axis alliance. War stopped play.

The 'success' of the Berlin Games and the world conflict that followed extinguished the IOC's biggest rivals. The international working-class movements that frightened Coubertin and his aristocrat friends in the 1890s had multiplied. They scorned the 'bourgeois' Olympics and created their own, much larger, genuinely universal sports festivals. The Workers' Games opened their events to anyone – even women! They truly valued participation above victory and records.

In 1925, a year after the Paris Olympics, 150,000 enthusiasts attended the first Workers' Olympics in Frankfurt. Six years later they mustered 100,000 worker athletes for their next festival, in Vienna. Again they gathered in 1936, this time in Barcelona, for their anti-Nazi games, but these were cancelled when Franco led his rebellion against the Spanish government. As a serious rival to the IOC, the Workers' Games were dead.

The IOC next met in Britain in 1948 for the first post-war games. While Londoners, their hosts, could boast an heroic struggle against evil, some of the committee had had a shameful war. Hitler's nominee, General Walter von Reichenau commanded the Sixth Army and in 1941, in Kiev, sanctioned what one historian has called, grimly, 'a stupendous massacre of Jews'. He was lucky; von Reichenau, a guardian of Olympic idealism, died before the war crimes trials that would have hanged him.

The IOC members were deaf to protests about their war record. The reformed Italian Olympic committee complained unsuccessfully that their country was represented by three noblemen, all former members of Mussolini's fascist party. They stayed, clocking up a total of seventy years' guardianship between them.

They were defended by a French member, another aristocrat who had just finished six months in jail under suspicion of treason.

At the committee's 1951 convention there were complaints from Dutch and Belgian members about the appearance of Germany's Karl Ritter von Halt, a Nazi party member and former storm trooper. Similar allegations were made against the Duc de Mecklenberg-Schwerin. Avery Brundage, soon to become chief guardian, leapt to von Halt's defence, calling him 'un parfait gentleman' and IOC president Sigfrid Edstrøm closed the discussion announcing, 'These are old friends whom we receive today.'

Mecklenberg survived on the committee until 1950, completing thirty years' membership. Von Halt did even better. Despite being denied a visa by the Norwegians for the 1952 Oslo Winter Games, he was elected to the committee's leadership cabal, terminating thirty-five years as a guardian in 1964. While the rest of Europe tried – with varying commitment – to rid themselves of old Nazis and fascists after the war, the Olympic committee provided a welcoming retirement home.

# CHAPTER 4

## *Sex, Death and Horst Pulls It Off*

When the Japanese went after the Olympics they didn't mess around. They weighed up the Olympic committee – and gave them what they wanted. Girls: big ones, small ones, all pretty and trained to perform like finalists in the SexOlympics. The members were seduced and reduced until they were hardly able to go back for more. Watching this libidinous festival was Tokyo-based journalist Eric Aldin who interviewed a senior official during the committee's visit to the city in 1958. When he asked how strong were Tokyo's chances of getting the Games of 1964, he was told to turn off his tape recorder.

They would win, the official revealed – but his explanation must be non-attributable. Then he laughed and divulged that each visiting Guardian of Morality had been allocated a female companion – most were university language students – to look after their every need.

This facility was exploited to the full; but for members who couldn't get enough, there were the professionals. Near the site of the future Olympic stadium, the official disclosed, was a five-star hotel reserved for the committee. It offered a unique service: elegant prostitutes, at no charge to the Olympians and their friends in the foreign press corps. Aldin checked – it was true, he says – and insists he behaved like a professional journalist, making his excuses and leaving.

'They really were top class,' he told me, 'they were so beautiful, so sophisticated, so intelligent. They weren't street girls, they were the cream of what Tokyo had to offer.' The IOC members had such a good time that they awarded the Olympic Cup to the city for 'their efforts in the successful preparation for the Games'.

And then it was on to Mexico and the laughter stopped – dead. If the IOC remembers Mexico at all, it's for Bob Beamon's epic long jump of 29 feet 2.5 inches, smashing the world's best by nearly two feet. Beamon admitted later that he feared failure – after a bout of energetic rumpy pumpy the night before. His first jump set the new record which lasted until 1991. His rivals were wiped out; he landed nearly three feet ahead of them that day.

The sanitised books and magazines that flow from the Olympic committee omit any mention of the greatest crime at an Olympics: nearly three hundred students were shot dead in Mexico City; another twelve hundred were wounded. Why the collective amnesia? Unlike the 1972 Games when eleven Israelis died in a raid by Palestinian terrorists, in Mexico the murderers were the IOC's friends, the government.

The victims were young men and women expressing their outrage at the corruption and misappropriation of public resources for a spectacle intended to enhance the image of a cruel regime. The protests had began a month before the Games, when 10,000 soldiers stormed the university campus – opposite the Olympic stadium – and arrested professors, students and even parents. A week later riot police fired thousands of rounds at another college.

Ten days before the Games opened the students met for a peaceful rally in the Plaza of Tlatelolco. As they were about to leave, the killing began. 'Within a few minutes the fleeing crowd was being mown down by machine guns and rifle fire,' reported a British journalist. To boost the body count, hand grenades were lobbed from a helicopter. Mexico City had been made safe for the Games.

'We have conferred with the Mexican authorities,' reported Avery Brundage, then the IOC's president, 'and have been assured that nothing will interfere with the peaceful entrance of the Olympic flame into the stadium nor with the competitions that follow.' The Mexican president's press secretary dismissed the massacre as 'a local affair'.

The government insisted only thirty-five had died. The Mexican General José de Jesus Clark, a member of the IOC's executive board, told his colleagues that more people were killed in traffic accidents in Mexico every day than had been shot in the square that night. Why all the fuss? After all, wasn't a show of force what the committee had demanded? He may have been right. 'Brundage had warned the President, Diaz Ordez, that if there were demonstrations at the Olympic sites the Games would be cancelled,' wrote the next IOC president Lord Killanin in his memoirs. 'The government strategy in the Square ensured that did not happen.'

Neither the army nor the IOC could stop Tommie Smith, the great black American sprinter. He set a world record in the 200 metres, ahead of Australian Peter Norman; in bronze position was a second African-American, John Carlos.

Smith and Carlos chose to take their hard-won places on the podium barefoot, an expression of solidarity with the millions of Black Americans struggling to survive

back home. They bowed their heads and raised black-
gloved fists during the American anthem. Peter Norman
joined his friends, wearing a civil rights badge. The IOC
and the United States Olympic committee were aghast;
the athletes had brought politics into the Games! Before
they could be thrown out of the athletes' village John
Carlos told the press, 'We are great American athletes
for 19.8 seconds; then we are animals as far as our
country is concerned.'

The pictures of their peaceful protest were published
everywhere – except in the US Olympic committee's
official report of the Games, where the incident didn't
merit a mention. They chose to recall Mexico with
pictures of a child and a bird captioned, 'The dove of
peace and the many smiling children were a cheerful
Olympic sign in Mexico City. Both mirrored also the
peaceful face of this proud nation.'

President Brundage dismissed the courageous protest
as 'a nasty demonstration against the United States flag
by Negroes'. It had nothing to do with sport, he said
and 'no more place in the record than the gunfire'.
The guardians could tolerate Nazis, after all . . . But
young blacks demanding civil rights? Well, that was
going altogether too far.

The athletes needed discipline, and Samaranch was
the man to impose it. At their Mexico convention the
IOC appointed him chief of protocol, and he watched
the exuberance of the closing ceremony with dismay. It
was 'a happy, joyous occasion when competitors from
all nations mixed in gay informality and enjoyed, yes,
enjoyed themselves.' reported a British journalist, 'while
the sour old men of the IOC looked down and frowned
on such conviviality.'

Samaranch put a stop to all that nonsense. His
protocol orders to the competitors four years later
at the Sapporo Winter Games in Japan smacked of

fascist-controlled sport in Spain. 'Strict but voluntary discipline must be observed by everyone. All participants should walk correctly,' ordered the man who still gave the straight-arm salute at home in Spain. 'Athletes are not permitted to wave handkerchiefs, flags, signs etc. It is forbidden to break ranks for any reason in the stadium. All athletes must keep their places until the end of the ceremony.'

Samaranch's over-zealous commitment to forty years of dictatorship made him an embarrassment during Spain's transition to democracy. 'One of the most important decisions of my life came when I realised my public life in Spain was finished,' remarked Samaranch later in what may be his only candid interview, 'not only politically but socially.'

But he had his insurance policy in place. Although he was offered an ambassadorship in Vienna he demanded – and got – a posting to Moscow. Few appreciated why he was so insistent on going off to live in a drab, communist citadel.

Brundage had retired in 1972, and Samaranch needed a new patron. Who could steer him to the top of the Olympic movement? Neither sports leader, nor even a member of the Olympic committee, the man with the power had trained as a shoemaker and now dominated the world's sportswear markets. Horst Dassler, boss of Adidas, never had time to become an IOC member; he was too busy controlling them from a discreet distance.

Dassler started off bribing athletes to wear his running shoes in the Games. 'Winners wear Adidas' ran the company slogan, and there it was on the television and in the press: those shoes with their three stripes, up on the podium, time and again. From Melbourne in 1956 onwards, Dassler was always there in the shadows with the black bag of money.

Sport was ridiculously under-valued. It sold itself cheap. Dassler sought out the leaders of the impoverished international sports federations and helped them create new events and championships. He persuaded sponsors to hitch themselves to soccer, track and field and swimming. He scanned the ranks of administrators and, picking men favourable to his plans, placed them at the top of their sports. Slowly he gravitated towards the IOC members, helping them with sports equipment in their own countries and winning their loyalty.

In time a word from Dassler could open the door to IOC membership – or close it forever. Most of the sports barons he promoted, cushioned now with vast and sometimes secret financial resources, are still in place, unruffled by elections or criticism. Dassler died suddenly in 1987 but the lucrative marketing contracts he created are still held by his heirs.

The supreme fixer, Dassler set up his team of company fixers; they became known and loved and sometimes feared in Olympic circles as the Adidas sports politics group.

'Nobody else had this political feeling for sport like Horst Dassler. Eventually almost every sport organisation had to deal with him,' remembers Christian Janette. 'He was a sort of secret co-ordinator. He had people working for him; at every sports politics meeting, people from Adidas were there.'

Janette helped organise the Munich Games and was then recruited by Dassler. Unwittingly, he became the link between the two most ambitious men in sport. 'In 1974 Samaranch knew that I was working with Horst Dassler and he told me that he would be interested to meet him and he invited us to Barcelona,' Janette told me in his Strasbourg apartment. 'At that time he was Governor of Catalonia and we spent two or three days there and then it started. I knew then Samaranch would like to be President. Horst liked him and later they became very good friends.'

Dassler had been doing business with the Eastern Bloc since the 1960s. He knew all the people that Samaranch needed to influence during his exile in Moscow. They weren't from the Foreign Ministry; they were the officials organising the upcoming 1980 Olympics and they were out of their depth. Staging a complex international event like the Games with the never-ending demands of the IOC and the sports barons was beyond most Moscow bureaucrats.

Now Samaranch, a senior IOC member, was in town and he wanted to help. He also wanted votes for his presidential campaign. And he had Dassler's backing. 'He helped the Russians with sponsorship, he was an important contributor to the success of the games,' says Janette. 'He did a lot for the Russians, they knew that and they never forget.'

While Samaranch and Dassler were helping the Russians clean up their act, the Russians were cleaning up Moscow for the Olympics. The capital was purged of anyone who might compromise the display of Soviet harmony. Leading dissidents like Anatoly Shcharansky and Alexander Ginzburg suffered show trials.

Poor health forced Avery Brundage's successor, the Anglo-Irish peer Lord Killanin, to stand down after only eight years. A new IOC president would be elected in Moscow. Samaranch began gathering his pledges. Dassler was crucial. He could deliver votes from all the sections of the movement: the Soviet bloc, the Latin world and much of South East Asia. He did – and Samaranch was elected on the first ballot on the eve of the Moscow games.

The new Olympic president was 'the kind of man who might emerge from an empty taxi', reported *The Times*. 'A man who can survive the Franco regime to become the first ambassador to the Soviet Union must have a mental agility out of the ordinary. He is an ambitious man and he has continued to be all things to all men.'

Not quite. When Spanish press censorship was lifted in 1977 a Catalan magazine profiled the former junior Führer. They too thought he was a 'chameleon' but added, 'he cleverly graduated the changes – but has not been able to deceive public opinion.' Maybe not in Barcelona, but Samaranch has bamboozled the wider Olympic world.

Christian Janette watched the partnership between the new Chief Guardian and the Supreme Fixer develop. 'I think that after being elected President Samaranch never did anything without advice from Horst Dassler,' muses Janette, 'because he probably wanted to run the IOC as Horst Dassler ran Adidas.'

In the next decade it would often seem that Adidas was running the IOC.

# CHAPTER 5

## Roll Up, Roll Up, Ideals for Sale

Tune in, slump back and welcome to the Olympic Global Bazaar! Candy bars blessed by Coubertin! Junk food with a moral message! Roll up, roll up, whatever you need, the Olympic bazaar has got it! And you can buy it all! Wander through the virtual reality aisles, pick up some five-ringed plastic at the money-lenders and fill those wire baskets.

Samaranch simultaneously proclaims the independence of the Olympic movement while giving his blessing to almost any commodity that pays a kick-back to the IOC. Hard liquor; sugary drinks with caffeine (prohibited by the dope cops); steroid-free beef steaks (ignored by some athletes); private detectives (they guard the box office); yuppie phones; fancy timepieces; leisure wear – and bras and panties to go underneath; computers, televisions, walking sticks for the infirm; there's a breathtaking everything.

Try and get away – you can't. Tune into American TV? They're screening Olympic *Wheel of Fortune* and Olympic *Jeopardy*. Want to blot it all out? You can do with a five-ringed product. Slip on the sanctified sunglasses, sip a preferred beer, swallow the approved painkiller.

No good? Need to escape? Take the Olympic route out; buy sponsors' gasoline to fill up your 'official domestic car or truck of the 1996 Games' – hurry, there's some Buick 'special-editions' left. Feeling flush? Buy a BMW, 'the official foreign-made cars of the Games'.

Can't afford a Beemer? Take the Olympic sanctioned subway to the airport, book with the ratified travel agent, fly with the endorsed airline, insure your trip with the recommended policy peddlers. If you don't like sport you can avoid the Games but you can't escape the Olympic Global Bazaar.

It was created by the shoemaker from Bavaria, the supreme fixer, the conspirator of the rings, Adidas's Horst Dassler. It happened so quickly and so smoothly that they must have been planning it for years. Dassler had manufactured the new Olympic president and now it was payback time. In the year Samaranch became ringmaster Dassler contributed an article to the IOC journal. Here was the new Olympic sage: Coubertin was flushed away forever as Mr Fixit laid out the new laws. The cherished Olympic homily of a healthy mind in a healthy body should be jettisoned, said Dassler. His recommendation? 'A bird in the hand is worth two in the bush.'

What did he mean? It was very simple: the Olympics should be auctioned off. As for the IOC, it must become 'an institution composed of representatives of sport and industry'. Astonishingly, none of the guardians objected that he was turning the Games into a commodity. And why should they? There was enough for everyone. So much, it didn't matter that Dassler, now the chief percentageman, would siphon off millions from the bazaar to his new Swiss-based marketing company. He would conduct the auction – and take a hefty commission.

The product was perfect. The Olympic rings, in the minds of billions of people, stood for something maybe hazy but altogether decent. The rest of the world might have gone to hell but the Games were good; they were moral, and every four years they offered a sense of spiritual renewal. Potential customers cared about them; that gave the rings the kind of value you could put in a bank. Dassler saw big bucks if he could sell global rights to a handful of the biggest players – the Cokes, the Visas, the Kodaks and the Panasonics. Any big corporation could send a large cheque to the Swiss accounts of Dassler and Samaranch and get a profitable slice of the Games. All that idealism, converted into just another commodity.

And boy was it profitable. Stuart F. Cross, Coca-Cola's vice-president for Corporate Marketing and Director of World-Wide Sports, explains; 'The strength of the Coca-Cola trademark coupled with the power of the Olympic image offers a dynamic combination.' What's the result? 'Interest in, and viewership of, the Olympics allows us to translate that powerful brand imagery into product sales,' purrs Mr Cross. Thank God for the Olympic Global Bazaar.

Samaranch was quick to point the way in the new world of the Olympics. When Daimler-Benz donated thirty Mercedes cars for the exclusive use of the IOC, he gurgled, 'Partners such as Daimler-Benz contribute a great deal towards the implementation of the Olympic Movement's objectives and ideals throughout the world.' Before anybody could ask him to prove this, Samaranch delivered his punch line: 'Together, the Olympic rings and the Mercedes star form a unique combination.'

To what purpose? What did this 'unique combination' offer the athletes? The partners required big viewing figures for their commercials. Really exciting sport meant record-breaking sport, and (though they may not know it) record-breaking sport means dope-fuelled sport. Oh, and that quaint old ban on professional athletes would have to go. It was time for another convention.

The deals were done, a year after Samaranch was put in place, at a congress of the Olympic Family – as he likes to call it – in autumn 1981 in the German spa town of Baden-Baden. They met in the casino and stayed in the Brenner's Park Hotel, remembered by committee member Dick Pound as 'surely one of the loveliest classical hotels in Europe'. Thousands of delegates flew in, not to debate the future of amateur sport, but to rubber-stamp their leader's decisions. Samaranch was up to his old fascist tricks. The congress was gagged and executive board members forbidden to express personal views. How would the committee vote? They'd been taken care of: for the first time their expenses were paid from IOC funds and a fabulous lifestyle beckoned once they had sold the Olympic birthright. It was an easy decision: the Olympic Charter became the promoters' charter.

Some feared that letting in professional athletes would kill the spirit of the Games. Samaranch promised, 'I wish to state clearly that we do not want the participation of avowed professionals.' But he'd kicked the door open and as each new Games came around, more professionals took part. Sponsors needed the record-breaking fix.

The committee that owns the Games and the sports barons who make the rules for the athletes were easy to buy off. This only left the little outposts around the world to sort out. These are the national Olympic committees that supply the competitors. Every country has one, the small British Olympic Association, the mighty USOC in America, the wealthy CONI in Italy; big at home, impotent in the politics of the IOC. They're denied votes at the Olympic committee and have one function: to deliver the athletes. They dress them up nicely in the uniform of a sponsor, frequently Adidas, and supply them fit to model leisure products before the cameras at the Games.

Would these hundred and fifty plus suppliers world-wide agree to Dassler's big deal? They did – and many did so because Mario said Yes. He's an IOC member now but it took a ten-year offensive to smash the committee's door down. Mario Vazquez Raña, millionaire, maybe billionaire; Mexican press and television mogul and friend of the little Olympic people. Nobody ever says why there's little love for Mario but many IOC members find him, well, a little unsettling. Mario is said to be indifferent to disapproval, even attacks, as long as it's always said in the same breath that he's rich and thus powerful.

Mario's so kind that when delegates can't afford to attend his conventions, he pays their fares to enable them to vote him extensions of what he calls his mandate. For longer than most can remember, he's been the president of the seriously unimportant Association of National Olympic Committees. It's the Olympic vacuum; it has no power, no point, no money other than what Mario chucks in the pot. That's why nobody outside Olympic talking shops has ever heard of it. But it provides Mario with a grand title and freeloading Olympic officials with even more trips and conventions.

But he can fix: Dassler knew he could bring in the little people. Many had fund-raising schemes in their own countries, selling the five rings to local companies. The big players didn't like that one bit. They wanted exclusive rights everywhere for their type of product. Coke wouldn't pay up if Pepsi was sponsoring indi-vidual national teams. Visa wouldn't play if American Express was in the team. The small committees could still sell the rings locally, but only if their clients didn't compete with the big boys. In return, they got a share of the global loot. This was the message that Dassler's hawkers took on the road. Who went with them? Mario Vazquez Raña.

The first target was the Latin American Olympic committees. After Mario had talked with them, they signed. It took longer to persuade Britain, America, Germany and Japan – and they extracted deals that cut into Dassler's profits in the early years.

He didn't have enough cash to buy them out so he quietly set up a partnership with Dentsu, the world's biggest advertising agency. Dentsu dominates advertising in Japan, and many newspapers, magazines and television stations censor themselves rather than run stories hostile to Dentsu interests. These Japanese partners wanted a stake in the new global sports market and they paid heavily for a forty-nine per cent share in Dassler's Lucerne-based company, ISL – International Sport and Leisure. What could Dassler offer Dentsu? His intimate links with the Olympic movement.

Their marketing programme was cockily styled TOP – The Olympic Programme. Dassler was now top gun in sports marketing. He had signed up the soccer world cup – proprietor-in-chief Brazil's João Havelange, also an IOC member – and would soon acquire world track and field – custodian Primo Nebiolo. Like Raña, Nebiolo had to fight a long war for his seat on the Olympic committee.

Dassler's competitors, who never got a chance to bid for the Olympic bonanza, were miffed. He dismissed concerns: 'What I do is best for the Olympic movement,' he said. 'I have no conflict of interest whatsoever.'

Samaranch and Dassler signed the TOP deal in Lausanne in May 1985. The decision was sprung on IOC members at their convention in Berlin a month later. A few were unhappy, complaining they had not seen the contract – which gave Dassler a twenty per cent cut of all sales of the rings – before it was signed. Why did this company they'd never heard of have so much influence over their committee? What was ISL, and who owned it? That was a secret, they were told. But in spite of the few who carped, the majority embraced the deal.

They soon got to know some of the demands of their new bedfellows. Dassler created a special TOP Sponsors VIP service which extended to sponsors privileges that previously only IOC members had enjoyed. During the first marketing campaign for the 1988 Games sponsors took 6,300 guests to Calgary and another 10,000 to Seoul. The barbarians were no longer at the gates: they were in the best seats.

Who would control the money? The IOC already had a small offshoot, Olympic Solidarity, which distributed some of the revenues from television and gate money at the Games. Samaranch took charge and installed Mario Vazquez Raña as his deputy. Between them, they decided which of the small committees in Mario's club would get handouts to train athletes and coaches and create sports facilities in their own countries. Since the mid-1980s, the duo have distributed around $100 million.

To look after the numbers Samaranch appointed a trusted old friend from his Franco days as director of solidarity at the IOC's head office in Lausanne. Curiously, Señor Anselmo Lopez wears a second hat. He is also treasurer of Mario's club of little Olympic Committees. That's the meaning of 'keeping it all in the Olympic family'; there are no conflicts of interest – it's merely sacred unity in action.

*

One of the great IOC myths is that Samaranch rescued it from near bankruptcy. Dick Pound, who oversees their taxgathering operations, claimed in 1992, 'Less than ten years ago you can say the IOC lived from day to day, without any major financial resources.' Samaranch's predecessor, Lord Killanin, tells a different story in his memoirs. When he took over from Avery Brundage in 1972, they had $2 million in the bank. When he retired eight years later, there was $45 million.

Soon the IOC had more money than it could spend. The trips, the galas and the heavyweight lunches came entirely from bank interest – and still there was cash to spare. Japanese member Masaji Kiyokawa warned colleagues to keep quiet about their $75 million surplus. But some of the little people were beginning to suspect. They struggled to supply the athletes for the money-spinning Games. Wasn't the IOC now swamped by the folding stuff? Couldn't they help a bit more? The big committee saw trouble coming. In secret it dismissed the little committees as 'greedy' and decided to censor all future information about its Swiss money mountain.

By the early 1990s the IOC controlled around $150 million, and with many services provided by sponsors or under-written by local and regional government in Switzerland, their overheads should be declining. Instead, they increase every year. And what really happens to their profits from the Olympics is an Olympian secret. If they had nothing to hide they'd be happy to open the books and disclose their bank accounts, payments slips and hospitality bills. Under the current regime, that's unthinkable.

# CHAPTER 6

## *It's a Tough Life*

If the IOC and all its overpaid and underworked *apparatchiks* just disappeared one day – *pouf!* – we wouldn't notice. They take the most from the Olympics and contribute least. They meet once every couple of years to pick a city to stage the games; after that – nothing. The real work is done by the organisers in Atlanta and continues in Nagano, Sydney and Salt Lake City. To fill the void in their diaries they fly first class from one obsequious bidding city to another. These cities lay on gargantuan free lunches, dinners, trips and presents, and some members of the Olympic family take advantage to seek business deals, solicit bribes or trade votes for sex.

The bidders bow and scrape to win over a majority of the committee; around fifty votes will put their city on the world map. Committee members are hailed as great Olympians, guardians of the moral values of sport and defenders, as their charter claims, of universal, fundamental ethical principles. The same chorus echoes from the sponsors, their friends in the press and minor Olympic officials world-wide.

Many don't believe a word of it, as I've found researching the Olympic movement. 'Don't quote me but . . .' is the regular refrain from officials who want the truth to come out but fear for their jobs. One who didn't worry was a director general of the English sports council. He went on the record recently about the IOC. 'They share the traditional prerogative of the prostitute,' said David Pickup, 'the exercise of power without responsibility.' He was crude, rude and one hundred per cent accurate.

The international Olympic movement is designed to centralise all authority in the hands of the IOC. The hundred-odd members are not accountable to the athletes, the sports federations, the fans or the national Olympic committees world-wide. They are not elected by their own countries so they can't be held responsible, anywhere, for their arbitrary decisions. To dodge any local flak they insist they are envoys from the IOC in their own countries.

The IOC myth is that they recruit the brightest and the best from world sport. In reality Samaranch selects new members who won't cause him trouble. He nominates and the committee rubber-stamps. Executive board members swallow their disagreements. Some are ambitious to succeed him; if they oppose him now, they may be marginalised and their support cut away.

What do they say at their annual convention? We're not allowed to know. All IOC meetings are private, followed by a stone-walling press conference. We can't join the debate about the future of our Games. They decide and the athletes and the fans learn from the press.

For 'the Olympic family', read, 'the families of the IOC members'. Some seats are inherited; the Garland family from America held a seat continuously for forty-six years. The Güell dynasty from Spain notched up even more – sixty-three years. The Grimaldis of Monaco have been members for three generations. When the current Prince Albert retires there will have been one hundred and thirty years of them on the committee.

Peru's Eduardo Dibos completed two-score years and handed on his seat at the banquet to his son Ivan who still enjoys every sumptuous outing – and business opportunity.

A newer dynasty is the ruling Al-Sabah family from Kuwait; Sheikh Fahd died in the Iraqi invasion – Saddam Hussein's evil son Uday is president of their national Olympic committee – and was followed onto the committee by his accident-prone son Ahmad. Keeping up the quota of nobles is Prince Faisal Fahd Abdul Aziz from the Saudi ruling family, whose attendance at committee functions is, well, uneven. (Even IOC nepotism hás its limits. Avery Brundage denied the existence of his two sons, born in the early 1950s to his secret mistress, as he hovered to become the next president. Disclosing two children outside marriage would have killed his elevation to Guardian of All Things Moral.)

It's an Olympic family dominated by men; ninety-three per cent of it, average age sixty-three and with a ripening cluster on the mortician's watch. Women were excluded until 1981 when Dassler and Samaranch went a-wooing the sponsors and their female customers. Suddenly, two suitable women were found.

Typical of the IOC woman with a tough job to hold down and a palace to clean and scrub is the Marquise de Marino, Princess Nora of Liechtenstein. She's a prime example of the rugged rules of selection – her father Prince Regent Franz-Joseph was a committee member before her. The IOC's rules state that members should live in their own countries. She does not. The Olympic interests of Liechtenstein are represented from her home, several mountain ranges and two countries away, in a Madrid suburb.

She's still a rare species on the committee. Since the first two women were recruited fifteen years ago,

Samaranch has appointed just six more. In the same period he's appointed seventy-six men. Ninety-nine male members are expected in Atlanta – and only seven women. Who's to blame? Venezuela's wealthy Flor Isava Fonseca explains. 'Since my election in 1981 only seven women have been appointed to the IOC,' she says, 'in spite of the known efforts of president Samaranch to motivate women in sport administration.' It's clear that women just don't measure up.

The old *apparatchiks* from the East have survived in a changing world; Romania's Alexandru Siperco and Mongolia's Shagdarjav Magvan will still be members at the millennium. Samaranch buttonholed Russian president Boris Yeltsin in order to retain old communist hack, comrade Vitaly Smirnov. The wily Muscovite, a staunch ally of the old Blueshirt from the early 1970s, has adapted well to the new political order, giving the declining Adidas the heave-ho, preferring the affections of Reebok. Only two of the old communist functionaries have disappeared, shoved aside to make room for Samaranch's nominees.

Yo-yo-ing is Ivan Slavkov's sport at the moment. One day the new Bulgarian government have him under house arrest; the next he's allowed out for IOC conventions. He's charged with embezzling Olympic funds and illegal arms trading, a non-Olympic activity confirmed to me by an Olympic official who declined his offer of an Uzi sub-machine gun. When Slavkov's not worrying about his own future, he must be concerned for his son, extradited from Switzerland on a rape charge.

Then there are the cosy public relationships with the partners. Kenya's Charles Mukora and France's Jean-Claude Killy are directors of Coca-Cola companies in their own countries. Other IOC members on the corporations' payrolls are Puerto Rico's Richard Carrion,

a director of Visa International in Latin America and
Israel's Alex Gilady, a vice-president for sport at NBC
who still takes part in the television company's contract
negotiations with the IOC.

The slightest ray of hope comes with the recent
appointment of Ukrainian sprinter Valery Borzov, who
took double gold in the Munich sprints. The IOC only
waited twenty-two years to recruit him. That's speedy
compared with Holland's Anton Geesink, who startled
world sport when he wrested the open judo medal
from the Japanese in Tokyo in 1964 – then waited
twenty-three years to 'qualify' for the committee.

However old, however indolent, the members still play
Olympic Games. In their version, they always pocket
gold. As part of his puffed up, aren't-we-important
strategy Samaranch has created a score of commissions to keep them busy. They travel first class to
meetings, collect their allowances in dollars and talk
long about little.

Samaranch picks the chairmen, none of whom dis-
agrees with him, and then he bins their reports. There's
a finance commission (it counts the millions); press and
television commissions (to manipulate media coverage);
commissions for culture, solidarity, Olympic memorabilia, the environment, studying Coubertin – and finally,
there's one for stamp collecting.

A favourite perk offers sun-soaked summer holidays
and the chance to influence the minds and bodies
of pliable youngsters. The Commission for the International Olympic Academy and Olympic Education
takes students to Greece to study Coubertin, Olympism
(whatever that is) and sacred unity. The budget for
this is diverted from funds supposed to buy sports
equipment for barefoot kids in the developing world.

But where's the time for sport? It's low down

Lausanne's priorities. Samaranch has set up an athletes' commission, and claims their suggestions matter. Their advice is often ignored, none more than their persistent demand to ban dopers for life. Samaranch wants to lower the penalty from four to two years. The reality is that athletes have no votes at the Olympic committee, no power in their own sport.

Completing the comedy is the Olympic Order. Once upon a time the list of the honoured sounded like an Olympic final; there was gold and silver, awarded respectively to retiring Olympic presidents and barons from the sports federations, and the bronze for athletes and lowly but hardworking (probably unpaid) officials. The stars who did the sweating – and were beloved by sports fans – got the least.

Discus thrower Al Oerter, who between 1956 and 1968 won four consecutive Olympic golds, was dismissed with bronze. The incomparable Jesse Owens was dispatched with silver. The much more important Mario Vazquez Raña has a silver *and* a gold; his brother Olegario, a baron at the international shooting federation and now an IOC member as well, has to be content with one.

Samaranch hands them out to anybody he wants to do business with – or suck up to. There's no other detectable logic in the selections. His honours lists are a jungle of trades, pay-offs and perhaps the occasional recognition of a decent human being.

Golds have been bestowed on Spain's King Juan Carlos (a trade for the Marqués title?); the King of Malaysia (baffling); Indian prime minister Indira Gandhi (influential third world leader); the Pope (big battalions); Boris Yeltsin (to win support for Vitaly Smirnov); former East German leader Erich Honecker (fellow despot); Romanian tyrant Nicolae Ceaucescu (despot); Bulgarian dictator Todor Zhivkov (despot) and French president François Mitterand (sucking up).

The one award that makes perfect sense is the gold to Japanese billionaire Yoshiaki Tsutsumi, who tipped $10 million to the committee. Oh, and perhaps there's one other; a silver went to Manfred Ewald, who oversaw East Germany's state doping system.

\*

Samaranch's problem, as his new partners hurl cheques at him, is to disguise the embarrassing truth: the committee – if needed at all – could get by with a couple of staff and a fax machine.

That would never do. Who would take seriously an organisation employing only two clerks? Which hadn't got enough staff to fill the seats in those free Mercedes? So they build more extensions to their Château de Vidy offices, buy more desks, install more computer screens, book more cars, more flights, seminars, conferences and photo-calls with anybody who might make a small headline on a soft news day in Patagonia.

Plus a swollen payroll; Samaranch has surrounded himself with a corpulent bureaucracy. There's the director general François Carrard, supported by a secretary general, and directors of operations, finance, marketing, legal affairs, computer services, sport, medicine, information, press services and of course, Olympic solidarity, all with their own expense accounts, personal assistants, secretaries, phones, fax lines, hard disks, floppy disks, laptops and ready-to-travel flight bags.

If all this vanished overnight there'd still be one monumental waste of money to cope with. It's Samaranch's last insanity, the Olympic museum he drove to completion even when the construction budget more than trebled from the promised $20 million. The unforeseen cost of this out-of-control white elephant has driven the IOC even deeper into the arms of its partners. Dassler's hawkers persuaded a multitude of sponsors to prop it up at $1 million a time.

The result is the longest museum name in the world, all squeezed on one prominent marble wall. Welcome to the Asahi Breweries, Sapporo Breweries, Kirin Brewery, Suntory whisky, Hitachi, Dowa Fire and Marine Insurance, Coca-Cola, Daimler-Benz and Mitsubishi Olympic museum. Take another breath . . . and enter the Kodak, Korea Times, Seiko, Adidas, Fujitsu, IBM, Toshiba, Bertelsmann, John Hancock and Japan Airlines Olympic museum. There's around a couple of dozen more. Even that wasn't enough, and they had to plunder solidarity funds to get the building finished. Again, less for the under-funded athletes of the supplicant countries.

And now you're inside, what do you find? A superficial, sanitised selection of Olympic memorabilia, second-rate sports art and lots of expensive video screens, so typical of Samaranch's world; all display and no substance. It doesn't justify the bus ticket to Lausanne – no secret to the IOC, who threw $600,000 at a firm of New York spin doctors to hype it. That hasn't worked so Samaranch has fallen back on another favourite trick: pay off the hacks.

'I thought I knew most of the tricks, subterfuges, scams, hypes, distortions, temptations and plain bribes employed to get journalists to say flattering things,' wrote the arts editor of *The Times* in his weekly diary, 'but this week I have come upon a delicious new dodge.' In his mailbox was a circular from the museum's promotion manager offering hefty cash prizes to journalists showing 'the Olympic Museum to advantage'. *Times* readers were warned to be on the look-out for hacks who had sold their souls to Samaranch.

Off the record, some IOC members admit that Samaranch's high-tech folly is an astronomical drain on their resources. The opening in June 1993 was comical. Some reporters queried why there was no drugs-in-sport exhibition. Primo Nebiolo brought as his guest former Italian premier Giulio Andreotti. As this book is being completed, Andreotti awaits trial for Mafia membership and conspiracy to murder. Two years earlier, Samaranch had given a gold Olympic Order. If he's convicted, will they ask him to return it?

But there was a bigger problem that day. The hacks in attendance knew about Samaranch's Blueshirt glory days. He won't tolerate discussion of the subject and his media massage team had a secret instruction sheet to help them dodge awkward questions. The one they feared most – and it's on page two of the briefing paper – was 'Why does the Museum not have President Samaranch's fascist uniform?' There it was, at last; the F-word. But they couldn't think of a direct answer – the only suggestion was a diversion to discuss Ben Johnson!

Among the exhibits is one selected personally by Samaranch. In late 1993 he acquired a replica of a statue by Arno Breker, Hitler's favourite sculptor, who decorated the 1936 Berlin Olympic stadium with fascist art. A fitting memorial perhaps to good friends and old Nazis.

# CHAPTER 7

## Spies, Lies and How They Nobbled a Princess

The enormous office complex on the corner of Normannen Strasse in East Berlin has new tenants now. The functionaries of the old Ministry of State Security have been evicted. But in the basement, nothing's changed. It's still the home of millions of confidential files compiled by the secret police over three decades of spying on the East German people, their western neighbours – and the Olympic movement.

Late at night, if you had a guilty conscience, you might imagine strange voices swirling up through the ventilation grilles from the depths. 'Please read me' demands the file on how the barons of bribes fix gold medals. 'No, no, read me first' rustles another bundle. 'I'll tell you how we worked for Samaranch to flatten that English princess.' A grunt of annoyance from another shelf: 'I'll show you how the Olympians rig elections.'

The building in former East Germany was one of the deadly spy centres of the Cold War. There are tons of files still to be read, indexed and revealed. Just another archive of Stalinist wickedness? Not exactly; these files tell it another way. 'OK, we may have been the bad guys a lot of the time,' they sniff, 'but read the ugly truths we dug out about the Guardians of All Things Moral. Were we any worse than they were?'

The East Germans did well at their final Olympics. When the medals were counted in Seoul the little nation of seventeen million had overtaken America and was hustling at the shoulder of its mighty neighbour the Soviet Union. Then the Berlin Wall came down and everybody assumed their officials would vanish from the face of world sport.

Not quite; the central committee may have gone but a few old *apparatchiks* still gorge at the top table of the international sports federations. One of the biggest Olympic sports is controlled by a decorated hero of those treacherous times and his secret files now beg to be read.

Karl-Heinz Wehr turned sixty-six in the May of this Olympic year and is a retired colonel of the defunct East German people's army. It may say that on his pension book, but he didn't do much soldiering. Comrade Wehr was too important for that.

The Olympic arena was the battlefield where the capitalists could be humiliated. Doping athletes was one obvious way of getting ahead in the sports war but Wehr's commissars were concerned with a more subtle art – manipulating the sports barons and, through them, the federations that ran sport. That was the way to gold medals. Wehr, with his determination and loyalty, was just the man to infiltrate one of the sports empires. And with that would go another job – working for the Stasi.

East Germany's secret police terrorised the citizens at home and spied and schemed abroad. All sports officials had to report to the Stasi after foreign trips and the more capable ones became registered informants. Their reports filled endless shelves in the Stasi basement. Some provided the knowledge to help them manoeuvre to win gold medals, to cover up doping and advance their nominees in the international sports federations. A lot of the files are just random tips and gossip but occasionally the information is devastating; secret truths the IOC would never want disclosed.

Karl-Heinz Wehr was signed up thirty years before the Atlanta Olympics. He became a real secret policeman with extra privileges in the East German egalitarian paradise. They gave him the codename *Möwe* – the Seagull – and a registration number, HA I 627/60. In 1972 the commissars sent him to the Munich Olympics to manage their boxing team and to stop athletes defecting, and their files on him record deep gratitude for the valuable intelligence he brought back. 'He has been a true member of the Party,' said one end of term report. 'His political reliability has been proved in very complicated situations in the German Democratic Republic and in the international sport movement.'

By the time the Los Angeles Games came around the commissars were delighted with their seagull. Wehr had come good; he was now a vice-president of international amateur boxing. They gave him the Citation for Struggle (bronze class).

In 1986 America's Don Hull stood down as president of international amateur boxing. Who would replace him? It had to be a stitch-up. Only the candidate backed by the Stasi – in league with the Adidas team of fixers – could win.

Professor Anwar Chowdhry, his beaky nose trained to sniff out black money, was a key member of Horst Dassler's legendary Adidas sports politics group, manipulating elections in the IOC and the Olympic sports federations, promoting presidents who would give contracts back to the company.

From his home in Sunnyside apartments, Karachi,

Chowdhry took responsibility for Asian sport, for boxing and for intervening in the federations, particularly swimming. Adidas paid him well. The censors who cleanse the Stasi files have almost obscured his salary with their thick felt-tips, but it looks like $100,000 a year.

Already amateur boxing's general secretary and ambitious to get his hands on the presidency, it was rumoured that Chowdhry the capitalist schemer cut a deal with Wehr the communist spook. If Wehr would help rig the election so Chowdhry got the plum, the spook could step up to be new general secretary, running the back office. This would suit the commissars back in East Germany fine. Let Chowdhry travel the world – 'Welcome Mr President, your car's waiting Mr President' – smooching the little people in the far-flung national boxing clubs to wear Adidas kit. They preferred their man to control the files, the money and the rule book.

The election took place in Bangkok in 1986. Any former official will tell you the rumours that some kindly soul came up with the money to fly reliable voters in from Africa, Asia and South America. They also say that a Korean millionaire donated money and 'hospitality' to help Chowdhry win. Wehr circulated lists of recommended candidates, Chowdhry was elected president and Wehr duly replaced him as boxing's chief functionary.

The East Germans had pulled off a remarkable victory. In a surreal alliance with a Korean capitalist, a dubious Professor and the Adidas fixers, they had captured the two top jobs and with them control of world amateur boxing. The Stasi poured money into amateur boxing's international magazines, featuring entrancing reports from the East Bloc; surely everyone wanted to read about the 'Boxing Championships of the Sports Committee of Friendly Armies'.

They gave Karl-Heinz Wehr a silver medal. He was to earn it. Later reports from their increasingly depressed seagull revealed that Chowdhry was impossible to control. He travelled the world seeking out the most luxurious hospitality, enjoying his expense account and boasted of plotting with the Adidas team to fix elections in the Olympic movement. He dodged difficult decisions and the mundane work of organising the federation, leaving these worries to the dogged Wehr.

Privately, Wehr had no illusions about his president. His Stasi reports bulge with tales of Chowdhry's boasts about his power, contacts and pay-offs from Olympic sport. Wehr learned even more when he visited Romania for talks with boxing officials. His host, Colonel Tudor Stanica, worked for the dreaded Romanian secret police, the Securitate and helped run Romanian boxing. 'Among other things we chatted about Chowdhry. The Romanian sports officials do not have a positive opinion of him,' reported the seagull.

Apparently Colonel Stanica had recently visited Pakistan. When his hosts discovered that he was vice-president of the Romanian boxing federation, they asked him if he knew President Chowdhry. Stanica said he did. They then asked if the sport did not have a more suitable presidential candidate. Wehr went on 'The Pakistanis said that Chowdhry should be stripped of his professor title, as he wasn't a professor but a normal teacher at the university. He was a completely unimportant person, who sold key-chains and other trinkets, climbing the ladder through corruption.'

If this was true, it was good news. A corrupt sports baron should be easier to control that an honest one. They couldn't have been more wrong. Chowdhry was uncontrollable – except by Adidas and Samaranch.

Now that Adidas's hired hand was boss of all Olympic

boxing, the company tightened its grip. Horst Dassler had built a luxury hotel and restaurant at his head-quarters in Landersheim in Alsace. It was just the place to seduce sports officials, and it became a second home to boxing's leaders. Wehr's reports show Chowdhry was a frequent visitor at planning sessions of the fixers – the Adidas sports politics team.

Within the closed world of the officials and the gents of the press it was common knowledge that Adidas had captured the boxing federation. Nobody complained. Nobody dared. It was Dassler's cash and connections that kept many of them in power, from Samaranch down.

Everything in the Olympic family was fine. Then Horst Dassler died. Cancer struck him down swiftly in his fifty-first year, in the spring of 1987. His loss to sport's leaders was immeasurable. The presidents he had created were left floundering without his guidance. So too was his team of Adidas fixers. Eight months passed before they could meet again in Landersheim to plot.

According to Wehr, the fixers feared losing their influ-ence over international judo and decided to support East Germany's Heinz Kempa 'so that he can remain the general secretary at the next election in two years time, although the situation in the leadership of this federation is out of control'. (Presumably, they meant out of Adidas's control.)

Also into Wehr's files went news that Samaranch had been ill and was ordered by his doctors to slow down. It must have been serious because Wehr reported 'his wife demands that he should immediately resign as IOC President.' Adidas had been down this path before. They put Samaranch in power. Could they control the process to produce his successor? 'The sport-politics group of Adidas spent hours discussing this development and a possible successor,' wrote our man in Berlin. The fixers identified three candidates, Australia's Kevan Gosper, Canada's Dick Pound and America's Robert Helmick.

But Samaranch's health appeared to improve, and the Adidas team diverted their efforts to other elections. Who would get the Winter Games of 1994? Sure that the IOC president was backing Sofia, they too backed the Bulgarians. But when the members voted, Sofia got a humiliating seventeen votes, departing after the first round. Anchorage went out in the next, leaving Lillehammer to defeat Ostersund in the eliminator. Chowdhry explained later, 'Sofia lost to Lillehammer, because twenty-four hours before the vote Samaranch changed his mind.' Had the Chief Guardian been reminded that Lillehammer might get him a Nobel?

The embarrassed Adidas manipulators wanted to know how the IOC members had voted in their secret ballot and Wehr's notes suggest they had access to the voting papers. He reported back that the East German member Gunther Heinze, had voted for Sofia. 'Adidas had proof of this,' he reported. Who told them?

Chowdhry felt his nose twitching. It was tugging his bloated frame towards Lausanne. Opportunity knocked. With Dassler gone, who would plot with Samaranch? Who would bring the lists of names to be promoted, others to be knifed, what vote needed rigging, back from the Olympian heights? Who better than himself? Chowdhry gleefully told Wehr that he was now 'being sought out by Samaranch'.

Wehr warned his commissars, 'Chowdhry has an influence which is not to be underestimated within the IOC.' He recalled being with Chowdhry when he called Lausanne to find out Samaranch's wishes. Would the Cubans boycott the Seoul Games? Chowdhry would insinuate himself into the Cuban camp to find out. Who should be the new IOC member for Taiwan? It turned out to be Dr Ching-Kuo Wu – a senior boxing official – and long before the public announcement, Chowdhry boasted to Wehr that 'he was very influential in this matter'.

But Chowdhry wanted more influence still. Wehr spotted his game. Why not work with Samaranch to deliver the skills of the Adidas team to Lausanne? They would be paid by the company – but connive for the Chief Guardian. If Chowdhry got his way, reported Wehr, the Adidas team would be run entirely 'in the interests of the IOC'.

Samaranch enjoys rubbing shoulders with his royals in public but betrays them cynically in private. He appointed Britain's Princess Anne to decorate the IOC and discovered too late that she wasn't his kind of royal at all. She refuses the endless gifts, ignores Olympic opening ceremonies when they clash with her work for deprived children and worse still, votes against his nominees for membership.

All this he could just about tolerate – until she innocently threatened to undermine his power over the sports federations. Karl-Heinz Wehr watched as always, and then wrote it all down for his commissars.

Princess Anne was president of equestrian sport in the 1980s and qualified for a seat on the association of summer Olympic federations, which shares out some of the revenues from the Games. In control since the association's creation in the early 1980s, is Primo Nebiolo, leader of world track and field and the most unpopular sports baron of all.

Nebiolo was imposed on track and field by the deft Dassler. It was a neat manoeuvre. The existing president sought re-election and Nebiolo was put up against him. Dassler quietly bought votes for Nebiolo, and, after the deadline for nominations had passed, warned the incumbent that he faced humiliation in the poll. He panicked and retired, Nebiolo was now the sole candidate, no vote was required and track and field woke up in mid-1981 to discover the unelected Nebiolo in charge. He's been there ever since and manages to deter – or buy off – all opposition. For his part Dassler was given the marketing rights to track and field's world championships.

Much of Nebiolo's power derives from a secret slush fund he extorted from the Seoul Olympics organisers. Cunningly, he presented them with finals times for track and field in Seoul that would have come up on American television in the early hours of the morning. NBC, who were offering $300 million for exclusive American rights, were devastated; viewers wouldn't stay up all night to watch and they'd read the results in the morning papers. Video tapes shown the next day wouldn't attract as many viewers – or advertisers. The value of the Games was about to plummet. Panic hit the Koreans. How could they get the finals times moved? Nebiolo played games with them for three years until they were desperate enough to arrange the transfer of $20 million to a bank account he controls in Monaco. Then the finals times were changed.

Nebiolo is crude, lewd – in 1995 he rounded on a Swedish television interviewer, demanding to know how many men she had slept with – and brings nothing but disgrace upon his sport. His claims to be cracking down on dopers are treated with scepticism. In the 1980s Italian sports officials accused him of being behind the doping of the national team and dope testers around the world say he delays and even tries to suppress positive results that would shame track and field.

All this made him amenable to Samaranch's scheming. Lausanne feared that the sports federations might demand a larger share of Olympic profits. The Chief Guardian cut a deal with Nebiolo. If he would keep the federations in line, there would be a seat for him on the IOC. Nebiolo agreed, and bought them off with the promise that although his sport was the biggest cash generator in the Games he would selflessly deny his federation the biggest share, splitting the money from Lausanne equally between every sport, big and small. Many were delighted: Nebiolo could afford the loss because track and field revenues were booming.

But the federation presidents still didn't warm to Nebiolo and his bombastic ways. The chance to dump him came in 1989. Nebiolo was in trouble; he had narrowly survived a medal-fixing racket organised by his own officials at his track and field world championships eighteen months earlier. The scandal left him vulnerable.

Several presidents moved to unseat him at a spring meeting in Barcelona; Nebiolo was up for re-election and his opponents needed a two-thirds majority to delay the vote while they found a rival candidate. By eighteen votes to seven, they succeeded. This was not the required majority, insisted Nebiolo, who was chairing the meeting. In the shouting that followed Princess Anne was heard to exclaim, 'Why is the chair persistently denying the will of the meeting? Why are we still talking? Why is the tail wagging the dog?' Over Nebiolo's frenzied objections, they agreed to vote for a new leader six months later in Budapest. Behind the scenes, the plan to save Nebiolo was put together. The architect was Samaranch.

Within a few months they had a fight on their hands. Princess Anne's allies let it be known that she would stand against Nebiolo if enough of her fellow sports presidents wanted her. Two (one of them a fellow IOC member) tried to rally support, but they were out of their depth. Up against them were the combined might of the Stasi and the Adidas fixers with Lausanne pulling the strings. Chowdhry gossiped to Wehr that he'd received a letter from Samaranch, instructing him to help rig the vote in Budapest. Later Chowdhry himself laid down the law to Wehr on how boxing's vote should be cast. They would support the 'one-eyed' candidate instead of the 'blind' one. The Princess was 'blind' to secret deals with Lausanne and for that, she had to be blocked.

'If an open ballot had taken place,' reported Wehr, 'boxing would have joined the majority of the international sport federations against Nebiolo.' This was an astonishing disclosure. Some sports presidents were prepared to betray their own athletes – as long as they were not caught.

Who would the other sports barons support? According to Wehr the judo federation (presumably back under control of Adidas) had agreed to vote against the Princess, along with some other, unnamed, summer sports federation presidents – but they were under pressure from their own sports to get rid of Nebiolo and could only support him in secret.

The British tabloid newspapers picked up rumours that Samaranch and Nebiolo were plotting against the Princess whose quiet commitment to good causes had earned her strong affection among the British public. Don't mess with our Princess was the message from the British press. 'Nebiolo, whose profligate use of after-shave and other potions is said to shorten business meetings in confined spaces by hours,' thundered the London *Daily Mail*, 'is the most hated man in sport.'

Just before the Budapest vote Chowdhry announced that another engagement prevented his attendance and

Wehr went in his place. On the eve of the decision the Stasi spook met with the Adidas team for the final horse-trading. Wehr agreed to vote for Nebiolo and against the Princess but begged one favour. Would they 'try to convince Chowdhry to present the boxing federation with his expenses claims as there was unrest internationally about them.' That wasn't much to ask. The Adidas team promised to put the complaint to Chowdhry without revealing the source.

Wehr doesn't reveal what pledges other sports presidents extracted but the Lausanne-orchestrated campaign paid off. The Princess was warned that officials who opposed Nebiolo in public would back him in a secret vote. She declined to stand. Even without a candidate, Nebiolo's remaining opponents still insisted on a vote and, the manoeuvring over, he was re-elected, by nineteen votes to six. Samaranch cynically told the press the result – manipulated to undermine one of his own Olympic committee members – was 'a great triumph for the unity of sport'. Franco's corpse must have convulsed with joy.

*

Samaranch let it be known that he would probably retire in 1993, after celebrating the Games at home in Barcelona. It was a ploy to force his rivals for Olympic power into the open, so he could cut them down. Without Dassler to guide them, the Adidas team fell for it and began building a power base for their candidate. Foolishly, they backed a man with the necessary ambition – but fatally flawed judgement.

Robert Helmick came out of the corn acres of Iowa and made his way up through the politics of swimming. Meantime he joined a law firm in Des Moines where he was praised by his senior partner for his 'creative mind', and got seriously rich. Helmick managed the US water polo team at the Munich Games and in an interview later indiscreetly revealed, 'I learned that I can pull and push under the water and sometimes not get caught.'

In 1991, the American press caught Helmick taking hundreds of thousands of dollars in consultancy fees from companies wanting to do business with the Olympic movement. Helmick was investigated by the IOC, but he was not charged with using his position to influence anyone on the US Olympic committee, nor were there any allegations of fraud. Nonetheless, he resigned his position in America and Lausanne and returned to the corn fields where he's now making oodles more money and threatening to sue anybody who's disrespectful about his Olympian record.

On his way up Helmick encountered Horst Dassler. Adidas wanted to push their new subsidiary, Arena swimwear, just as Helmick was rising to become general secretary and then president of the international swimming federation.

In the mid-1980s Helmick took over America's Olympic committee and soon Adidas got the contract to clothe US athletes at the Games. Helmick claims it was already negotiated before he took office. But Helmick's time at the swim club had to end; its rules demanded a change of leader and Wehr reported Chowdhry working the corridors at the Seoul Games for Adidas's candidate, Mustapha Larfaoui from Algeria. Larfaoui was elected swimming's president and is now an Olympic committee member.

Helmick was recruited to the IOC in 1985 and in 1989 he declared himself a candidate for the committee's executive board. There are two versions of what happened next: Helmick's – and that of Karl-Heinz Wehr. 'A further activity initiated by the Adidas sports politics group,' Wehr reported to his commissars, with what authority we shall never know, 'is to have the president of the national Olympic committee of the USA, Helmick, elected as a member of the Executive of the IOC. Everything is already arranged, so that Helmick will be elected.'

If this wasn't enough, Chowdhry let slip something even more astonishing. The Adidas fixers held a meeting in Landersheim at the end of May 1989 to finesse the election plan and Wehr noted, 'Also invited was Robert Helmick, President of the national Olympic committee of the USA.'

Adidas seemed desperate to position Helmick on the executive board; without that senior status he couldn't launch a credible bid to succeed Samaranch. 'This is the reason why Helmick was invited to Landersheim,' observed Wehr. Chowdhry also told him that the fixers were researching how IOC members were likely to vote.

Wehr was able to report, 'The election to the various committees of the International Olympic Committee resulted much as Professor Chowdhry has been prophesying for some time . . . the relatively new member of the International Olympic Committee and president of the US Olympic committee, Robert Helmick, was voted into the Executive Committee.'

It seems that Helmick was appreciative of the Adidas support. Wehr added, 'Chowdhry sent a telex from Puerto Rico informing me that the elections, managed by the sports political group of Adidas, went as planned. Bob Helmick thanked him personally for his support in his election into the IOC executive.'

The former American sports leader says that Wehr has completely misunderstood what was really going on in Landersheim. 'I have never known the Adidas company nor their top corporate officials to be "keen" to have me elected to anything! Ours was a somewhat strained relationship,' claims Helmick: So what was he doing with the Adidas team in Landersheim in May 1989? 'I was invited to stop by Landersheim in May of 1989 for an occasion with others to discuss various sports organization matters. They suggested they could provide me with useful information. It was suggested by them that they could provide me information that would help the candidature of Atlanta and Salt Lake City. They had always been proud of the fact that they and Horst Dassler were very instrumental in having Samaranch elected IOC president,' says Helmick.

'They offered to assist in my election which only indicated to me that my election was assured. Their offer seemed somewhat superfluous since it was well known that Samaranch fully supported my candidature. In his view, it was important that a member from the USA, with its large marketing capabilities, be on the Executive Board.'

How did Helmick respond? 'I merely listened. It seemed to me that it was an attempt to have me think they were somehow instrumental in something which then was quite assured. I thanked them for their views on the various individuals involved in international sport decision making.

'To my knowledge, nothing ever came of the meeting. I heard nothing following the meeting. Therefore, there was no "success from the meeting".'

I also asked Helmick his view of Chowdhry. 'I knew Mr Chowdhry through social occasions at international sports meetings,' Helmick responded. 'I have never had an occasion to form any opinion with regard to Mr Chowdhry.'

# CHAPTER 8

# If You Know the Right People, You Can Buy a Gold Medal

Whenever Karl-Heinz Wehr walks down Normannen Strasse, past the building bursting with the secrets, fear surely rises. He can't shrug it off. Every time he recalls that his reports from the Seoul Olympics are still filed there, the fright must grip him. Wehr filed these disclosures in the months after the 1988 Games assuming they would never be read by unfriendly eyes. Boxing would be the pariah of world sport if the reports got into the wrong hands. The scandal could destroy the credibility of the Olympics. If only he had managed to shred two crucial pages before the West Germans arrived with their new locks and new guards and new clerks to index and open the files to enquiring journalists.

Several years have passed since then and some of his files have been opened. But the truth about the bribes paid to win medals – and the subsequent cover-up – still hasn't been made public. Wehr can walk on, jauntily. He's off to Atlanta soon. Let the good times roll. Those dumb Americans never guessed what really happened. It's business as usual.

The team of young American boxers who travelled to

the Seoul Olympics expected to meet tough opposition – and hoped to overcome it. What they didn't know was that some of them, however skilful their footwork, however fast their hands, however courageous they might be, could not win. They were never going to be able to beat judges and referees who took bribes.

As fighter after fighter was robbed in that Olympic ring many in the boxing world were convinced that the officials had been bought. Usually, these things can't be proved. Nobody keeps a record of such duplicity. Except that this time, someone did. The whole conspiracy was recorded and filed away by the meticulous Karl-Heinz Wehr. Every dirty detail is there, from the cheating itself through to the negotiations to ensure a cover-up. There is a list of who paid the money and the middlemen who filched most of the bribes for themselves. These secret documents also make clear that at least one IOC member – and possibly several more – knows the full story.

If Karl-Heinz Wehr is to be believed, a Korean multi-millionaire captured the leadership of the international boxing federation, bought medals for his national team and enjoyed humiliating America into third place in the final medals table, behind the two leading Soviet bloc countries.

The Koreans believed that they had been robbed four years earlier at the Los Angeles Olympics and pointed the finger at their American hosts. Before leaving Los Angeles the president of their boxing federation, multi-millionaire Seung-Youn Kim, known as 'Dynamite Kim' after his family munitions company, offered a short Olympic homily the gist of which was that in America, the Koreans had learned about hometown decisions. In Seoul, he implied, the Americans may learn even more.

Because of the rows in Los Angeles the international

boxing federation planned a special competition before the Seoul Olympics to test their judges and referees. It was hi-jacked by the Koreans. 'All the Olympic judges and referees were in Seoul in March 1988,' I was told by a boxing official. 'They were entertained lavishly, given presents, taken to night clubs – anything they wanted. When the games came along, the Koreans expected their payback. Chowdhry promised them gold medals. Even Wehr was worried.'

I've handled one of those presents; a gold crown embellished with jade in a glass case labelled 'Seung-Youn Kim, Korean Amateur Boxing Association'. These were given to at least 100 boxing officials. 'The hospitality was phenomenal,' said New Zealand referee Keith Walker. 'You can read what you like into that.'

In early September the Olympic family began arriving in Seoul. There was good news for boxing. One of their officials, Major General Francis Nyangweso of Uganda, was elevated to join the Olympic committee. He joined two others, Dr Ching-Kuo Wu from Taiwan and Paul Wallwork from Western Samoa. Whatever was about to happen in the Seoul tournament, there were now at least three IOC members with inside knowledge of the frailties of Chowdhry and some of his gang.

Over the next few weeks Olympic morality reached its nadir. The tournament was such an horrendous experience that even Karl-Heinz Wehr needed a month to recover before he could tell all to his commissars back in East Berlin. So much had gone wrong, it had all been so unbelievably crooked that Wehr's reports repeat themselves as he struggles to accept that his sport had been hi-jacked by gangsters. Wehr, of course, did not see himself as one of them. Yes, he wasn't against cheating to win medals for his political allies. But the Koreans were so unsubtle about it.

He was astonished to find the Koreans outwitting him at a game he'd thought the Soviet bloc ruled – rigging fights. 'We had decided that all boxing judges should stay at the same hotel to limit the influence of the Koreans,' reported Wehr. 'We put two boxing judges in each room so that they were constantly controlled. On arriving in Seoul the organisers disregarded the lists. The judges were roomed together as the Koreans wished, ruining our plans.'

Wehr might have been able to handle the problems caused by the Koreans in Seoul – with Chowdhry's support. As usual, Chowdhry was more profitably engaged. 'In the first weeks, during many international congresses, he tried to force through Adidas' interests,' reported Wehr, who was left to handle all the organisational headaches alone.

No sooner had the Games begun than Wehr discovered that his officials were letting some boxing judges get away with murder in the early rounds of the tournament, handing out victories to fighters who had clearly lost. He intervened, suspending the worst of them – and suddenly, the Koreans weren't lavishing gifts on him any more. 'In the first days of my stay in Korea I could move about relatively freely,' he wrote. 'Later, the Koreans did not miss a chance to try to corrupt or influence me. They repeatedly attempted to persuade me to take back my decisions punishing judges whom they seemed to have an interest in. There were always judges prepared to declare a South Korean boxer victor, even if this was completely ludicrous.'

Wehr continued weeding out the worst officials, enraging his hosts. 'It's difficult to relate the brutality with which the Koreans tried to get their judges back in service,' he complained. 'For days there were Koreans constantly at my office, in the boxing hall, and at the hotel trying to influence me to reverse my decisions.' When that had no effect, they resorted to death threats.

But the pressure worked. The first American boxer to have his medal chances sabotaged was Anthony Hembrick. He arrived in good time for his bout, unaware that the Koreans had had it rescheduled. By the referee's reckoning he was a few minutes late – and the penalty was disqualification. American officials lobbied the appeals committee and they voted 2–2 to allow the fight to go ahead. It didn't happen; the chairman, Taieb Houichi from Tunisia, cast his vote against Hembrick. The Americans sought out Chowdhry and Wehr. 'We appealed to their sense of fair play, sportsmanship and Olympic camaraderie,' said one. Apparently, he wasn't joking.

America's Olympic leader Robert Helmick asked Samaranch to intervene with Chowdhry, to 'push for the spirit of the games'. With his intimate knowledge of the debts Samaranch owed Chowdhry and Adidas, Helmick might have guessed that such a protest would be fruitless.

The Hembrick affair made minor headlines. But the next scandal was the most shameful sports spectacle ever seen on television. Bantamweight Alexander Hristov from Bulgaria and Korea's Byun Jong-il brawled for three rounds and New Zealand referee Keith Walker twice penalised the Korean for using his head as a battering ram. It cost him the fight. As the Bulgarian celebrated victory Korean boxing officials piled into the ring and started throwing punches. 'Lee Hong Soo, a trainer coach, and another coach, backed Walker into a corner and punched him before other referees rushed to his aid,' reported the *New York Times*.

Walker groaned, 'Korean coaches were kicking and punching and pulling my hair out. I was punched in the back by their head coach.' A security officer threw off his blazer, jumped into the ring and pummelled Walker as another security man tried to kick him. Officials hurled folding chairs into the ring. As a pale and shaken Walker headed for Seoul airport and home, Byun sat in the ring for sixty-seven sulky minutes of silent protest.

Who was to blame for this outrage? And whatever happened to the Seoul Olympic slogan of harmony and progress? Wehr pointed unhesitatingly at the president of the host boxing federation: 'Seung-Youn Kim had invested an incredible amount of money in the preparation of his boxers and wanted to see it repaid in medals.'

The officials of Wehr's international federation were little better. The executive committee dealt with the scandal in private. Secret minutes of the executive committee reveal that when Chowdhry asked Bulgaria's Emil Jetchev, who had been at the ringside, to name the rioters, Jetchev replied that 'he felt unable to do so. He said he was filling in score sheets at that moment and did not see anything.'

Worse was to come. Today Roy Jones is the IBF super middleweight champion of the world. Then a light middleweight, he went to Seoul as one of America's brightest medal hopes. There were two conspiracies bubbling; the Koreans wanted golds and the Soviet bloc wanted to deny America medals. Together, they crushed Roy Jones.

Korea's Park Si-Hun had been extraordinarily fortunate on his route to the final. Sceptics called his lucky streak a series of hometown decisions. Park won his first bout when Abdalla Ramadan of Sudan doubled up in the second round from two low blows. His second opponent was one of the favourites. East Germany's Torsten Schmitz. Most observers thought Schmitz had won but Park got the decision. Wehr blamed both the Koreans and Bulgarian Emil Jetchev who chaired the committee responsible for controlling the judges. Back in Berlin he commented, 'It became clear that Jetchev was under pressure and had no interest in changing the situation.'

Park then fought Italy's Vincenzo Nardiello who was ahead with all five judges after the second round. Two gave Nardiello the third round as well. The other three decided that Park had won the final round by such a wide margin that they gave him victory. Nardiello, astonished, fell to his knees and pounded the canvas with his fists. Then he jumped out of the ring and screamed at the judges until his coaches hauled him away.

When Park met Jones in the final *Boxing News* was at the ringside.

> Although Park was taller, the American was much faster, sharper and skilful. The Korean, unlike many of his compatriots, was not a crude slugger, but he was made to look something of a plodder as he chased ineffectively after Jones, who whipped in long left hooks from range to pick up the points in the first.
>
> Going into the third, Jones appeared to be two rounds to the good and assured of victory barring a disaster. He landed a good long left hand at the start of the round and was soon scoring at will as Park, a 22-year-old university student, kept advancing. When the final bell went, Jones walked around the ring, arms raised in victory to be booed by the predominantly Korean crowd. There seemed to be no argument about who had won.

Judges Zaut Gvadjava of the USSR and Sandor Pajar of Hungary agreed. Both gave Jones victory over Park by

65 to 60. The other three judges had been watching a different fight. Hiouad El Arbi of Morocco and Alberto Duran of Uruguay scored 59–58 for Park; Bob Kasule of Uganda scored the bout 59–59, advantage to Park.

This was laughably at odds with the score on NBC's computer, which showed that Roy Jones landed eighty-six scoring blows and the Korean only thirty-two. Even more devastating was the average number of blows landed each round. Park scored 10.4: Roy Jones achieved 28. 'I thought I had beaten him to a point where I couldn't be robbed,' said Jones, ruefully. 'Unfortunately, I was.'

After the fight Chowdhry was surrounded by furious American officials. Coach Ken Adams shouted, 'You wouldn't dare give the decision to the Korean!' Western European officials joined in, describing Park's victory as 'criminal', 'disgraceful', and 'shocking'.

The Moroccan judge, El Arbi, improvising hastily, told a French journalist that he voted for the Korean because he thought Jones would receive a 5–0 result and was afraid that might provoke the partisan crowd. He added, 'It was a terrible thing. The American won easily, so easily that I voted to make it 4–1 not to embarrass the host country.'

Fifty thousand Koreans called up their national TV station to protest at the way they had 'won' the gold medal and even Park himself proclaimed Jones the victor when, at the medal ceremony, he grasped him around the waist and lifted him high. Park admitted later to the *Korea Herald* that Jones had beaten him.

The only person who thought Park deserved to win gold was 'Dynamite' Kim, who insisted, 'Today's decision is very, very fair. There is no scandal today. I cannot understand why foreigners have such prejudice against Koreans.'

They had now won two decisions against the Americans. There was one last chance to steal a medal from

an American boxer. *Boxing News* spotted what was
going on:

> The referee nominated for the plum job of hand-
> ling the prestige super-heavy final was none
> other than Gustav Baumgartl of East Germany,
> who fully lived up to the expectation of his masters
> and did a job on the American Riddick Bowe.
>
> As all insiders know, the main chance for Lennox
> Lewis of Canada was to catch Bowe early on,
> and by the second [round] Lewis was rapidly
> tiring from the clinches, was taking stick and
> looked ready to go. But the GDR ref invariably
> found an excuse to interfere, continually harassing
> Bowe with unwarranted cautions, breaking up his
> rhythm and getting his mind off the job at hand.
>
> Then, as soon as Bowe got hit as a result, though
> remaining untroubled, the Third Man stepped in.

Referee Baumgartl grasped his first opportunity and
stopped the fight, awarding victory to Lewis.

Both men were good fighters but few doubt that Bowe
was robbed. The final Seoul medals totals were thirty-
six for America and thirty-seven for East Germany.
Had Roy Jones and Riddick Bowe won the medals
they deserved, America would have overtaken the East
Germans – but still been far short of the USSR's total of
fifty-five.

The boxing world wanted action over the Seoul
scandals and an investigation was promised, beginning with a meeting of senior officials in Frankfurt.
It was a farce. Emil Jetchev, who had to answer for
the behaviour of his judges, arrived too late. According to the confidential minutes of the meeting, when
America's Paul Konnor raised the Jones–Park fight, he
was told by Australia's Arthur Tunstall OBE, 'that the

shortcomings in officiating observed in Seoul should not be over-emphasised. There had been similar incidents in Los Angeles. In Seoul the overall result was not bad.' In public, the federation announced that tough disciplinary measures would follow a second meeting planned for Nairobi, Kenya, the following spring.

Wehr went back to Berlin and told his commissars that the Nairobi meeting would be a waste of time.

There are two versions of what happened in Nairobi. The version to fool the public was reported in the federation's *World Boxing* magazine under the stultifying headline 'Kenyan Amateur Boxing Association hosted a significant world federation meeting from 13 to 20 March 1989.' What had gone wrong in Seoul? Not a lot, it seemed: just 'different viewpoints' about how to score fights.

This was the message world boxing was supposed to swallow; some of the judges had been a bit careless – that's all. Chowdhry and Wehr told the world, 'We cannot tolerate that the efforts undertaken by both athletes and coaches are wrecked thoughtlessly.' It was fiction and the officials knew it. A small cabal – a handful of the top officials of the boxing federation – conspired to hide the truth from the world and several dozen other officials at the meeting.

Chowdhry spent much of the time shut away in his suite at Nairobi's Intercontinental Hotel. The conspirators joined him to stitch up a compromise. According to the confidential minutes, Uganda's IOC member Nyangweso felt that any punishment inflicted should have an 'educational effect'. Tunisia's Taieb Houichi played down the scandal and a Moroccan official also argued for leniency. But even these secret minutes don't record the truth.

Fortunately, Wehr did. His explosive disclosures are on two pages of his Stasi reports, dated 29 March 1989. Wehr names the guilty officials and the money they pocketed to pervert Olympic sport.

He warned his commissars, 'What I am about to relate exists in no published documents. Only Günther Heinze (the IOC Member from East Germany) has been informed verbally.' So at least one Guardian of Olympic Truth knew that medals had been bought.

How had Roy Jones been robbed? Wehr discovered the judges had been more than 'thoughtless'. Tantalisingly, the censor has scored out the names of the crooks – but the identities of some are only half-obscured. We'll call them X, Y and Z.

In plain language Wehr reported, 'During the discussion about the punishment it became known that X had received $10,000 from the Korean organisers. He gave three African judges $300 each to give the victory to the Korean.

'Y of the South American federation, had received $5,000, of which he gave two ring judges $500 each with the instructions that in every bout the Korean should be the victor.'

An African representative on the executive committee – we'll call him Z – 'possessed an affidavit from his judge, stating that he had received $300 from X with the above mentioned directions'.

That was it: officials had taken money to rig Olympic medals. Despite the censor's penstrokes, it's not hard to work out who laundered the bribes to the ringside judges. They all hold senior rank in the boxing federation.

Wehr's reports read like the minutes of a Mob conclave, fixing a Vegas championship to clean up on the betting. These were leading members of the Olympic family who had taken an oath to uphold the rules and

the 'true spirit of sportsmanship'. Now they faced the
ultimate Olympic crisis.

According to Wehr the Koreans admitted paying the
bribes. Now it was down to a simple choice; ban the bent
officials for life – and tell the world why – or cover it up.
Which way would they go? Would amateur boxing's
leadership take an Olympian deep breath, confess all
and clean up their federation? Of course not. These
crooks were going to put themselves first and the
athletes and sport last.

Five officials were suspended for two years. They
included Bob Kasule of Uganda, Hiouad El Arbi from
Morocco and Alberto Duran of Uruguay – which par-
tially addressed the Roy Jones scandal. But to confuse
the public, the list included Sandor Pajer of Hungary
who had voted 60–56 *for* Roy Jones!

A further thirteen officials were suspended from
officiating at the next world championships and among
them was Zaut Gvadjava from the Soviet Union who
had also voted 60–56 for Roy Jones. So the two honest
judges in the Jones bout were given the same treatment
as the crooks! Boxing's bosses chose to turn a blind
eye to the corruption, merely refusing the Koreans
permission to stage international competitions for a
year and suspending six of their lowly officials for
eighteen months.

Back in Berlin, Wehr felt vulnerable. 'I am not sure
if those who have knowledge of these events will keep
their mouths shut. Only Chowdhry and I discussed
these plans. I don't know who he spoke to. (IOC member
Gunther) Heinze is of the opinion I did the right thing.
We cannot risk such a scandal.'

And they didn't. Boxing's barons had taken bribes and
covered up to protect the reputation of the Eastern bloc
and their Adidas-employed president. Did the United

States Olympic committee stand up for their athletes? Er, no. They allowed Karl-Heinz Wehr to publish his lies in their monthly magazine. For decades America's Olympic bureaucrats grew fat off dollars donated by the public to beat the communists. Now the enemy was given a platform to mock them.

The July 1989 issue of the American Olympic committee's magazine, *The Olympian* carried a misleading apologia from Wehr for the Seoul robbery. Readers were not told that the article had been lifted from the Stasi-funded *European Boxing*, hot off the East German presses.

For the few in the know, it was comical. Readers were assured that Chowdhry had done his utmost to make Seoul a magnificent tournament. So why had it gone so badly wrong? Why was Roy Jones in tears after he lost his rigged bout? Wehr offered Americans a thin answer. Some bouts involving Koreans 'did not correspond to the modern concept of amateur boxing'. He let slip an oblique clue about the bribes – 'officials revealed a disparity between their real abilities and the way they judged certain bouts' – but nobody pursued it.

Chowdhry and Wehr then visited Atlanta where the bid team for the Games of 1996 had worrying news for them. They'd been tipped off by the US State Department that Wehr was a suspected Stasi agent. But no-one was really bothered. There were chuckles back in Berlin.

But the East German party was nearly over. On 9 December 1989, a month after the Berlin Wall fell, Wehr had a last emotional meeting with his boss, Oberstleutnant Radeke. Wehr made a final request: Could the Stasi guarantee that his files would be kept secret? Radeke promised they would. His dirty deals were safe.

\*     \*     \*

The boxing federation resisted the tide of change that swept the old Eastern bloc. Chowdhry and Wehr are still president and general secretary respectively and the crooks named in the Stasi files still hold their jobs. They will preside over the medal hopes and the physical risks faced by boxers in Atlanta. The federation's three IOC members – Francis Nyangweso, Dr Ching-Kuo Wu and Paul Wallwork – seem happy enough and Samaranch was so delighted he awarded Chowdhry an Olympic Order in 1992, praising him for his 'respect for the rules' and for being 'an ardent defender of fair play'.

# CHAPTER 9

# Spooky Mickey Kim, Chief Guardian-In-Waiting

The entourage of black belt instructors trails a squat figure as he wanders genially through clusters of Olympic delegates enjoying their coffee break at an Olympic convention. Kim Un Yong has every reason to be cheerful; his sport, taekwondo, has just made it into the Games and will debut as a gold medal sport in Sydney. Twenty years of dirty tricks – and God knows how many pay-offs – have come good.

Kim isn't just smiling for the sake of taekwondo. Today's a personal triumph. Now he's the only candidate for Samaranch's throne who leads an Olympic sport. In two years' time, when they get to Atlanta, he will be the old man's deputy and poised to take over. After that, it's up to the IOC members – so he beams at every possible voter, at his allies, at his fellow sports barons gathered here in the autumn of 1994 under the domed roof of Paris's La Défense convention centre to debate the future of the Olympic movement.

Kim plans to be that future – and why shouldn't he? Like the current Chief Guardian of Olympic Idealism, he's also got a history he can't talk about. In the dusty old files of America's intelligence agencies are sleazy revelations about one Mickey Kim, a very savvy spook.

Can this be the same benevolent sports leader Kim Un Yong, honoured at the heart of our Olympic movement? You won't find any mention of 'Mickey' Kim in his official IOC biography. Perhaps, as with Samaranch and his fascist past, it's slipped Kim's memory.

Politics Korean-style is a dirty business and Mickey Kim has spent a lifetime up to his neck in it. He's survived war, coups and dictators. Every corrupt regime has found a use for him; each bloodthirsty general who seized power could count on his loyalty. The military spotted his potential in the 1950s and sent him to university in El Paso, Texas. College records don't confirm his claim to have graduated but he returned to Seoul ready to be trained as a professional intelligence agent and, like Samaranch, his long-term job would be to manipulate sport for cruel dictators.

Kim's first patron, General Park, seized power in a military coup in 1961. To suppress dissent and block demands for democracy Park set up the Korean Central Intelligence Agency, combining foreign espionage with savage repression at home. The General installed Mickey Kim as personal aide to the chief spook. Kim performed well and won a posting to head the protocol office of the prime minister – a watching brief for a trusted spy.

'Park was so paranoid that he needed his own man as watchdog,' a former Korean diplomat told me, 'to know everything that happened.' Congressional hearings in the 1970s into Korean intelligence activities in America – where Mickey Kim pops up several times – heard that General Park and his junior officers ran Korea like a military prison camp. The KCIA was his 'powerful enforcement mechanism', crushing all opposition.

The first international enforcement came when a team of KCIA agents and taekwondo instructors kidnapped more than thirty Korean dissidents in Germany, smuggled them back to Korea, tortured them all and hanged three of them. Mickey Kim, rising KCIA agent, was in Europe that year under diplomatic cover, escorting the new Korean ambassador to an audience with Queen Elizabeth at Buckingham Palace.

Mickey Kim was always on the move. A posting to the Korean embassy in Washington in 1963 was followed by another to Korea's mission at the UN in New York, and then a spell at the London embassy. 'This is strange,' the former Korean diplomat told me. 'Kim did not work for the Ministry of Foreign Affairs so he must have been there for the KCIA. Normally a diplomat does a tour of duty and then they go home to catch up on government thinking. In London I think he would have been watching colleagues, Koreans in commerce, students and of course dissidents.'

More promotion followed. Called home briefly, Kim was made deputy head of the Presidential Protection Force. This was more than bodyguarding. Park ran his own private team of spooks, loyal only to him, and Kim was trusted with special assignments, freelancing in and out of America for three decades, as a diplomat, working with KCIA front organisations, being exposed in a conspiracy to pay and extort bribes and spouting Olympic idealism. He must have had a different hat for each day of the week.

Bribe the US Congress, General Park was screaming, incensed by White House orders to reduce American troops in Korea. Only Congress could block this, so it must be bought. The corruption was orchestrated from the Korean embassy in Washington. Crooked politicians on Capitol Hill pocketed large wads from a $1 million slush fund and other big bribes went in from a corrupt Korean businessman liaising with the KCIA.

The embassy instructed Kim to work with the Reverend Sun Myung Moon (banned as an undesirable from Britain in 1995) whose Moonie cult was frightening America's parents. They believed the Moonies kidnapped their children and turned them into zombies, programmed to raise funds for his private business empire. It was the usual kind of religious stuff, controlling banks and manufacturing grenade launchers, machine guns and anti-aircraft weapons.

Kim must have felt at ease with the Moonie leadership; they backed General Park, did deals with the KCIA and were happy to spend some of their wealth meddling in American politics. He also benefited from a dubious Moonie front organisation, the innocuous sounding Korean Cultural and Freedom Foundation.

The FBI seized its books when they stumbled over the embassy-inspired bribery plot. Who had been on the cultural foundation's gift list? Mickey Kim of course. Here was evidence that Kim was now a very high-ranking spook indeed. In the foundation's accounts was a note: 'A gift [$100] to an important Korean government official, Assistant Director Kim Un Young (Korean Secret Service) on the death of his mother.'

The American press savoured another Mickey Kim scam, discovered by House Committee on International Relations investigators. He'd tried to shake down Colt Industries, suppliers of rifles to the Korean army, for a contribution to General Park's rigged election campaign of 1971. Company lawyers advised Colt to refuse – and Mickey Kim was shown the door.

As the scandal unravelled in Washington, Kim left town. He showed up at little-known Maryville College in St Louis and, overnight, was reborn as 'Dr' Kim Un Yong, 'a model of involvement in the intellectual, diplomatic and cultural life of the Republic of Korea' according to the Maryville professors. Did Kim pay for this honour? 'I don't know anything about that,' former college president Harriet Switzer told me, primly.

The good doctor was summoned to get his new orders from General Park. He'd tarted up his own image – now he must do the same for the evil regime. Get us some nice headlines for a change, was the instruction. What was the remedy? Hiring expensive New York spin doctors? Releasing political prisoners? Holding free elections? Out of the question. What else might succeed? It worked for Hitler and for Samaranch when he did his meagre best to put a gloss on General Franco's rule. Off the all-purpose tyrant's shelf came state-sponsored sport. Almost overnight Mickey Kim was repackaged as a revered sports leader. General Park imposed Kim on the Korean Olympic committee, tossed him some instant honours to add to his instant doctorate – and gave him a challenge. Taekwondo was unique to Korea. If Kim could build it up into an international sport, credit would flow back to the regime and it might be a launch-pad to greater things.

Unfortunately taekwondo was already controlled by somebody who didn't bow to the dictatorship. General Choi Hong Hi was a career army officer who'd devoted his life to studying martial arts. In the 1950s he'd created taekwondo, devising its name and techniques, and soon his new sport had several international affiliates. But he wouldn't play with General Park – or Mickey Kim. They wanted the status of owning an international sports federation: Choi just enjoyed the sport. And he didn't like their other, secret agenda.

'Park wanted access to the international federation,' says Choi. 'He saw it could be a powerful muscle for his dictatorship.' Choi was threatened with jail when he refused to hand taekwondo over to the KCIA and fled to Canada, taking his international federation with him. Back in Korea, Park took his family hostage.

Kim took over, setting up his rival World Taekwondo Federation and installing himself as president. Its inaugural meeting empowered Kim to select all the officials – and taekwondo went into action for the Seoul regime. They sold Kim's version of the sport world-wide as a noble art – and clandestinely exploited it to keep General Park in power.

Exiled Korean dissidents who embarrassed the Seoul regime with their campaigns against its cruelty were pursued by an alliance of spooks and terrifying martial arts experts. 'Intelligence agents were planted under cover of diplomats and taekwondo instructors were sent abroad to set up schools,' says a former Korean diplomat. 'They were later used as auxiliaries. The KCIA would fly in and use these people and their local knowledge.'

In May 1973, when Korean opposition leader Kim Dae Jung tried to speak in San Francisco, ten taekwondo experts led by a KCIA officer turned up to disrupt the meeting. Local police prevented them. They tried again three months later, kidnapping him in Tokyo and smuggling him back to Seoul and five years in jail.

But repression at home and state-sponsored terrorism abroad brought unfavourable headlines, threatening foreign aid and contracts for Korea's sweatshops. What would be good for business? Korea needed the Olympics. The Nazis had manipulated the Games, for their own ends in 1936, the Mexicans had done the same in 1968 and the Soviets were getting ready for 1980. The KCIA turned on the charm and set about wooing the Olympic family.

Guns and sex were the weapons of seduction. Seoul bid successfully for the world shooting championships of 1978 and showed that Korea had what it took to stage a big event and keep the officials happy.

'Girls were available for anyone who wanted them.

One visiting official opened his bedroom door late at night to find a beaming hostess,' recalls a British sports official. 'Foolishly, he didn't say no, he got rid of her saying he had a meeting with a colleague in half an hour. Thirty minutes later there was another knock on the door – there were two girls! Everything was on offer. When we left I saw people at the airport with video recorders, radios, even fridges.'

Everything was on track to launch a bid for the 1988 Games. Then General Park was gunned down over dinner by his secret service chief for an insane order to fire on 30,000 rebellious workers in the southern city of Pusan. Within weeks General Chun Doo Hwan had seized power, backed by the corrupt commander of the Seoul garrison, General Roh Tae Woo. The slaughter went on. In May 1981 the army shot pro-democracy demonstrators in the city of Kwangju. The government said only 200 were killed: local people claim thousands died. That got more bad headlines; the more dissidents they gunned down, the more the generals needed that unique festival of peace.

Why shouldn't they be given the Olympics? For a quarter of a century successive juntas had sent government puppets to Lausanne where they'd been welcomed with open arms. These were Korea's great Olympians, the men whose personal integrity set the style for the KCIA's bid to stage the Games of 1988.

South Korea's first IOC member, Lee Ki-Poong, a senior member of the first post-war dictatorship was appointed in 1955, served a few years – and then disappeared. IOC histories don't reveal why – it's too embarrassing. 'Lee Ki Poong and his wife and two sons were found shot to death in a suicide pact,' reported the Associated Press in April 1960. 'Mr Lee, the controversial and disavowed vice-president-elect, was chief target of anti-government demonstrations, sparked by charges that Mr Lee's lopsided victory in the March 15 election was rigged.' Lee's over-enthusiastic falsifying of the ballot brought down the military junta and left him friendless. Despite his crookery, Lee got the usual IOC send-off. President Avery Brundage mourned, 'It is a loss to the IOC whose members have in their few contacts learned to respect him.'

The next regime provided a new candidate, Dr Lee Sang-Beck, in the words of one former Korean government official, 'a stooge of the junta, manipulated by the Korean intelligence agency, Park's control mechanism.' He died after only two years on the IOC and in came Chang Key-Young, who lasted a decade.

Chang was too busy conducting shady financial deals and running his own newspaper empire to make much mark on the Olympic committee – except as a crook. Brundage's successor, Lord Killanin, remembered Chang sending a flunky to see him in Lausanne. 'This emissary announced that he knew I had a problem paying my expenses (which was not the case, I assured him) and that Mr Chang wished to give me a present,' recalled Killanin in his memoirs. 'He held out an envelope, which I refused to accept. "Oh," he said casually, "it's only a thousand dollars!"'

Chang died in 1977 and Korea was immediately given a new IOC member, Kim Taik Soo, described by one Korea expert as 'having no known accomplishment in any field including sports before the military coup. But he was a fanatic supporter of General Park.' The regime gave him various sports posts, but he too died without making any contribution to the Olympic movement.

The generals soon supplied a replacement. Park Chong Kyu joined in 1984 and Samaranch boosted him as a statesman with a track record in political science and international affairs. But what a record:

Park's only international achievement was his role in America's KoreaGate scandal. In May 1974 as John Nidecker, a special assistant to President Nixon, was on his way to Seoul airport, an envelope containing $10,000 was thrust into his hand. Nidecker sent it straight back to the generous man whose name was on the envelope – Park Chong Kyu.

Park didn't just offer bribes – he also sent his troops out fishing for them. Congressional investigators reported that when Mickey Kim tried to shake down Colt Industries for campaign funds, he was acting under orders from the statesmanlike Park Chong Kyu.

What was the Olympian-to-be Mr Park doing slipping bribes to White House aides and soliciting illicit pay-offs? It was his job. Park Chong Kyu was the head of General Park's presidential protection service and described to me by a former CIA analyst in Seoul as 'a deadly and very dangerous man, Korea's Number One Thug'.

When Park Chong Kyu died from cancer after only fifteen months on the IOC, Samaranch gave him a posthumous Olympic Order. The choice to replace him in 1986 was Park's deputy at the presidential protection service, the trusted servant of successive brutal, fascist regimes, Dr Mickey Kim Un Yong.

Winning the Games of 1988 was easy. Korea's sleazy IOC members must have tipped off their colleagues about how best to score votes. 'Seoul gave away, quietly, two first class round-trip tickets to each IOC member,' recalls Peter Ueberroth who presided over the Los Angeles Games. 'The tickets were easily redeemed for cash; many were.' What else might influence the Olympians? Five Korean Air stewardesses and three Miss Koreas spearheaded the Korean's bid team for the vote in Baden-Baden in 1981. 'They were graceful, attractive and enthusiastic,' recalls Mickey Kim.

Whatever needed doing was done and Seoul trounced its only rival, Nagoya from Japan, by fifty-two votes to twenty-seven. Helping out where cash bribes and lovely women couldn't was Adidas's Horst Dassler. Korea was a major supplier to Adidas and Dassler made it his business – literally – to support the bid. Dassler got his payback later when Seoul signed him to handle their merchandising, licensing and sponsorship.

Mickey Kim was far from relaxed at the convention. Babbling that 'the Olympic movement stands for a better and more peaceful world' alternated with organising his strong-arm thugs to keep everybody smiling. General Choi, the man he had ousted from Korean taekwondo, was rumoured to be on the warpath and might show up in Baden-Baden to stage an anti-Seoul demonstration. 'I called five taekwondo instructors to stand by the entire time,' says Mickey.

More of his Olympic values surfaced over the selection of a committee to organise the Games. 'Bureaucrats, the military, police, intelligence agents, sportsmen, press, broadcasters, diplomats and even businessmen' were Mickey's choice.

The regime practised its own style of training. As the Asian Games, staged as a dry run for the Olympics, opened in October 1986, police and military arrested a quarter of a million Koreans, to shield Samaranch and other guests from embarrassing pro-democracy demonstrations. The people fought back: within weeks the biggest-ever protests were breaking out in the capital. The dictatorship put 70,000 police and troops on the streets, and despite all the killing, gassing and beatings they inflicted this time it wasn't enough.

The protests continued into 1987 and with the Olympics just over a year away President Chun produced his personal version of the Olympic Truce. The people wanted the constitution changed: Chun ruled it out. The people wanted him to talk with the opposition: Chun refused. Nothing, Chun insisted, was going to change until after the Olympics. He intended staying in power for ever.

The people wanted democracy and an end to corruption, military dictatorship, torture and repression, and pinned their hopes on elections scheduled for later in the year. Chun and his ruling clique were horrified at this prospect and outside Korea he appeared to have only one supporter, IOC president Samaranch. Twice in 1987 Samaranch wrote privately to Chun, urging that elections be postponed until after the Olympics.

The demonstrations went on. Chun gave way, announcing that his successor would be General Roh Tae Woo, one of his strongest supporters and president of the Seoul Olympic organising committee. The riots intensified. Roh, seeing his chances of power slip away, stole several opposition demands and announced, dramatically, that there would be elections and some reforms.

At the end of the year Roh won thirty-seven per cent of the vote and was declared president-elect. The dictatorship would have a new face for the Olympics. The demonstrations diminished, but the police state went on full alert for the festival of peace. In preparation for the Games Seoul was again cleansed of alleged criminals, political dissidents, even beggars and blind people.

Political demonstrations were banned in most of Seoul during the Olympics. New president Roh, enforcing this decree with nearly 90,000 troops, declared the city a 'peace zone'. Samaranch rewarded him at the end of the Games with the gold Olympic Order, declaring Roh to be 'the real inspiration behind the Games'.

Roh appointed Mickey Kim as a special roving ambassador in 1990. In October 1995 Roh wept on Korean TV as he admitted pocketing $650 million in kick-backs from Korean businessmen during his short time as president. 'I am ready to accept my punishment,' he said as they led him off to jail. His mentor and predecessor General Chun was arrested three weeks later for the crimes he had committed while in power.

KoreaGate was soon forgotten and so was the tawdry image of 'Mickey' Kim. He was unstoppable. A year before going to Baden-Baden for the vote on who would stage the 1988 Games, Kim had steered his world taekwondo federation to official recognition by the IOC.

But how did he get into the IOC? A member of its executive board told me, 'Whatever issue came up, Kim was saying "Yes" to everyone, so he would be invited to join.' Kim must have said 'Yes' a lot of times to Samaranch. Mickey Kim became a Lord of the Rings at the IOC convention in Lausanne in 1986. Nine days later he took over control of all world sports, Olympic and otherwise, capturing the presidency of GAISF, the General Assembly of International Sports Federations. Such promotion was unparalleled in the career of any sports politician. But there was more to come: within two years Samaranch shepherded Mickey on to the IOC's executive board.

The former Washington shake-down artist is now a respected international sports leader. His power in the sports federations and at the IOC props up Samaranch's 'unity' of sport. Mickey receives honours from the Belgian, French and Spanish governments and Samaranch praises him as his 'most important assistant'.

It's been a long climb to the Olympian heights from the spooky gutters. Mickey now looks at Samaranch, notes his age and infirmities, and dreams: Will I be the next Olympic president?

# CHAPTER 10

## *Black Belts and Dirty Money*

What a proud moment it will be for the young tae-kwondo fighters as they stand before the mat in Sydney, ready to compete for their first Olympic medals. Mickey Kim will look down at them with even greater pleasure. The world will see athletes determined to bring honour to their country, their sport and Olympic idealism. Mickey will see dollars, deutschemarks and pounds sterling. Every athlete, every referee, every official has had to pay him for the privilege of competing in the millennium Games. It's another Olympic racket and Mickey's monopoly has the blessing of IOC president Samaranch and national Olympic committees everywhere.

Winning the exclusive franchise for Olympic tae-kwondo was a dirty business. Around three-quarters of the sport's world-wide competitors have been excluded and a rival sport roughed-up and jump-kicked to Olympic oblivion. The rules and practices of Mickey's World Taekwondo Federation make a mockery of the Olympic charter. Senior IOC members confirm this – off the record. They believe that his federation is linked to crooked politics in Korea and suspect that he runs it as a personal intelligence network, helped by Olympic sports officials. Nonetheless, they extend concessions to

Mickey's version of taekwondo denied to every other sport in the world.

The art of kicking and punching made its Olympic debut as a demonstration sport in Seoul. Every host nation – up until Atlanta – has been allowed to show off its own sports and nobody objected when the Koreans chose taekwondo. A thousand fighters performed at the opening ceremony. But Mickey overdid it in the sport itself; Koreans took all but one men's title – the heavyweight final – and although Samaranch went out of his way to bestow the medals personally, the rest of the world saw nothing but a local sport, dominated by local athletes and their local judges, that had little place on the Olympic programme.

That might have been the end of Mickey's schemes to lead his fighters into the Games but Samaranch gave him a second chance. In Barcelona – against all Olympic precedents – taekwondo was allowed back as a demonstration sport for a second time. Mickey learned the lesson from Seoul and left most of his best fighters at home. Medals went to several countries and taekwondo was a step nearer to the real thing.

Not all the action in Barcelona was on the mat. In the privacy of the IOC convention Mickey administered a crippling blow to the only other sport that might beat taekwondo into the Olympics. Combat sports – fencing, boxing and judo – were already well represented at the Games. If there was room for another, it surely had to be the hugely popular sport of karate.

Three years before Kim launched his tiny KCIA-sponsored world taekwondo federation in 1973, the world union of karate federations – WUKO – was formed by Jacques Delcourt from Paris. Karate was off on the long road to the Olympics.

Delcourt lobbied the IOC in the early 1980s for

official recognition. But by this stage Mickey Kim had made his presence felt in Lausanne with a seat on one of Samaranch's Olympic committee commissions and recognition for his taekwondo federation. He was one step ahead – but under threat from a bigger, respectable rival sport. What happened to karate then was more out of the spooks' manual than the Olympic Charter.

WUKO's application for recognition was opposed suddenly by a rival karate federation, the International Traditional Karate Federation – the ITKF – a small, purist group with only a few thousand members, many of them professional instructors, who practised their own version of the sport. The ITKF had affiliates in only six countries, against WUKO's eighty-five.

Samaranch promptly became the great democrat, unctuously concerned for the rights of minorities. There would be no IOC recognition unless the giant WUKO merged with its tiny, distant and unfriendly cousin. The two got together in Cairo in 1983 and signed an agreement – which the small federation soon tore up.

Delcourt pressed ahead and karate's case was heard at the IOC convention in East Berlin in 1985. It would probably have got nowhere but for a surprising intervention from Louis Guirandou-N'Diaye, the IOC member from the Ivory Coast. A fourth Dan karate black belt, N'Diaye spoke up for WUKO. He knew the background to the karate wars. The small federation, he claimed, had gone its own way after failing to take over the large one. Much worse, it had breached UN rules on sports contact with South Africa. Recognise WUKO, urged N'Diaye, and the IOC membership agreed. They also backed his argument that unification of the two karate federations was not essential to the Olympic future of the sport.

Samaranch had to concede recognition – but he still backed manoeuvres to undermine WUKO. Meetings were called, letters sent recommending the merger, despite the IOC having accepted N'Diaye's argument. The rows continued through the late 1980s and Delcourt claims his federation was being persecuted by the IOC. He was right: suddenly Lausanne toughened its stand and demanded a merger. In desperation Delcourt called on Mario Vazquez Raña to mediate with the ITKF. More agreements were signed but the ITKF wouldn't budge.

Delcourt went to Belgrade in 1990 and put his case, again, to the IOC's executive board. They promised a detailed study – but secretly prepared a shroud for WUKO. A year later came an abrupt instruction from the executive, of which Mickey Kim was now a member, for WUKO to merge with its midget cousin or be expelled from the Olympic movement.

The coup was completed on the eve of the Barcelona Olympics. While the fans chanted the Barcelona slogan 'Friends for Life' Samaranch quietly organised a death in the Olympic family. WUKO's status was not even on the agenda of the IOC convention, so few members were aware that they were about to banish around forty million athletes from their movement.

Delcourt claims he was unaware karate's future would be discussed. The execution took only three minutes. Samaranch arranged a report which claimed that the dispute between the two federations was 'damaging to Karate as a whole' and recommended withdrawing IOC recognition. The Olympic committee, to their shame, obeyed him and WUKO – which claims to be the tenth largest sports federation in the world – and its 152 national affiliates were cast out into darkness. Kim's version of taekwondo now had a clear run at the Games.

Delcourt was outraged; he condemned the one-sided decision as a 'Stalinist trial' and demanded the right to appear with a lawyer before the IOC. He claims that Samaranch made it known that if this happened, they would refuse to recognise WUKO for ever, and give the case to their legal experts. It would last ten years and cost millions.

'Corruption and blackmail,' exclaimed Delcourt, adding, 'the rumour is that it's a plot between Samaranch and his friend Kim. Karate is ten to twenty times more important than taekwondo in the world and should have priority in the Olympic Games, but this does not suit Kim's sordid business. An IOC member has told me, "Kim is protected by Samaranch, no one can touch him."'

General Choi discovered that for himself. The exiled father of taekwondo and leader of the International Taekwondo Federation went to Lausanne in 1984 to lobby Samaranch. He was accompanied by one of America's top taekwondo instructors, Chuck Seref, an eighth Dan, then highest rank achieved by a non-Asiatic. A big man with gnarled hands from smashing bricks and planks, Seref has travelled the world with the General. 'I first encountered him in 1968. He was treated like a God by anybody involved in the sport,' he says. But not by Samaranch. 'When we met Samaranch,' recalls Seref, he assured us, "Taekwondo will never be an Olympic medal sport unless the ITF and the WTF merge – even if only for the Games."

'The General said he had pursued negotiations because he thought it more important for taekwondo to be recognised than him holding out personally,' Seref continues, 'and Samaranch said it was "a terrific idea". As soon as the meeting was over we sent letters to the WTF requesting a dialogue. They didn't answer.'

Instead, the response came from the spooks. 'The KCIA contacted all our Korean instructors around the world, maybe twenty or thirty, maybe more, and pressurised them into joining Kim's federation,' says

Seref. 'Then they put pressure on our taekwondo schools. Here in Denver the WTF opened up a rival school just five blocks away from one operated by one of my best instructors. One of his students went and asked, why open here, so close to an ITF school, and the guy replied that he was instructed to do so. There were lots of instructors who arrived, set up schools, lost money, damaged existing schools and then moved on.'

Choi battled on but Mickey Kim now had Samaranch's support. Lausanne parroted Kim's offer to let Choi's members join his federation if they chose. Just as the bigger karate federation had been told they must merge with the little one or be expelled from the Olympic movement, now Choi's older and larger group was being told they should dismantle their federation and join the smaller, younger KCIA offshoot.

A few months before taekwondo's premiere in Seoul Choi wrote to Samaranch, begging him to look again at Mickey Kim's sports federation. 'The WTF is managed and controlled by politicians and Korean CIA officers, rather than taekwondo leaders,' the General asserted, 'and its constitution stipulates that the headquarters will permanently be stationed in Seoul. It is nothing but a quasi-governmental organisation of South Korea and not an international sports organisation.'

And did they even practise the genuine sport? They used 'any taekwondo, karate, judo, kung-fu or hapkido instructors' claimed Choi, simplifying the complicated moves into a full-contact sparring event convenient for Olympic bouts and television coverage.

Kim's federation meetings would make wonderful comic television. Around sixty delegates assembled in Seoul in October 1989, claiming to represent thirty million members. Shouts of 'bitch' and 'bastard' echoed around the federation's office when a delegate's wife clashed with one of Kim's officials. Inside the assembly the comedy continued. Kim told them they must have a 'sense of mission' and was promptly re-elected unopposed as president. Most of the officials stood to applaud him and Kim thanked them for their trust.

Then the meeting moved smoothly into a display of the kind of spontaneous democracy that makes rulebooks unnecessary. They were supposed to ballot secretly to elect six vice-presidents, a general secretary, a treasurer, twenty-two council members and an auditor. What a waste of time for busy men!

An Egyptian member leapt up and urged that Mickey Kim should be given a free rein to select all these officials himself; he was immediately backed by three colleagues. Kim asked delegates to stand up if they 'wished to delegate power to me to appoint all officials'. Fifty did and Kim was given supreme authority. Seven from Europe sat tight, opposing him, and four delegates abstained.

Mickey presides over a money-making machine. It starts at entry level to the sport. The only way to train and learn is to sign up with a professional instructor. Sang Lee, former leader of Mickey Kim's USA affiliate, runs his school in Colorado Springs and charges $2,365 for a three year black belt course. If students want to pay in instalments, interest charges bring the total to $2880.

Athletes who want to aim for the Olympics have to spend more money. There are two ways Mickey pulls in the cash. His WTF in Seoul is based in the Kukkiwon building. But the Kukkiwon is also the name of a separate organisation – and it's a money-spinner. To get the essential grading certificates to compete in the Olympics you have to buy them from the WTF – if you're a member – or the Kukkiwon if you're not. Send money to Mickey and hope for gold. Don't – and stay home and watch the sport on television.

The Kukkiwon system was attacked by American grandmaster Sang Kyu Shim just before the Barcelona Games. He denounced the WTF as 'a profitable quasi-franchising business collecting hundreds of thousands of dollars in examination fees from its US black belt candidates alone.' The grandmaster added, 'One wonders where this money is going'.

He published his critique with a drawing of a cash register labelled 'Kukkiwon' sucking in the dollars, concluding that the WTF is like an 'outmoded socialist economy – gigantic and uniform but monopolistic, inefficient, inflexible and stagnant'.

Others say it's corrupt. Allegations abound that taekwondo rankings can be bought. A dozen master instructors in Georgia claimed in 1994 that the Kukkiwon was selling certificates to unqualified competitors. This was backed by grandmaster Chung Eun Kim of *Taekwondo Times*. He estimates that up to $1 million a year flows from America alone to the Kukkiwon in Seoul for grading certificates. 'It seems to me that WTF leaders just want to keep all the power and financial benefits for South Korea,' says Chung.

The Kukkiwon has set two levels of fees for certificates: in the late 1980s foreigners had to pay up to five times as much as Koreans. One master who broke away from Mickey Kim says this is financial exploitation. It's a monopoly that is said to generate up to $30 million a year in remittances to Korea.

Taekwondo experts who've been inside the Kukkiwon say that Kim and many of his officials take no salary from the WTF. 'They've got private money from somewhere,' one told me.

Taekwondo in Britain is split. Mickey's WTF affiliate

claims 15,000 members – but his critics suspect it's lucky if it's got as many as 9,000 fighters. Frozen out of the Olympics is the British Taekwondo Council which claims 25,000 registered and insured members. When trials were held to send a British team to Seoul in 1988, none made it who weren't affiliated to Mickey Kim. Four years later no British fighters went to Barcelona, critics say because the Koreans declined to invite them.

If the IOC allows Mickey to stage contests in all the usual weight divisions at the Sydney 2000 Games there could be sixteen golds to be won. Cynics predict that Korean WTF members, judged by Korean WTF officials will take all the medals, pushing Korea to its highest ever total of golds and elevating Mickey Kim to heroic status at home.

Abroad, there are already calls from within his own ranks for Mickey to step down. In a 'meeting of the masters' debate, published in *Taekwondo Times*, one of America's leading instructors commented politely 'Dr Kim has excellent management skills, but is not a real trained master in taekwondo.'

That was the courteous give-away. General Choi devised the sport, and even in his eighties still tours the world giving seminars, based on his fifteen-volume instruction manual. Could Mickey Kim do as much? 'He's never even wrestled on the mat,' says Chuck Seref, dismissively. Taekwondo masters I've spoken to in Britain and America agree. Mickey was put in place – because he was a trusted spook – by a corrupt military regime more than twenty years and backed by their successors, he's stayed there.

After taekwondo's second demonstration in Barcelona Mickey Kim took his campaign for Olympic recognition to New York's Madison Square Garden. Nine IOC members accepted invitations to the eleventh taekwondo world championships and then it was on to Paris where, in September 1994, the IOC voted to stage his version of taekwondo at the Sydney Games.

In private, Mickey Kim is not loved at the IOC. One member of the executive board told me, 'I think he is a combination of thug and spook. There's great speculation that he runs the Korean CIA. He certainly trained with them. He's pretty opaque. He's very ambitious. He's got this network of taekwondo which is totally supported by the Korean Government and that's his job. He's a braggart and a bully. He's everything you would think about somebody from that part of the world, in a position of power.'

At least one member of the executive appears to know about Kim's spooky history. An unexplained footnote in Dick Pound's account of the politics behind the Seoul Olympics baldly refers to the KoreaGate scandal in Washington in the 1970s and the 'illegal activities of the KCIA'.

Kim won't say if he's a candidate for the succession – but nobody ever does. In late 1994 he commented, 'I believe it is about time for the end of the Western world's hegemony of the IOC.'

Samaranch for one has no doubts about Mickey's federation and his version of taekwondo. He says that within the sport are 'principles which come close to, one might say merge with, those advocated by the Baron de Coubertin'.

# CHAPTER 11

## No Lady, No Vote: Rubbing Up and Shaking Down On the Bid Circuit

Three hours north-west of Stockholm the train slows. Over the tree tops looms the ski-jump tower at the Lugnet winter sports centre. Cross-country and biathlon trails loop away into the pine forests. Every winter they fill up with skiers; everyone is there, from international stars to local sports fans. For nearly half the year Sweden is snowbound and the people get out there and revel in it. The Vasa long distance ski race is their greatest endurance event, ice hockey rivals soccer in popularity and the Swedes have hauled home bags of medals since the Winter Games began. They're among the most enthusiastic competitors but it seems they'll never be the hosts.

The train stops: we're in the small town of Falun, once a candidate for Olympic glory. 'I gave the best years of my life to campaigning for the Winter Games,' laughs Lars Eggertz, the local politician and businessman who led two successive bids. 'Promises, handshakes, we heard it all. Unfortunately we believed too much in honesty and fair play.' Eggertz and his team competed from the late 1970s until they hit rock bottom in

1986, insulted, exploited and discarded by an Olympic
movement they discovered was corrupt. So welcome to
Falun, the graveyard of Sweden's Olympic dreams.

Awarding the Games to Seoul and Los Angeles had
been low-key affairs compared to the campaigns that
followed. The television rights soared in value, Horst
Dassler's salesmen jacked up the price of the rings and
cities everywhere were tempted. They fell for the dream
that the Games might pay for themselves without tax
money. They could be the centre of world attention for
a fortnight and enjoy the legacy of new sports facilities
for years to come. Just play the Olympic Game, pander
to the IOC members, let them molest your daughters;
wine, dine and suffocate them with hospitality until
around fifty votes are in the bag. That's Olympic
campaigning today, where the winners end up paying
a high price for the Games and the losers disappear
instantly after the vote; used, abused, with so many
sour stories to tell.

Olympic bid campaigns are run increasingly by private
corporations or government quangos and the bills,
receipts, secret correspondence, records of deal-making
and plain corruption are hidden forever. That suits the
IOC, knowing as they do what many of their members
get up to in bidding cities.

What would happen when Swedish values collided
with the Lords of Lausanne? Unlike the secretive
Olympic committee, the Swedes believe in openness; it's
a safeguard against corruption. Lying in the basement
of the Falun city archive are the carefully filed debris
of the city's Olympic dreams. Brochures, invitations,
banquet seating plans; hotel bills; begging letters from
IOC members; letters from around the world marked
confidential; notes of off-record conversations – all the
things the Olympians wouldn't want us to know. Lars

Eggertz pointed me to the shelves and walked away, smiling.

The Swedes bid twice in the 1960s, twice more in the 1970s and then cranked up yet another campaign for the Games of 1984. Would this be the winning bid at last? Poring over their plans in the long winter nights, they'd come up with a new, cheap blueprint for small countries to host the Olympics. Spreading the sport across four cities and using existing venues was very Swedish, very sensible, very rational and of no interest to the IOC who gave the games to Sarajevo and its government chequebook and tossed just ten votes to the Swedes and their new model Olympics.

Sweden came bouncing back with a new bid for the Winter Games of 1988. Åre in the mountains to the north would host the alpine events and everything else would be staged in Falun. They rushed to prepare for the vote in Baden-Baden in 1981. Senior IOC member Raymond Gafner and his wife were cosseted over a five-day visit and Lars Eggertz and his team made long-haul trips to lobby IOC members. The vote again went against them, but in a straight fight Calgary, the favourite, won forty-eight votes and the Swedes secured a healthy thirty-one. They went home, followed by a symphony of inducements from the Olympic movement. Into the Falun archives went unsolicited letters from IOC members prompting another bid. Samaranch encouraged them to try again; Canada's James Worrall urged, 'Next time, I am sure you will be successful' and soccer supremo João Havelange promised, 'You will have my full support.'

The Swedes fell for it. Lausanne encouraged them to believe the slogan 'It's time for Sweden', and the Swedes thought that meant the Olympics would be theirs in 1992. The government came up with the all-important guarantee for the budget and the Falun team went on the road. For the next few years some of them more or less lived with their passports in their hands, showing up at every Olympic convention, every sports federation meeting, handing out modest gifts and fact-filled brochures.

Weren't they perfect candidates? Hadn't they paid their dues? Sweden had been a founder member of the IOC and had won nearly ninety medals at past Winter Games. Stockholm had hosted the most successful of the early Summer Games in 1912 and in 1956, when Melbourne was unable to stage the equestrian events, the Swedes stepped in with an alternative venue. With five failed bids behind them, how could they lose this time?

King Gustav formally announced Falun's new bid at the Sarajevo games and the team were heartened by the influential Marc Hodler, president of international skiing and IOC executive board member, telling them that this time, it really was Sweden's turn. Lars Eggertz' bid team went lobbying. The visa stamps piled up; if Mario Vazquez Raña's Association of National Olympic Committees wanted to meet in Seoul, a polite Falun official showed up to earnestly lay out the bid's budget and facilities. African Olympians met in Adidas Ababa: the Swedes were there, complimenting them on their idealism.

It was the same in Taipei, Bangkok and Mexico City; Lisbon, Budapest and Bahrain. There were so many factions to be appeased, so many pompous Olympic power-brokers needed reminding of their own importance. Thirty months of passport controls, strange hotel rooms and jet lag but always rewarded with the drip, drip of hints, nudges and winks that when they got to Lausanne in October 1986 for the vote, Sweden's Olympic dreams would come true.

The Falun team were smart enough to know that

Samaranch and his Olympians love rubbing shoulders with royalty so King Carl Gustaf and Queen Silvia, along with Prince Bertil and Princess Lilian were deployed to grace a Falun exhibition at the Los Angeles Games. It seemed to work. Samaranch turned up to be photographed with them and put on his public face of smiles and encouragement.

If the Swedish Royals had known what the IOC were saying in private, they might have taken the next plane home. Earlier the previous year Samaranch's executive board had decided to encourage as many bidding cities as possible for 1992. World-wide enthusiasm to host the Games would encourage the TV networks to make higher bids for Olympic rights.

More reassuring letters went into the archive. 'I strongly believe that 1992 will be the year of the winter Olympics in Falun,' purred Yugoslav IOC member Boris Bakrac. 'If not – there is no justice at all . . . Sweden deserves to be the host in 1992.' Samaranch was at it again, gushing to Falun officials, 'You have very strong support from your Royal family' – which he seemed to think was the plus point of their bid.

Behind the aloof pomposity of the Olympic committee were the parasites in the shadows. A record thirteen cities were chasing the Winter and Summer Games of 1992, and all were vulnerable to hucksters claiming they had Samaranch's ear and could control blocs of IOC members' votes. Consult with us, they whispered, you are outsiders; we understand the labyrinths of Lausanne: you don't – just give us money and you'll get the Games.

Dick Angell was on the team from Anchorage, Alaska, making a first attempt for the Winter Games. In 1985 he lobbied the sports barons at a meeting in Amsterdam. Victory could go to the Americans, was the confident message from the president of international boxing, who appeared to be up to his old tricks.

'I got talking to Anwar Chowdhry who told me that he was one of the people who helped Seoul get their Olympics,' recalls Angell. 'He said that if we wanted to hire him on a quiet basis he would be more than happy to help us get the Games. He told us he was involved in the Korean thing – it was generally rumoured that the Koreans had paid bribes – and was responsible for them getting it.'

The Anchorage team were taken aback. Nobody had told them about the seamy side of Olympic bidding. They thought you just went out on the road and promised a great Games to everyone. 'We were a little surprised,' says Angell. 'We were not in the position to pay – nor would we. It was obviously going to be a lot of money but this was suggested in a round about way.' Adidas's Horst Dassler showed up at the Amsterdam convention, keeping an eye on business. 'I told Dassler about Chowdhry,' says Angell. 'He laughed and changed the subject.' The Anchorage lobbyists weren't to know that Chowdhry was one of Dassler's team of sports political fixers, doing a little freelancing on the side.

Chowdhry didn't even have a vote. Some of those who did, the Olympic committee members, had discovered fringe benefits in the new desperate, well-funded campaigns to get the Games. 'This guy took a trip from his home in Africa to Paris, then Toronto, then Anchorage, then South Korea, back to Paris and then home,' recalls Dick Angell. 'He then billed all of us for first class return tickets for him and his wife as if they had taken separate trips. He must have cleared $25,000 profit.'

How could Angell prove this? 'Our committee checked with Toronto and Seoul and he had played the same trick on them. We reported this informally to two senior IOC employees – so it would get back.' Angell also named another IOC member 'who did the same thing'.

Angell added, 'We did not report this officially. The moment you report this to the likes of X [Angell named a senior IOC member] you're dead. Bidding cities cannot afford to upset IOC members who vote. And the IOC would only cover up and deny. After we had been around for a while we realised that there were people using the Olympics to feather their own nests.'

Probably the best-feathered nest belongs to the Takac family; Olympic insiders, fixers, warm hand-shakers at the conventions, sleeve-pluckers in the corridors, profiteers to the core. Longest in the game is Artur Takac, who turned up in Falun wearing his Olympian hat as the highly paid sports adviser to president Samaranch. Artur had worked his way around the Olympic circuit since he left Yugoslavia. He had been a technical adviser to the Mexico and Montreal Games and now he operated out of an expensive, IOC-funded office back in Belgrade. Although he was in Falun to assess the facilities for his president, Artur had time for other, unofficial ventures.

'He told us it would be profitable to meet his son Goran,' recalls Lars Eggertz. 'He indicated he was a specialist and it was suggested his involvement would help us win.' Goran, trading on his father's links to the IOC, offers himself as a consultant to bidding cities. He's given hard-to-acquire accreditation for Olympic meetings – which gets him alongside the full wallets – and also runs a publishing business in Lausanne. Samaranch gives him exclusive rights to produce the official books of results and pictures after the Olympics – he scored with Albertville and Barcelona. He touts his expertise at putting together the all-important bid books that every candidate has to send to the Olympic committee.

Artur thought this could be helpful to Falun. 'He encouraged us to use his son to produce the book for our presentation,' says Eggertz. 'We went to Lausanne, had lunch and talked about this book but we declined the offer.' Goran's seductive pitch didn't work with Falun but he still managed to sign up several other competitors. Sofia, Lillehammer and Cortina employed him to boost their hopes for the winter event and Brisbane hired him to hone their pitch for the Summer Games. They all lost.

Papa Takac was at it again with the Anchorage team. It was the same old tune. 'When we were at an IOC meeting in Portugal in 1985 we met Artur Takac,' remembers Dick Angell. 'He sat us down and told us about his involvement in the Games going to Sarajevo. He said we should talk to his son.' The Anchorage team passed on Goran that time round but Artur was lying in wait for them when they bid again for the Winter Games of 1994.

'Artur Takac said, "I would like to have a meeting with you at ten at the office of my son,"' recalls Rick Nerland, executive director of the Alaska team. 'Artur said on the way to the meeting, "I'm introducing you to my son. I think he has some suggestions to help you. I'm doing this because I really like what you did. But if you do business with him it's up to you!" He introduced us to Goran and then got up and left.' Goran shook them down for $10,000 a month for a year, and then Anchorage cancelled his contract. 'We achieved what we were looking to achieve and at a certain point we were not getting a return on our investment,' said Nerland.

Still working for Sofia, Goran was comforted by Bulgaria's IOC member. 'Goran is a good professional and one of the best sporting consultants,' said Ivan Slavkov. 'We are friends.'

Another friend of competing cities was Fékrou Kidane, an Ethiopian exile and freelance sports reporter who got lucky when Kuwait's Sheikh Fahd put up some cash to publish a newsletter, *Continental Sports*. It was a mediocre effort but Kidane used it to shake down the unwary.

He contacted bid cities, boasting that the newsletter was 'distributed to all national Olympic committees, international federations, Ministries of Sport and the international press.' *Continental Sports*, he wrote to Eggertz, 'is the best means to promote Falun.' Then he hit the button. 'Your sponsors' participation is needed to finalise the project.' Falun's bid, like most others, was backed by local and national companies, either for sentimental reasons – or hopes of business if the games came their way.

If Falun's sponsors would buy $55,000 worth of advertising, it would be 'fantastic'. What could he offer them in editorial coverage that might impress the Olympic community? How about an interview with Sweden's Queen Silvia? Kidane sent some of his probing questions in advance. 'It would seem your personal life is linked with Olympism' was one toughie the Queen had to face. Another was 'it seems you are very much involved in the bidding efforts of the city of Falun.'

Kidane enjoyed a six-day trip to Sweden, paid for by the Falun team. Filed away in the archives are scribbled notes of his advice on how to handle the Olympic voters. Soccer boss João Havelange could deliver members from South America, North Africa and Malaysia. China's Zhenliang He was 'no problem'. Crucial of course was the man from Adidas. 'We need Mr Dassler's support and we might have it – but Dassler's name shouldn't be mentioned officially,' counselled Kidane.

Kidane chided his hosts for their naivety. Wise up, he instructed. 'The ones who decide where the Olympics shall take place are big companies like Coca-Cola, ABC TV, Adidas. It's what makes the movement and its members the most earnings who decides. Falun should establish good contacts with these companies in order to get the Olympics.'

Fékrou Kidane had sometimes written critically of Samaranch and the IOC. But unfortunately for him *Continental Sports* collapsed and Sheikh Fahd died in the Iraqi invasion of 1991. Kidane needed a new patron. His editorial view changed and by 1995 he was listed in the IOC Directory as 'Chef de Cabinet of the President and Director of International Co-operation'.

The biggest ordeal for Falun was always going to be the inspection trips by the IOC members. Thirty-seven IOC members, wives, children and hangers-on boarded a chartered plane to Sweden direct from their 1985 convention in East Berlin. Peruvian member Ivan Dibos brought two friends; last to arrive at Berlin airport was the patrician Ashwini Kumar, his wife and two daughters, with a police motor-cycle escort for their limousine.

The visit began on a Friday night with a dinner in Falun hosted by the King and Queen. For two IOC members, Hamzah from Malaysia and Ali from Pakistan, that was the beginning and end of their interest in Falun's facilities. They departed the next morning having cost the gritted-teeth Falun team a considerable amount in travel and hotel bills.

Lars Eggertz and his team had wised up by now to the indolence of many of the Olympians. For those who did have a passing interest in sport there was a tour of the Falun facilities followed by an eighty-minute helicopter trip north to Åre to view the downhill runs.

Alternatively, they could spend their time shopping, sightseeing and playing golf.

Late on Saturday afternoon the members were flown to Stockholm and installed in the city's most expensive hotel. That evening the Falun team with eleven hostesses entertained their guests on a boat trip around the Stockholm archipelago. Most left at the end of the weekend. Months later, when Lars Eggertz got the bill, he discovered that one member and his wife had invited themselves to an additional week in the costly Grand Hotel.

Eggertz had been too busy at the time to keep the freeloading in check. He'd spent the Sunday morning consoling one of his hostesses who'd discovered late on the Saturday night that an IOC member thought he could get anything he wanted in return for the promise of his vote. The member – let's call him Mr Wandering Hands – had spent his evening chasing Falun's team of hostesses for sex. What could the Swedes do? A public complaint to Lausanne would have destroyed their hopes of the Olympics. Privately a senior member was informed and then the issue was dropped. Long after the votes had been cast, it would rear its head again.

Sex wasn't the only commodity the members were after. Businessman David Sibandze from Swaziland busied himself trying to fix a university place for one of his offspring. In the Falun archive is a list of the modest academic achievements of Sibandze's son Cecil Sibuisso. Attached is a school certificate showing young Cecil's very average grades. Also in the Sibandze file is a grovelling letter to him from a senior Swedish sports official. 'You informed us that your son would like to continue his studies in our country,' it begins, pointing out that the deadline had passed for admissions to Swedish universities for the coming academic year. 'However,' it continues, 'I have some good and friendly contacts in our Ministry for Foreign Affairs as well as in the Immigration Office and in the Ministry of Education. I will do my utmost trying to persuade the authorities concerned to accept an application from your son.'

Lars Eggertz completed the story for me: 'David Sibandze enquired whether we could arrange a place at a Swedish university, preferably Uppsala, for his son. The matter was eventually arranged and Sibandze was informed. We learnt later that all the bidding cities had been asked the same question.'

What bothered Eggertz much more was the upward spiral in the cost of schmoozing the Olympians. Samaranch brushed him aside, saying that bids brought cities good publicity and reminding him: 'IOC members ought to have rather better gifts than other people.'

Lausanne picked some members who had empty diaries, constituted them as an 'evaluation committee' and dispatched them to freeload off the bid cities. Falun knew the ropes by now, arranging a social programme with dinners, skiing and, of course, lunch with King Gustav. At the end of their extended, round-the-world holiday trip, they wrote a report on the candidates. 'It was full of padding,' despaired Eggertz when he got his copy, 'it said nothing and made practically no comparisons.'

It was the same with the winter sports federations. Falun was equally unimpressed by their efforts. 'Their reports on the visits to the candidates contained no real evaluation,' says Eggertz, wearily. 'Appointing every possible commission from the Olympic movement to visit and report on the various candidates is an unnecessary and meaningless occupation. The question is whether they are even read.'

The last thing Samaranch wanted was a stark evaluation of the bidders' merits. They all had to be kept on their toes right up to the vote; kept sending the gifts, kept spending silly money on IOC members. The members didn't want to be corralled into voting for the best-qualified candidate. Other, much more important considerations applied when it came to the ballot.

Samaranch was now aged sixty-six and looking to his retirement years. His reputation in Barcelona was still clouded by involvement with the Franco dictatorship. What might win him grudging tolerance from the Catalan nation? At the end of the dictatorship Barcelona, like most of Spain, was run-down, its infrastructure poor. One infusion might transform its creaking frame: Olympic investment.

Never mind that tax bills would loom into the next century: the Olympic hype machine would tell Catalans that their city was one of the chosen few; merchants and property developers would be enriched; there would be jobs and prestige and the old Blueshirt could take the credit.

So Barcelona simply had to win the Summer Games of 1992. Then Paris announced its bid. Catastrophe! The French sweated their assets to the full. IOC members in need of a vacation were sent airline tickets and lodged at the opulent Hotel de Crillon. Gifts included coats and perfumes and discounts in the better boutiques. Those who didn't shop until they dropped whiled away evenings at Maxim's or the Tour d'Argent – with the bill taken care of.

How could Paris be stopped? Its powerful bid had one flaw. Albertville in the French Alps was also bidding for 1992. It was impossible to give France both the Summer and the Winter Games.

Albertville's chances weren't rated: the venues for each sport were so spread out across the Savoy region that they were offering a series of mini-games, semi-detached from each other. Falun, the front runner for the previous two years, didn't feel unduly threatened. After all, France had hosted previous Winter Games in Chamonix and Grenoble and so it was time for Sweden.

Slowly, they picked up signs that Samaranch was backing Albertville. He avoided Falun, saying 'I do not visit candidates for the Olympic Games.' Then he made a high-profile trip to Savoy for the world free-style skiing championships and was conspicuous in the company of Albertville's joint bid leader Michel Barnier. The international press began to carry rumours of Barcelona and Albertville creating an axis to defeat Paris and Falun.

An IOC member from Norway, Jan Staubo, spotted that the voting was being rigged. 'There are now rumours of coalition and pre-arrangements being made between candidate city organisers and others,' he wrote to Samaranch, 'to get members to vote for a particular city for the Winter Games in order to influence the selection of the city to host the Olympiad.'

This was code for Barcelona and Albertville. Two months before the ballot in Lausanne Staubo pointed out that with the exception of the vote in 1981, which gave the Games to Calgary and Seoul, the IOC had always decided the summer host first and then the winter. He continued, 'I consider that we must abide by Rule 33 of our Charter and vote *firstly* for the city for the Olympiad and subsequently for the city to host the Winter Games. The IOC voting procedure must remain sacrosanct.'

For Barcelona to win the Summer Games, the vote for the winter host had to be staged first, so that if Albertville won, Paris's hopes went down the tubes. And it was. Eggertz' fears for the outcome deepened when they arrived in Lausanne and were invited, with other bidding cities, to lunch with Samaranch.

'You can imagine our astonishment when Samaranch, who is usually very careful about etiquette, chose to place Albertville's Michel Barnier next to him,' he says. 'Our Prince Bertil ought to have had that place.' The Swedish Royals had served their decorative purpose during the campaign but now that Samaranch had Albertville to support, they were past their sell-by date and could be safely snubbed.

Suppressing their gloom, the Falun team lobbied non-stop. Bjorn Borg was enlisted to play tennis with IOC members. Another golf tournament was organised but only Mbaye, Herzog and Coles took part. Prince Bertil and Princess Lilian hosted meals and photographers were hired to take pictures of each IOC member with Queen Silvia.

The Swedes showed off their 'Four Seasons Pavilion' with changing themes every day, matched by seasonal food and drink. Similar stunts were laid on by the other dozen candidates, the gifts rising from knee deep to chest height.

Inside the convention Kenya's Reggie Alexander one of a few members critical of Samaranch's devotion to power, money and personal prestige, told of his nightmare at their founder's grave. 'It opened up before my eyes: de Coubertin's hand reached out, grasped the Olympic rings and pulled them down into the ground,' he said, dramatically. 'Then the Baron said to me, "You can have these back only after you have stopped misbehaving yourselves."'

The Falun team made one last effort, lining up outside the convention centre after breakfast; a last chance to eyeball the nearly thirty members who'd promised it would be Sweden's turn this time. 'We felt powerless, inadequate and drained,' says Eggertz.

'Most members walked straight ahead without looking around or greeting anyone.'

Five hours later the contenders were summoned inside. The eighty-five members present arranged themselves on the stepped stage, providing a backdrop for their president. By the time he arrived, nerves were close to snapping. Eggertz remembers, 'When Samaranch came in everyone rose and applauded. It was a little too much for some people and one of the Falun team refused to stand up.'

Samaranch tore open the first envelope: Barcelona had won. Then the second: Albertville, with fifty-one votes. Falun, who'd captured thirty-one in the previous contest, scored only eleven.

German IOC member Willi Daume said after the vote, 'It was a political choice. Everyone knew that if Albertville was chosen, no one could threaten Barcelona.' The members had given Samaranch what he wanted, the best Winter Games candidate had been tossed overboard; and Albertville would turn out to be not only an unremarkable Olympics, but a burden on the French taxpayer.

Thirteen bidding cities squandered $100 million to ensure Samaranch had a safe retirement home. Tens of thousands of air-miles were clocked up by supplicants and years of tireless commitment wasted. It wasn't even a fair fight: Eggertz heard a rumour that a few days before the vote, Samaranch had told a group of IOC members, 'Morally Falun should have the Games, but Albertville must win.'

There was still the matter of Mr Wandering Hands. Neither Lars Eggertz nor the hostess he had consoled in the Grand Hotel back in 1985 had forgotten this great Olympian. He'd certainly put himself about that Saturday night. He'd approached two of the Falun hostesses and had been turned down each time. Rejection seemed to make him even more eager. He'd tried it on a third woman, coming on stronger. He caught her in the lift with the demand whispered by someone in nearly every bidding campaign: Get your clothes off and I'll vote for your city. Don't – and I won't.

'He was told clearly that that was not how things worked in Sweden,' recalls Eggertz with a flash of anger. 'There was a stormy scene with a clear decision. No lady, no vote.' But although Eggertz did report it to a senior IOC member, nothing appears to have been done. Mr Wandering Hands still represents the Olympic committee around the world. The hostess still calls her experience 'Olympic dirt'.

I pressed Eggertz for the name of the member and eventually he told me. Eggertz also told the story – and gave a strong hint to the man's identity – in a book he wrote about Falun's experiences at the hands of the IOC. It was published in Sweden in late 1987 and translated into English by the IOC themselves. By chance their executive board met in Stockholm in April 1988, ironically in the Grand Hotel where the sex-for-vote incident had occurred three years earlier.

Samaranch was furious: not about the outrageous behaviour of his fellow Olympian – but at Eggertz for disclosing it. He suggested they write to the Swedish national Olympic committee, expressing their surprise and dissatisfaction. He was calmed by Dick Pound who advised that it would be wise to take no action. The rest of the board, including Kevan Gosper, Judge Kéba Mbaye – a vice-president of the International Court of Justice – and the Prince de Merode concurred. The incident was buried – but not forgotten.

The Eggertz claims were put to leading IOC members later in 1988 by an American reporter. 'I think the gentleman who wrote this book is a bad loser,' responded Raymond Gafner, who had been at the Stockholm meeting which resolved to do nothing. 'I hear these charges usually from losers, losing bidders,' said Dick Pound, adding, 'they say these things and we bring them in and say, "Who did this? Which country was he from?" They say it's not worth it.'

Pound claims that the IOC seeks to take action when allegations are made to it, but this sits uneasily with his earlier reaction to the Falun scandals. After the Lausanne vote of October 1986 the secretary of the Swedish Olympic committee wrote to Pound about the incidents that had upset the Swedes.

Pound's confidential reply can be found in the Falun basement archive. On 4 November 1986, he wrote, 'It is always with regret that I hear that some IOC members may have made improper personal requests from candidate cities. I expect that if specific examples of this (with names) were reported to the IOC, the IOC could then be in a position to take appropriate steps. Without formal requests, however, it is very difficult to do anything. That is a judgmental matter which I leave to you.'

# CHAPTER 12

# *Move Over Reverend King, Billy's Had a New Dream*

No doubt Atlanta will scrub its face, shine its shoes and present itself as a hopping, healthy, homely city for the Olympics, welcoming the world with good old-fashioned Southern hospitality; pecan pie, whiskey and rye – not forgetting the spiritual side. Visit the Jimmy Carter centre or the tomb of Martin Luther King; re-live his dream of ending oppression – all in the city that escaped the worst of racial conflict because Atlanta, as they say, is too busy to hate.

It's a good story but life in Olympic city isn't that simple. Look down as your plane circles Hartsfield airport. From above you see a spread-out, thriving city. What you don't see are the invisible boundaries that divide the have-a-lots from the don't-have-very-much-at-alls.

Atlanta is a small, poor town of 400,000 people, surrounded by three million more in the prosperous suburbs. The city's broke, barely capable of providing a decent life for the majority of its citizens. Roads and bridges are crumbling, half the adult population is usually without work and thirty per cent of all households are likely to be on welfare. Crime rates are among America's worst. What does it have that makes it a likely Olympic city? It just happens to be the headquarters of the giant Coca-Cola corporation, the IOC's favourite partner.

Parachuted into the heart of the city is the cuckoo in the nest, the white business-inspired Olympics; gleaming new sports centres and their $1.6 billion budget slap up against the city's seventy per cent black community.

Up on Williams Street, with a view over the midtown, live the Dunwoodies – during daylight hours. They're the overwhelmingly white folks, many from the suburb of Dunwoody, who created and control the centenary Olympics. Bustling around their Atlanta 96 offices are the highly-paid suits essential to the modern Games, taking care of external relations, physical legacy, communications, human resources, creative services, hospitality and all those other imaginative job creation schemes that sop up the billion plus they've raised from selling, selling – and they'll still be selling the five rings desperately to anyone who'll buy them right up until the torch arrives in town and Samaranch steps up to the podium.

In charge, meeting and greeting, making the big speeches, insisting they will raise enough money is Billy Payne. Caught between the demands of the Lords of Lausanne, the grasping sports federation barons, the we-want-full-value-for-our-money sponsors and a city that's wondering if it's going to have to fork out money it hasn't got to stave off Olympic bankruptcy, Billy has braved two heart bypass operations and more headaches than a punch-drunk boxer.

The folksy story of how he dreamed up the city's Olympic bid is churned into every press profile. Billy, a bulky former college football player, now bespectacled real-estate attorney and conservative businessman, had just finished fund-raising for his church and itched for a new challenge. He called a few chums and they embarked on the crazy dream. It's as simple as that.

He's told the story so many times because Olympic groupies love to hear that getting the Games is about faith and idealism and not all to do with knowing how to work the system. Again, like most things in Atlanta, it's never as simple as the spin doctors would have you believe. America is full of former football jocks turned lawyer. Billy's different: he had the direct line numbers of the men who matter in Atlanta.

When the epic idea bowled Billy over in February 1987 he hollered to his wife Martha in their kitchen in the leafy suburb of Dunwoody. Martha cooed back, 'You've gotta call Peter.' Billy's best friend, Peter Candler, is a grandson of the Coca-Cola founding family. A large cheque and a phone call from Peter to Horace Sibley followed. Horace is another man who matters: he's a partner at Coca-Cola's Atlanta lawyers, the powerful can-do firm of King and Spalding. Horace joined the fledgling Olympic dream committee and brought in another K&S attorney, Charlie Battle. Charlie's clocked up a lot of air miles since. The good news was that he'd have to travel the world. Then he found out that being in charge of international relations meant having to clasp hands and bare his teeth with the Lords and their hangers-on.

These were the big guys: next Billy networked his neighbourhood, and came up with lots more plain church-going folks like him and Martha. There was Cindy Fowler, a wow at corporate hospitality and Ginger Watkins, now Billy's well-rewarded chief of staff. Ginger is well-liked by the international press but bothered one Atlanta hack who found her, well, addicted to corporate-speak. 'She said it was going to be fun working with me,' he wrote. 'This was the fourth or fifth time I'd heard this influential person say something that was either wrong or baffling or both.' They weren't all close neighbours but Billy's dreamers would soon become known as 'the Dunwoody Mafia'.

Billy dug out his list of direct line numbers and hit more buttons. His immediate need was money for his first campaign, persuading the US Olympic committee that Atlanta should be America's candidate for the Games of 1996.

One call ensured that the people of Atlanta would be told the Olympic dream was good for them. Cox Enterprises, owners of the city's only daily paper, the *Atlanta Constitution-Journal*, and a couple of TV stations put up $200,000 and the use of their corporate jet.

Over on the west coast they also wanted the nomination. San Francisco's city hall told America's Olympic committee that it would back a bid if the committee would accept gay members on its executive board and give money to gay sports organisations. That left only Minneapolis-St Paul to beat. Atlanta and the Twin Cities battled it out at a USOC summit in Washington in April 1988 – with dinner plates.

Minneapolis entertained the US Olympic committee with 'foods from around the world', courtesy of the Hilton's pantry. Atlanta rented a private house laying on fresh tuna carpaccio, seafood pate au cognac, pastrami salmon, caramelised pecans and rich deserts. The committee burped Atlanta the winners.

Now the Dunwoodies had to take on the world and the international front-runners, Athens. The Greeks had the scenery and they used it. A bunch of IOC members with knives and forks in their top pockets jetted in to enjoy dinner in the shadow of the Acropolis, played a little golf and flew on to inspect the ruins at Olympia. To recover, they cruised back to Piraeus via the Gulf of Corinth and the temples of Delphi.

Atlanta chafed when Samaranch announced in Athens,

'I don't think the other candidates should worry you. If you work hard, I can tell you that Athens will be the host country.' The Americans didn't yet understand that all the girls get this treatment. There was similar alarm in Melbourne, who never really got into the contest for 96 and Belgrade, also a bidder even as the Serbs were planning a new cemetery map of Yugoslavia.

Manchester, a real contender, was treated shamefully by the IOC. With its great character, vibrant professional and amateur sporting traditions, and the best pop music in Britain, this soccer-mad city had everything an Olympics needed. But the boutiques didn't impress the Olympic wives; it was too far from London to offer their kind of interesting alternatives to the sport and the people had an unsettling habit of electing left of centre politicians, not at all to Samaranch's liking. Bob Scott, who led the city to two successive defeats in the Olympic lottery, was the only winner to come out of Manchester's bid, picking up a knighthood. It's the British way.

Toronto was the big gorilla; on the same time zone as Atlanta it also offered the American networks easy prime time viewing. A cosmopolitan city with every kind of restaurant, a good sporting record, a great lake-front – and crippled by its own openness. 'Atlanta had a major, major advantage with a controlled press, a big advantage over Toronto,' moaned Paul Henderson, the Canadian bid leader. 'You have a monopoly newspaper there while we have four very strong, competitive dailies here.' Toronto also had another disadvantage; lively and enquiring politicians.

As Atlanta was winning the US nomination, the Canadian city elected a clutch of anti-poverty organisations, neighbourhood groups, greens and socialists to city hall. Let's just look at the impact of your plans on our city, they asked sweetly. The syndicate

of local businessmen drumming up the bid bristled:
like Atlanta, they were pushing a business-knows-best
agenda and objected to nosy politicians scrutinising
their plans.

At street level in Toronto opponents angered by
plans to divert public funds from housing and welfare
created the Bread Not Circuses coalition, demonstrated
against visiting IOC members and staged an 'anti-
Olympic' torch relay through poor neighbourhoods.
'The Olympics generate millions of dollars,' explained
an activist. 'It just fails to get to the people who
need it.'

That wouldn't happen in Atlanta. If they won there'd be
'a legacy of facilities and housing which will benefit this
community, its young athletes and citizens for decades
to come,' promised Billy Payne. Simultaneously, Billy
unveiled his slogan for the city's bid: 'Atlanta and the
Olympics: Yes. Partners With the World.' The Olympic
world began to arrive on Atlanta's doorstep and first to
make his inspection was its Leader. His priorities were
clear. Samaranch went straight to Coca-Cola's head
office, laid a wreath at Martin Luther King's tomb and
then sped off for Washington in a Coke corporate jet to
chat with President Bush.

Next came Prince Albert of Monaco and three other
members, flown in by the Cox company jet to inspect
Atlanta's plans. Entertaining them cost $100,000 and
they were made to feel more comfortable than they'd
been in Toronto. 'The organisers tried to shield visitors
from press questions,' noted a local reporter. Whatever
the gulfs that divided the community, the Dunwoodies
would show the Olympic committee a united Atlanta.

Days later children singing an African welcome song
and handing out roses greeted two dozen IOC freeloaders. Shamelessly, Atlanta played the Martin Luther

King card. Mayor Andrew Young told them Atlanta was 'the human rights capital of the world'. Czech member Vladimir Cernusak claimed 'the teachings of Martin Luther King are very much the same ideas upheld by the Olympic movement – the principles of peace and non-violence.'

The Reverend King had given his dream to the people, not sold it to Coca-Cola, but his aura was wrapped around Atlanta's campaign. Forget King the revolutionary, demanding a 'reconstruction of the entire society, a revolution of values'. That's all in the past, said the spin doctors; the man is marketing magic. Billy granted himself King's posthumous blessing, promising that the leaders of the poor, black neighbourhoods 'will be instrumental players in staging the Olympic Games'.

Whatever kind things were being said by IOC members on tour, Samaranch told his colleagues 'it is time to be harsh on the candidate cities' and proposed raising the IOC's cut of the millions the movement raked in from auctioning the rings. That was kept secret.

In the spring of 1990 another wave of Olympic committee freeloaders arrived at Hartsfield airport and were met by a motorcade of Cadillacs. Then it was off to the seaside in a fleet of corporate jets to inspect Savannah's Olympic yachting facilities. Lest they got peckish there was caviar and mint julep, and to save on washing up, they kept their silver julep cups.

After a trip on publisher Malcolm Forbes' fabulously appointed yacht, the *Highlander*, they sailed back to fireworks spelling out 'Welcome IOC'. Four years later and twenty-two months before the Olympic yachting began, Savannah witnessed another historic first; the local yacht club admitted its first black member.

The Olympic committee had some odd ways of

checking out Atlanta's proposed facilities. A gang of golfers disappeared off to Augusta with Billy Payne to test the Masters' course although golf wasn't scheduled for the Games, while Samaranch's wife went off to grace a cultural festival in a neighbouring state. France's Maurice Herzog laid his wreath at the King tomb and made a pointed comment which must have chilled Toronto. 'We hate choosing a city where there is some difference of opinion over the Games,' he warned. 'We need consensus. From what we've seen here, it's one hundred per cent.' It was so easy for Atlanta. There were no differences of opinion because there had been no consultation, no city-wide debate on whether they could afford the Games – or even wanted them.

Atlanta and its rivals all heard the same sweet nothings from the Olympic committee. According to Karl-Heinz Wehr in his secret Stasi files, Samaranch's initial choice was Athens. But they were handicapped by politics. Greece had a socialist government, and Wehr reported that Lausanne would not do Olympic business with the home of the ancient Games unless the right-wing opposition won the next election.

He also talked to Greek sports officials and back to the Berlin archives went the claim that the Greek opposition was already offering boxing supremo Anwar Chowdhry a hefty bribe to push Athens' bid. 'They are prepared to increase this sum,' said Wehr, 'if he doesn't ask too much.' If Wehr's reports of Chowdhry's gossip are true, all the bidding cities were keen to get the influential sports president on their side – and they could if they came across with his minimum fee. 'Chowdhry confided in me that they had to offer him more than $100,000.' This amount had already been offered by one bidder, he claimed.

Wehr also reported Samaranch's change of mind

after his initial enthusiasm for a centenary Olympics in Athens. The Olympic president had confided in Chowdhry who reported back to his colleagues at the Adidas sports politics group that Toronto was now favourite, followed by Atlanta. Melbourne was judged 'a distant third' followed by Athens, Belgrade and finally Manchester, 'without a chance'. His files show that as late as 1989 the Stasi were still active conspirators in the Olympic Game. Then the Wall came down and comrade Wehr's reports stopped abruptly.

Atlanta may not have been invited to contribute to Chowdhry's personal pension plan but they learned the rules of the game fast. 'Remember there are ninety votes and those people are not all of the highest integrity,' they were warned by Peter Ueberroth who had presided over the Los Angeles Games. 'Some are entirely principled people, and some are not.'

Dunwoodies attended every international sports politics convention and visited nearly every IOC member at home, exceeding the efforts of their most determined rivals who through tight lips, described them as 'talented gift givers'. This round of global partying – soon to be overshadowed in excess by the campaigns for the Games of the year 2000 – came to an end when the Olympic committee, gorged and again weighed down with presents, arrived in Tokyo in September 1990 for the vote. Belgrade went out in the first round, followed by Manchester and then Melbourne. Toronto went next, before Billy's boys saw off Athens by fifty-one votes to thirty-five.

A victory for Coke, howled the world. 'To charge that the Coca-Cola company influenced the site selection process for the 1996 Games is an insult to the integrity of the IOC,' insisted the fizzy drinks men, 'and the hundreds of Atlantans who worked on behalf of the Atlanta organising committee.' And of course to all the folks on the bid team who were friends of the company.

The losers left for their disconsolate home towns, asserting unblushingly that their failed bids had nevertheless put them on the world map and wondering privately how Atlanta had pulled it off. With cash bribes, free gold credit cards, free hospital care and college scholarships for IOC members' offspring, declared the German news magazine *Der Spiegel* a year later.

As Atlanta and the IOC fulminated at the allegations the Olympic committee's reputation dipped further. Toronto's defeated bid leader Paul Henderson disclosed that an IOC member had tried to shake them down for a free college place for one of his children and there was talk that another member had reported a theft of jewellery from his hotel room and left town in a huff when the bid committee declined to compensate him for it.

Billy Payne damned the *Spiegel*'s report as false, irresponsible and reckless. *Spiegel* declined to retract despite Samaranch's support for his freeloaders. 'I trust them, I trust them 100 per cent' he vowed – but it was a different story behind closed doors in Lausanne. Some of his executive board were embarrassed by the drip of stories about members' crookedness and pinpointed one racket. In particular several members were in the habit of visiting all bidding cities in one global swoop, usually on bucket shop tickets – and then billed each bidder for two first class return tickets from their homes.

The hand of the few reformers seemed strengthened when the angry Athens teams announced they would consult all the other losing cities to discover what rackets had been worked on them. Lausanne hurriedly summoned all the candidates for 1996 – Athens refused to attend – and heard a list of complaints. It was an empty gesture. Whatever was said, a Lausanne mouthpiece claimed the complaints were so minimal that it wasn't even necessary to report them to Samaranch, leaving him in the clear to repeat that he had never heard any bad things about his boys.

Having won the Games all Billy had to do now was to raise the one and a half billion dollars needed to stage them. It gets tougher for each city. Each time round the Lords of Lausanne help themselves to more from the money pot. Samaranch gave his home town Barcelona two-thirds of the television revenue but Atlanta has got less. Around $120 million will disappear into the IOC maw.

No problem, insisted Billy's team, this is America, we've got a great product, we'll have money to spare. Coke pitched in first with their $40 million in sponsorship – and then it went very quiet. Money was tight and when the multi-nationals did sign up, several offered a mix of cash and services when what Atlanta craved was big bundles of dollars to build venues for the sport.

Everything in the Olympic catalogue went up for sale. Any hustler with a chequebook could paste the five rings on his product. Barbie dolls and sports bras have them. So do jalapeno cheese biscuits and salad dressing. After that you'll need a toothpick – and Billy's got an Olympic holder for them. Turn on your computer, there's an Olympic screen saver. Park your car, switch on the Olympic anti-theft device. The Olympic global bazaar has turned itself into a dime store.

TV games shows *Wheel of Fortune* and *Jeopardy* are now an extension of the Olympic Games – but none of this is tawdry or cheap. Train tickets with rings are exciting and dynamic. General Motors celebrates its status as the Official Domestic Car and Truck of the 1996 Olympic Games. Spin doctors say they're thrilled their product is now Olympian – 'an important part of our corporate strategy to expand our global retail business.' They all get large blocks of Olympic tickets for their corporate clients.

Billy's hustlers have had an even tougher time selling their mascot, Izzy. A bug-eyed creature – a scrawny version of the Michelin Man – Izzy came out of a computer graphics programme and goes back frequently as the boffins attempt to make him loveable. Mascots are supposed to be cuddly and end up under kiddies' duvets: this monster is the stuff of nightmares.

Billy's nightmare is what the foreign media will make of Georgia's state flag. Above all the hype about peace, brotherhood and love will flutter a symbol of hatred and oppression – and he can't do anything about it. As de-segregation rulings were handed down by the courts in the 1950s the good ole boys showed their defiance, adding the Confederate banner of cross and stars to the state flag. It's still there, an embarrassment to Atlanta, 'the human rights capital of the world', but out in the redneck rural state it's political suicide to call for change.

'A state flag that is like flying the Confederate swastika,' says Maynard Jackson, Atlanta's first black mayor, is 'a constant reminder of negativism and hatred, castration, lynching, constant rape.' Billy's media mouthpiece didn't seem to understand what the fuss was about.'The state flag is the legal flag of Georgia,' he pointed out. 'End of story.'

The civil rights baloney of Atlanta's bidding years has steadily come unglued as they move towards the opening ceremony. As soon as they averted their eyes from the flag the homophobes of the suburbs struck. Politicians in Cobb County, directly to the north of the city and the venue for Olympic volleyball, passed an anti-gay resolution. Billy's boys switched volleyball to a more liberal location. Where were the Lords of Lausanne during these well-publicised squabbles? 'It is an American problem,' said Samaranch, evading the issue of the Cobb county gay-bashers. 'I think you would be very disappointed if people from abroad come here to teach you how to solve this problem.' What about that racist flag? It's a 'local situation' said the Guardian of All Things Moral and sped off to Paris to celebrate the centenary of his Olympic committee, assuring his guests, 'in the future, as in the past, Olympism will show its force for conciliation and its humanism in promoting peace and understanding.'

Meanwhile, Billy's search for hard cash led him into another fiasco rooted in the racism of the South. If golf was rushed into the Games, he figured, and staged at the famous Augusta Masters' course there could be another $20 million in television revenues and new marketing opportunities. Lawnmowers, water sprinklers, golf clubs, bags and balls, plaid trousers and silly hats could all be plastered with the five rings. Billy announced that Olympic golf would 'leave a Southern mark' on the Games – and he was right. Augusta had just one black member – and no women.

The Lords in Lausanne couldn't see any problem. They'd enjoyed free golf at Augusta during Atlanta's campaign. 'I didn't realise then there was any problem,' said the eminent Judge Kéba Mbaye from Senegal, 'because I didn't feel something when I was there.' Mbaye is said by the Olympic committee to have been a great fighter against apartheid, but it didn't seem to bother him in Georgia.

It took a hostile resolution from Atlanta's city council to put Billy and his friend Juan on the spot. The Olympic leader was suddenly otherwise engaged, a media massager saying on his behalf that it wasn't the IOC's place to delve into the club's membership practices. As anger grew Samaranch told an Italian sports paper that Olympic golf was now 'a slim possibility'. Billy was left wrong-footed, wailing, 'I don't know why president Samaranch made that statement. I plan to see him soon and ask.'

Billy's private bid team stayed private. His buddies who campaigned for the Olympics got nice new jobs with big pay packets to organise their Games. 'Atlanta's Olympic effort is being spearheaded by a tightknit group of friends, relatives, and business associates,' reported the local press. Decisions were taken in private. To help with the networking, Billy hired the mayor's sister and the City Council president's wife. Coincidentally, contracts were given to two council members. 'We must simply face the fact that Atlanta still has a good old boy network,' said another council member, 'and does business that way.'

Before speeding home to the safety of the suburbs the Dunwoodies can gather at exclusive watering holes like the century-old Piedmont Driving Club. Just twenty-one months before the Games opened the Piedmont admitted its first black man, but with a membership fee of more than $20,000 the club is unlikely to be swamped by applications from the neighbourhoods. Twenty-four months before the Flame was lit, the Piedmont admitted its first woman.

As the Dunwoodies leave town each night for their comfortable homes they'll pass the homeless sleeping on the pavements. There's a lot more of them now since a city-centre park, named after Coke's longest-serving boss, was cleared to be remodelled for the Olympics and equipped with benches that can't be slept on. 'Woodruff Park became a day shelter for homeless people because appropriate shelters do not exist,' commented Robert

Cramer of Atlanta's task force for the homeless. 'For far too long Atlanta has been home to sweeping attacks on homeless people.'

In case such Olympic undesirables creep back into sight, Billy's created a refuge from them. If you're an Olympic visitor with money to spend, head for the $100 million Centennial Park, billed as 'a festive gathering place for all'. Not quite all. A chain-link fence will exclude the poor and the ticketless.

Chain-link fences will be a more appropriate motif for Atlanta's Games than the five rings. Billy's Olympic committee is staging a private Games and it's tough for anybody who gets in the way, like the residents of Summerhill, the city's oldest, and maybe poorest, black neighbourhood. They're used to being trodden on. First the city drove an expressway through their community, and then took more space for the Fulton County stadium, home of the Atlanta Braves baseball team. That'll be a warm-up area for athletes during the Games.

Three-quarters of the Summerhill folks exist on welfare – which gives them time to watch construction of the latest intruder, the new Olympic stadium. They tried to fight it: early in 1991 a group of protesters travelled out to the affluent suburbs, held a candlelight vigil outside Billy's Dunwoody home and sang, 'We Shall Overcome.' They didn't. Residents of a more prosperous suburb had better luck. Billy was persuaded to move a planned tennis complex because these folks didn't want the extra traffic in their neighbourhood. Clearly there are neighbourhoods and neighbourhoods.

More protesters camped out the night before the groundbreaking ceremony at Billy's stadium. 'We are not influential or wealthy and are comfortably ignored by the powers that be,' said one of them. 'We wish to share in the benefits of the upcoming Olympic experience, not watch others benefit at our expense. Neighbourhoods are perfect examples of how low-income African–American communities are bulldozed solely for the profit, usage and fun of others.'

A handful of Summerhill's apartments and shops are getting a paint job before the Games – but not for the sake of the residents. 'It's always frightened me,' explained a relieved city official, 'that an international TV crew would be able to photograph the new stadium and, without changing its position, pan down to a slum house.' It's going to be nicer for visitors too. 'It would be a shame for people to leave their hotels and enter a community with overgrown grass lots and dilapidated houses,' said another official, welcoming the construction of a 'gateway' of Victorian-style homes on land between the stadium and the prosperous downtown.

Billy, who is paid $670,000 a year to organise the Games, has given much thought to these problems. 'We must be global in our approach and keep a close relationship to the ideals of Baron Pierre de Coubertin,' was his message to the neighbourhoods, with the after-thought, 'no-one has a right to demand participation, to share in the economic largesse.' Activist the Reverend Timothy MacDonald knows what Billy means. 'Five years ago, I had high hopes for what the Olympics could do to benefit the community,' he says. 'It's a dead issue now.'

*

As the construction and the disruption of Atlanta neared its end, the tickets went on sale. Sports fans were forced into a lottery. The entrance fee was upfront payment for the events of their choice; losers got their money back later. Many federal, state and city politicians didn't have to worry about not getting seats. In private, they were invited to jump the queue and order tickets they didn't have to pay for until later.

When news of the private deal leaked out a spokesman for Billy Payne said, 'I make no apology for this. These are our tickets.' Public watchdogs Common Cause savaged him: 'This is elitism, and it's buying favours with the very people who approve the expenditure of taxpayers money which has made the Olympics possible.'

Billy was silent for a month as the row grew. Then he offered his Olympian thoughts: critics, he said, just don't understand how private ventures operate.

# CHAPTER 13

## *The World's Richest Man Wins Olympic Gold*

'Sorry sir, this is a restricted area,' says one of the phalanx of police officers stationed near the entrance to Birmingham's five-star Hyatt hotel. 'But we are accredited press,' says one of us. 'I'm sorry sir, but they don't want you in there.' Above us flutters the Olympic flag. The International Olympic Committee is back in Britain for the first time in nearly half a century. A lot has changed since the spartan post-war Games staged in London in 1948.

A fleet of gleaming white limousines, all conspicuously marked with the five Olympic rings go to and from the Hyatt, driven by identical blonde, long-legged young women. They deposit a stream of well-dressed people, mostly men, at the hotel door. The ninety-odd members of the Olympic committee have jetted in first class for their 1991 convention.

The police relieve these very important people of their luggage, and escort them through the security controls. The shiniest and most stretched limousine arrives with an escort of police motorcycle outriders. It's the sort of car Birmingham council could put a homeless family in and still have room for the relatives. Engulfed in the back of this monster, a Rover Regency, is Olympic president Samaranch. He's here to preside over the committee's annual convention and most important of all, the choice of a host city for the Winter Games of 1998.

The Hyatt's post room is already overflowing with gifts from the five bidders. It's the last legal gift-fest: the rules will change in the battle for the Games of 2000 but for now the committee members get Vennini glass, Gucci handbags, personal computers, watercolours, limited edition prints, silk scarves, ties, books and stetsons.

'There was so much stuff coming into the post room that the girls there spent the entire week simply delivering gifts to the IOC members' rooms. It was incredible,' says Shirley Hunt, one of a clutch of students glad of the temporary work. 'The gifts started to come in around mid-day and from then on the post room was just heaving with bags and gift-wrapped boxes of all descriptions. I know that Princess Anne returned all her gifts but I think she was the only one.'

The members also like their comforts. The Hyatt's 300-plus rooms were block-booked exclusively by the Olympic committee for a full week in June: the bill is £277,512. In the penthouse suite at £595 per night is president Samaranch. He can entertain private guests around the twelve-seater dining table, relax in one of the many deep settees by the fireplace in the lounge, luxuriate in the jets of the jacuzzi built into the huge sunken bath tub, tap out a tune on the keys of the baby grand piano or simply take a nap in the four-poster bed.

'The IOC arranged all the room allocations,' says Catriona McFadden, the Hyatt's spokeswoman. 'They're very protocol conscious . . . They took a blueprint of all the rooms, their sizes and did the allocating. They then visited us about once a month to liaise and see that all was well.

'Lausanne faxed us with all the room allocations.

They changed pretty regularly. At one stage they were faxing us so often that we didn't even bother to enter them into the computer! I've never seen anything quite like it and I doubt I will again. The nearest I've come to it is a Tory Party conference – but that didn't really match anything like this. These people act more like heads of state.'

Birmingham city council picked up the bulk of the tab – and considered itself fortunate. They'd failed in recent years to win the Games but won the sop of hosting the Olympic convention. The media cheer-leaders reckon this will benefit future British bids. Birmingham was lucky: they had to battle with Moscow, Belgrade, Nairobi, Riyadh, Monte Carlo and Budapest for the privilege of entertaining the Olympians.

As with the contest for the Games themselves there were separate rounds of voting with the bottom city dropping out until the winner had an overall majority. On the last round it was Budapest versus Birmingham. One of Budapest's supporters, the committee member from Kuwait, decided to pop out for a quick smoke. In his absence Birmingham won the nomination – with a majority of one.

In the Hyatt foyer the Olympic deal-makers are at work. Committee members, sponsors, marketing men, national Olympic committee chairmen, spivs and inter-national federation presidents meet and greet, sur-rounded by potted palms, trees in oversized terracotta plant pots, floodlights and fountains. A string ensemble appears. They play 'Take Good Care of Yourself'. There should be no worries on that score.

The hangers-on press the flesh in the lobby, circling the pool like piranhas, waiting to nibble at any little morsel. Behind the neo-classic columns in the main reception area and at corner tables in the restaurants are huddled groups of marketing men and agents with ideas to sell and business to do. The hotel staff move discreetly around constantly spraying and polishing the glass-and-marble-effect table tops.

In one corner Kuwaiti television are filming the young Sheikh Ahmad. Gold thread runs through his robes and he carries a gold-topped walking stick. His father, murdered by the Iraqis in the invasion barely a year earlier, had been a member of the Olympic committee. The young Sheikh has taken his father's place as head of Kuwait's national Olympic committee and expects to succeed his father on the IOC. Everything he does is filmed. The Sheikh stands up. The camera starts running. The Sheikh sits down. The camera, still running, captures his every movement. The Sheikh orders tea. The camera never seems to stop.

In the bedrooms at the Hyatt are complimentary flowers, wine and fruit. Another welcoming gesture is boxes of chocolates from the local manufacturers, Cadbury's. Suddenly there's turmoil along the corridors. The chocolates are snatched from the guests' hands! Mars have paid tens of millions of dollars to be the official Olympic world-wide snack food sponsors and they must not be upset by a rival. 'A special welcome to the IOC Marketing Department,' says a specially printed note in the Hotel's Brasserie menu. A special welcome indeed.

Primo Nebiolo, supremo of world track and field and desperate to join the Olympic committee, descends the hotel stairs. He moves around the lobby as if on castors. He embraces Charles Mukora, Coca-Cola's man in Kenya and now that country's IOC member. Mukora is also on Nebiolo's federation council. One pace behind the president is one of his press handlers. There is much exaggerated hugging and kissing.

Wives and children have been brought along too. For them there's a week-long 'Social Programme', including a connoisseurs' trip around the Worcester Royal porcelain works, a visit to Shakespeare's birthplace at Stratford-upon-Avon and an antiques tour of Shropshire. These outings come on top of a special performance of Swan Lake, a concert by Birmingham Symphony Orchestra – and the banquets. Samaranch will host one, Her Majesty the Queen another.

Then there's the dinner thrown by the British Olympic Association. This glittering occasion was hosted by BOA president the Princess Royal, Princess Anne, at Warwick Castle, one of the finest medieval castles in England. Three hundred guests attended to a champagne reception in the Great Hall; followed, in a marquee erected in the Castle grounds, by a feast of iced watercress soup, whole salmon trout and strawberries with brandy snaps and cream.

The guests of honour that night were Samaranch and his wife. Mrs Samaranch stepped gracefully from the rear of their chauffeured limousine and in a reflex action smiled and waved her hand to the crowd – even though there wasn't one.

An armoured knight on horseback and a marching pipe band greeted the rest of the committee members. A lone piper played from the floodlit battlements as they left for home three hours later. When thanked for his hospitality the following day, a senior BOA official replied, 'You're welcome. We like to keep it simple.'

Before they get down to their secret discussions, the committee demands a grand opening ceremony and insists it is hosted by the local head of state. So at 3 o'clock on Wednesday 12 June 1991, in the new £160 million International Convention Centre, accompanied by a fanfare from the trumpeters of the Life Guards, President and Mrs Samaranch followed the Queen and the Duke of Edinburgh into the royal box. Behind them were seated the IOC members.

Also in the royal box – and breaking all the protocol regulations of the IOC – was Primo Nebiolo, there at the personal request of Samaranch. Some IOC members were put out by the Italian's presence but, as they later conceded, 'How can anyone tell the IOC President who he may or may not have in the royal box at the opening of his own IOC session?'

After the obligatory references to the foresight of Baron Pierre de Coubertin Samaranch told his audience that 'Olympic sport must not become mere show business.' The way to prevent this, he suggested, would be to 'convince the mass media to help us give more importance to the ethical values of sport'. He took a quick diversion through the ethical problems of doping and then spent rather more time reporting on the progress of his Olympic museum.

The Queen then told Samaranch, 'The eyes of the world will be on the results of your deliberations. I am confident that the movement will continue to thrive under the direction of those who, like you, serve its cause with such devotion.' And with that the Queen declared the 97th session of the International Olympic Committee open.

Madame Verdier controls everything. A trim woman with a pale complexion framed by dark wavy hair, who dresses in dark suits and sensible shoes, she protects her Olympic charges like a Dobermann. She is the official IOC filter. Under Madame Verdier's regime the day's agenda is always the same. At exactly 8.45 in the morning she escorts photographers and television crews into the hall for a photo opportunity. Here they may take pictures of the committee as it prepares to discuss the great issues of the day.

On the platform sit some of Samaranch's inner cabinet. There's Dick Pound and Mickey Kim, Australia's Kevan Gosper and China's Zhenliang He. This 'opportunity' lasts exactly fifteen minutes. Then Madame Verdier, who has been hovering anxiously, escorts the photographers and cameramen out and shuts the doors firmly behind them. The world must not be allowed to join in the Olympic debate.

The media centre is alive with the logos and the products of the paymasters. It's awash with free Cokes and Mars bars, electronic typewriters from Brother and fax machines by Ricoh. Each journalist eagerly accepts a free briefcase from Adidas; it's part of the bonding process. The press become part of the Olympic family – part of the Olympic team.

At the end of the morning session there's a press conference, chaired by Madame Verdier, flanked by two giant Olympic flags. The journalists listen to her brief account of the proceedings. If pressed on any awkward point she retreats behind 'That was not discussed at length' or 'I don't believe that was on the agenda.'

A handful of more robust journalists complain. They've been kept out of the Hyatt. They can't get in to talk to individual members to find out what really went on inside the closed session. But Madame Verdier sees the problem differently. Two Japanese journalists had the temerity to approach one senior member at the end of a session before he could escape to the sanctuary of the Hyatt. As a result, the security outside the meeting hall has been extended to prevent a repetition.

After two days of haggling, Madame Verdier announces a compromise. We will be granted a special pass system. But only forty will be available for the five-hundred-strong media squad. The next day a notice from Madame

Verdier appears in the media centre: 'Please do not abuse this system or the privilege will be withdrawn.'

Only on the final day does Samaranch himself appear to address the world's media. He is asked about Catalonia and Gibraltar, both pushing for independent recognition by the Olympic committee. Samaranch says he has just set up a commission to look at the question, headed by IOC vice-president Kéba Mbaye. 'I will ask him to comment on this,' says Samaranch.

Mbaye looks perplexed. He replies, 'I can't tell you anything – I just took up the job this morning.' The problem of a recent doping scandal is raised. Will Samaranch set up an inquiry? 'No,' says the president. 'This is a matter for the International Amateur Athletic Federation.' So much for that.

Getting specifics is difficult, generalities abound. But few of the journalists press him hard. After forty-five minutes Samaranch declares the press conference over. As he makes his departure a sizeable section of the press stand and applaud him. Some of those remaining in their seats frown. Journalists applauding the subject of their story? It's simply not done – not in the free world.


The hacks have their own way of serving the Olympic eminences. Others didn't have any choice. 'They all thought they were important. They were all clearly used to being waited on hand and foot,' said one of the hotel waitresses later. 'But they weren't polite. A couple of them were for ever clicking their fingers in the air, which is something I hate. I'm not a dog.'

The whole Olympic committee had become accustomed to being waited on hand and foot. They'd just completed yet another circuit of attentive and deferential bidding cities, all hoping for the Winter Games of 1998. This time the bidders were Aosta in Italy, Jaca in the Spanish Pyrenees and Östersund, keeping alive Sweden's hopes. But the front-runners were always Salt Lake City, which had as good as built all the facilities, and Nagano, three hours' journey by train from Tokyo in the Japan Alps – which hadn't built anything. You would never have guessed that their bid was little more than a set of plans still on the drawing board if you'd seen the show they put on.

The Nagano team booked five hundred hotel rooms in Birmingham and filled them with lobbyists. Some ran their hospitality suite, others put on daily demonstrations in the square outside the convention centre, lined up in martial formations, waving umbrellas robotically to taped music.

Everybody who mattered from Nagano and indeed Japan seemed to be in town – with one exception. The man behind the bid, the man likely to make the biggest profit if they won, the man who already had the biggest personal fortune in the world, stayed home.

Three years earlier *Forbes* magazine estimated that Yoshiaki Tsutsumi was worth around $19 billion. But nobody knew for sure. His holdings in land, railways, bus companies, hotels golf and ski resorts were concealed behind a labyrinth of companies and many Japanese commentators guessed he could be worth twice as much.

Tsutsumi owned seventy per cent of Japan's huge ski resort industry and was always looking to expand, especially if the Japanese taxpayer could be made to share the cost. His family's seamless ties to successive governments helped him stay ahead of his rivals, and when he put his weight behind the town of Nagano, it was guaranteed to emerge as a leading contender for the Olympics.

Three rival candidates for Japan's Olympic bid for 1998 were swiftly dispatched and then it was down to the Japanese Olympic committee to support Nagano's bid. Who should emerge as its new president? None other than Mr Tsutsumi. But as complaints from environmentalists about his plans for the region grew he resigned. Sceptics said he preferred to work in the shadows and had never wanted the position in the first place.

Japan's poor showing in the Seoul Games helped. Their four golds – against neighbouring Korea's twelve – instilled some popular jingoism into the bid. The political establishment joined in and Tsutsumi's bid acquired endorsements from past and present prime ministers. The politicians promised to invest $671 million from public funds – against only $218 million from business – in facilities and roads and infrastructure improvements. There would also be a 'supreme class' hotel for the IOC.

Samaranch must have been tickled to be approached by the richest man in the world and the business and political leaders of the most powerful economy. And there was another important connection that few others noticed. The Nagano bid was backed by Dentsu, the advertising giants who owned forty-nine per cent of the Horst Dassler-created International Sport and Leisure company, holder of the Olympic marketing contract.

Samaranch took his executive board to Tokyo in the autumn of 1990. There he acquired yet another honorary degree, Japan's highest civilian award from the government and a private audience with Emperor Akihito. The real business was done at Tsutsumi's New Takanawa Prince Hotel, on land once part of a royal estate. Slipping away from the lavish reception Samaranch went with Tsutsumi, an interpreter and a grand tea-master to a private ceremony in a secluded lodge. Afterwards the rumour in Tokyo was that the Olympic president had offered the world's richest man a seat on the IOC and that Tsutsumi would eventually succeed him.

The following year the Olympic committee members made their earnest inspection visits. They stayed in Tsutsumi hotels and were welcomed in Nagano by thousands of locals mobilised by schools and employers, and were accompanied by 'hostesses' throughout their trips. The Olympians relaxed in hot springs, were entertained by geishas, and, according to Japanese reporters, were given valuable paintings worth many millions of yen. This is one of Japan's traditional routes for laundering money from business to politicians.

Samaranch went back to Japan in May 1991 – a month before the vote in Birmingham. He was the centre of attraction at a reception in one of Tsutsumi's biggest Tokyo hotels where he gave his host the gold Olympic Order 'for exceptional service to the Olympic movement'.

The next day together with the governor of Nagano province and the city's mayor, they boarded a specially chartered former imperial train for Nagano. The trip reputedly cost the bid city nearly £1 million. According to a Japanese investigative journalist who tracks Tsutsumi's activities, in the privacy of the rail excursion Samaranch asked the billionaire to help out with the vast deficit looming on the Olympic museum in Lausanne. How about $13 million? Tsutsumi agreed, came across with $10 million from his own business empire and helped encourage another seventeen Japanese companies to cough up $1 million each. On a previous visit Samaranch had asked Japanese prime minister Toshiki Kaifu to give special tax breaks to companies which contributed to the museum. Allegedly, Samaranch then asked Tsutsumi to invest in resort developments in Barcelona.

Arriving in Nagano, Samaranch was put through the

rigours of a tough press conference. The first question was 'Would you like to make a statement?', followed by 'What was your impression of Nagano?' On auto-pilot, he told the locals, 'Maybe never in my life have I been given such a warm welcome.' Similar warmth must have enveloped one member of the Olympic committee's inspection team who turned up, flew over the as yet vacant sites in a helicopter and announced, 'The hosts are very well prepared.'

Japanese opponents of the bid hadn't much hope against the combined forces of Samaranch, Tsutsumi's billions, the entire Japanese business and political establishment and Dentsu. But they tried. Between Samaranch's two visits an anti-Olympics campaigner, Mrs Noriko Ezawa stood against the incumbent mayor in Nagano's council elections. He romped home with 103,000 votes but she discovered she was not alone in her protest; 15,000 local people backed her.

'These games are nothing more than an event to help corporations make big money,' said Mrs Ezawa, pointing at Tsutsumi's empire, Dentsu and the Japanese state television network NHK. She was supported by Japan's Fathers of the Catholic Council of Justice and Peace who claimed that opponents had received death threats, local welfare budgets would be cut to provide the cost of new facilities, and that illegal women immigrants from poor Asian countries would be exploited in menial jobs and in the night clubs.

They were joined by environmental groups, claiming the Olympic developments were bringing a 'massive rape of mountains, forests and rivers and the displacement of local farmers'. The Nagano area already had one hundred and twenty ski runs and fifty-eight golf courses and Tsutsumi's opponents claimed the delicate Alpine environment couldn't take any more.

The protesters – who revealed that construction work at one downhill ski run had exposed soil with high asbestos content – achieved an early success. Tsutsumi planned new ski runs in a National Park, home to rare Asiatic black bears and the last forty pairs of golden eagles in Japan. When the protesters won the support of the Japanese branch of the World Wide Fund for Nature, he backed off. But for Tsutsumi, there were compensations. The new bullet train from Tokyo would stop at the door of one of his new resort hotels. Whatever happened at the Birmingham vote, the billionaire was already a winner.

'I said to Samaranch on the day before the vote in Birmingham,' one long-serving IOC member revealed privately, 'that the best technical bid is clearly Salt Lake City. They have everything in place. I asked him can you still give it to America after Atlanta? Do you vote on ability to deliver the Games or politically on this? He said gruffly, "We can't give it to the Americans again." Then he changed the subject.'

The Utah state capital had built the Salt Palace, a vast convention and press centre; a 50,000 seat Olympic stadium; an Olympic village for 4,000 athletes and all the ski venues. They had 50,000 hotel rooms ready. The skating and ice hockey sites were under construction and due for completion in less than six months. The bid team were keen to show it all off to the Olympic committee. 'Our goal is to bring 50 to 60 IOC members here to visit. But that is going to cost over a million dollars,' ran a fund-raising ad in a local paper.

'Got a calculator handy?' asked Utah's *Park Record*. 'Assuming the full 60 members come, and the figure doesn't surpass a million bucks, the cost per IOC member is $16,666. Let's knock off $1,666, for first class air fare. That leaves us with a nice round sum of $15,000. Subtract another 100 bucks for Salt Lake City '98 sweatshirts, caps and gym bags, and $700 for a week of first class accommodation and that still leaves $14,200 to spend. Which raises two questions: What do IOC members eat? And how do I join the IOC?'

Back in Birmingham the five rivals set out their stalls in neighbouring suites in the Hyatt. Salt Lake City brought in pine trees and singing cowboys. Östersund operated out of what looked like a Swedish pine kitchen, offering glasses of vodka, loganberry juice and pastries stuffed with smoked reindeer meat to passing Olympians.

'We visited eighty-seven IOC member in their own countries and brought seventy-two to visit Östersund,' said their Mr Borg. 'Too many gifts are now being given. We give each IOC member a gift on our personal visits, a gift when they visit our city, a gift when they visit our hospitality suite and a gift every day in the hotel. We give little things like glass and Swedish handicrafts. The girls in the hotel who have to deliver the gifts were complaining yesterday. Some of the gifts are just too big.' Not to worry. Extra suitcases are on order for the Olympians to carry away their harvest.

Nagano's suite is decked out as a Japanese tea room. Meeting and greeting is mayor Tasuku Tsukada. He listens impassively as the young translator interprets a question about their gift giving. He nods wearily, and with a resigned look disappears behind a shelf in the hospitality suite. When he reappears, he is clutching a box of beautifully wrapped sweets. The question has been interpreted as only a bidding city knows how.

There's one question he doesn't answer. Hired to advise their bid is Goran Takac, son of Samaranch's sports advisor Artur Takac. Mayor Tsukada declines to reveal Goran's bill. He may be aware of a little spat inside the Olympic family. The usually oleaginous *Sport*

*Intern* newsletter has diverted in its latest issue from praising Samaranch to a sharp attack on the Takac family. 'Takac junior has for years been bleeding the candidates for the Winter Games,' writes publisher Karl-Heinz Huba. Goran seems unworried, on semi-permanent posting in the Hyatt foyer, looking out for clients and new business. He didn't have the same problems as the media in getting access. Huba is in another part of the hotel, collecting stories that will fit his newsletter's blend of sanitised, Olympic family reporting.

As dusk falls mayor Tsukada leaves each night for the leafy suburb of Moor Green, home of Nagano's secret hospitality offensive. For £500 a night they've rented Highbury House, a sumptuous mansion bequeathed to the city council by a former millionaire politician. 'When I got up there I was amazed,' says student turned waitress Shirley Hunt, who also worked at Highbury that week. 'The Japanese had flown in their own chefs, serving girls, waiters, everything. The chefs had done an incredible job, salmon and prawns and all kinds of seafood set out in a beautiful ice display. It was wheeled round to each of the guests who made their choice and then watched it fried in batter in front of them. It was a spectacular show.

'There was also a full bar with wine, spirits and saki. The spirits were served by eye. We were told not to bother to use measures. Most of the guests were pretty merry by the end of the evening. A couple were obviously well over the top and kept demanding more drink. It was really embarrassing.'

Salt Lake City also hired a hospitality house but the vote had been as good as decided before their arrival in England. For all the millions of dollars they'd spent building facilities, they nearly went out on the first round. With Aosta they scored the lowest equal vote of just fifteen out of the eighty-eight votes and had to overcome the Italian city in a run-off before the voting proper could continue. Out next went Jaca, which surprised nobody, and then it was the Swedes versus the two big boys. That didn't last long and as expected the Americans faced the Japanese in the final round. Tsutsumi's investment paid off with forty-six votes for Nagano, four more than Salt Lake City.

Yet again the Swedes went home with nothing, the Americans were furious and Samaranch embarrassed. It was obvious that many of his Latin members had given sympathy votes to the no-hopers Aosta and Jaca in the first round, rather than make an effort to choose between the better contestants. One less vote and Salt Lake City, the best equipped bid, would have been eliminated and the IOC seen as foolish and irresponsible.

There was one other round of voting in Birmingham and it caused as much controversy as the Winter Games ballot. Samaranch wanted Mario Vazquez Raña, boss of the impotent Association of National Olympic Committees admitted to the IOC. The problem was that his members didn't. They had resisted in 1984 when Samaranch tried to slip Raña – and track and field boss Primo Nebiolo – into the committee as *ex-officio* members. Now there was a vacancy for a new member from Mexico.

Samaranch proposed four new members; Germany's Thomas Bach, Switzerland's Denis Oswald, the Belgian Jacques Rogge – and Raña. Raña's opponents were ready and waiting. 'The idea was to get enough people to push Samaranch into a secret ballot,' disclosed one IOC member who opposed Raña but was only prepared to talk about him anonymously. 'Some of the most senior people in the IOC thought there should be a secret vote but the agreement of twenty-five members would be needed. I was shown a list of supporters with around twenty-five names on it.

'I said I was not prepared to ask for a secret ballot but I was prepared to open the batting and to say "Mr President, will you assure us that your nominees have the support of the present IOC members in that country?"'

To show there was nothing personal against Raña, the question was put when the first nominee, Thomas Bach, was proposed.

'Samaranch didn't answer me, he just went on with the business and called out "Vazquez Raña". I am convinced that, having been put down once by him, he thought that I wouldn't ask the question again. So I pressed my buzzer once more, and if it hadn't been for Carrard, the director general of the IOC, drawing his attention to the light on my desk I think Samaranch would have ignored me. I said "Mr President, I have to repeat the question." Whereupon he became very angry and said in outraged tones "Is anybody against?"

'Obviously I put my hand up because I was against him going ahead. All six women put up their hands and four of the men – Philipp Von Schoeller, Prince Albert of Monaco, Pedro Vazquez and Tay Wilson.'

At that point in the plan, Anita DeFrantz, one of the two American IOC members, should have asked Samaranch for a secret ballot. But the American didn't get up. 'I was caught by surprise by the fact that Samaranch called for the vote so quickly,' DeFrantz said afterwards. 'He did it before there was a chance to call for the secret ballot.

'I think a secret ballot would have been desirable; then people could have voted how they wanted without worrying. But when you take the oath on becoming an IOC member you swear to uphold the principle that IOC decisions are made without appeal. So now

Raña's elected there is a problem with talking about any opposition there might have been.'

'He handled that so cleverly, he was such a brilliant technician,' says another IOC member. 'Thirteen people voted for him, ten voted against him and there were sixty abstentions. Can you imagine getting into a London club with sixty abstentions? A number of the members came to me afterwards and said "We support what you did but we were in a rather difficult position."'

Then it was time to go home – and one member couldn't resist a little racketeering at the expense of his hosts. All members who wanted them had been given free air tickets from Birmingham to London. The organiser of the week's activities was Denis Howell, then a Birmingham Labour MP and former leader of the city's bid for the Summer Games of 1992. 'The night before everyone was leaving,' recalls Howell, 'someone came to me and said that one particular IOC member had a lot of luggage and wanted a car to go to London airport. Our transport man pointed out that given the traffic in London and Birmingham it would be much better to take the Heathrow shuttle from Birmingham Airport.

'I spoke to our people and asked if we had any cars, we were totally stretched that departure day. Finally we got two cars. It had been put to me that this IOC member was getting on a bit and didn't want the bother of flying from Birmingham.

'We were absolutely astonished to be told by the drivers afterwards that as soon as the cars left the Hyatt Hotel this member instructed them to go to Birmingham Airport. The drivers said, "But we thought you were going to Heathrow." "Yes," came the reply, "but I want to go and cash in these tickets." So they went out there to cash in the London to Birmingham section and then drove down to London!'

The Olympic committee members bade fond farewells as they left the Hyatt. 'See you in Albertville next year – and then we're off to Barcelona' was the merry cry. And they did – except for one member who before the year's end had left the ranks of the guardians a great deal sooner than ever he imagined.

Lawyer Robert Helmick seemed poised to bid for the leadership of the IOC whenever Samaranch decided to quit. He was head of America's Olympic movement, had presided over the International Swimming Federation and was on the IOC's executive board. He went home from Birmingham looking forward to more advancement.

Then he got a call from *USA Today*. The reporters didn't want to know about his ambitions; they wanted to talk about his Olympic business interests. They'd obtained a confidential dossier of the consultancy fees Helmick had received from companies wanting to do business with the Olympic movement.

It seemed his law firm had been receiving fees from Ted Turner's television companies, always keen to get a share of broadcasting the Games. Then there were consultancy fees from golf and bowling associations hoping to get into the Olympics. Helmick was on the IOC's programme commission, advising the committee on which new sports should be allowed into the Games. On top of that were fees from sports marketing companies. During the first week of September 1991 the newspaper alleged they totalled $127,000.

The disclosures came on the eve of an American Olympic committee meeting. 'Any inference or allegation of an appearance of impropriety is unwarranted,' insisted Helmick, but one of his vice-presidents announced, 'We intend to have a bare-knuckles discussion with Bob.' After the meeting Helmick seemed less sure of his position. 'I want to make it clear that I apologise for any actions that I have taken, or that I have failed to take, which could have given an appearance of conflict,' he said.

A few days later deals worth another $150,000 more were disclosed, and by the middle of September there was another statement from the Des Moines lawyer. 'With deep regret I am resigning my position as president of the US Olympic committee, effective immediately.' Could he, would he remain on the IOC? They set up an inquiry, led by Judge Mbaye. On 3 December 1991, having checked the temperature at an IOC executive board meeting in Lausanne, Helmick decided that his Olympic Game was finally up.

At one in the morning he pushed a resignation note under Samaranch's door. 'I believe it is the decent thing to do,' wrote Helmick. 'I want to strongly reassert my belief that I have done nothing ever of harm to the Olympic movement . . . I regret the situation that has arisen as a result of how my actions have been interpreted by others.'

The IOC's inquiry report has never been disclosed. Whatever they found out – if anything – or what their recommendations were, remains buried. It was all smoothed over quickly; fellow executive board member Kevan Gosper said that Helmick's resignation was 'an elegant solution'. Helmick still insists there is no evidence (indeed, nobody has ever suggested that he used his position to influence or attempt to influence the USOC or the IOC) that his firm's consultancy deals influenced his decisions in the Olympic movement.

# CHAPTER 14

# *An Old Blueshirt Comes Home*

Albertville wasn't so much an Olympic Games, more a series of individual winter sports championships scattered across thirteen locations in the Savoy region. It lacked the closeness and warmth of a compact venue, with athletes from different disciplines unable to congregate and create any real Olympic buzz. The Swedes in long forgotten Falun muttered 'we told you so.' They'd been told that one reason for their defeat by Albertville was the eighty-minute helicopter flight to the Alpine skiing events further north in the mountains. 'What eventually led most people not to vote for Falun was the matter of the distance between the sites,' argued Dick Pound after the votes that gave the Games to Barcelona and Albertville. It didn't make sense in Sweden.

Holding the Games in Savoy didn't make much sense either to the French taxpayer. They went over budget and central and regional government picked up the excess of $60 million. This didn't stop Samaranch announcing 'We are all winners, but above all, Savoy.'

So began a year of the Olympic movement appearing to help itself to taxpayers' money in France and Spain and squandering Olympic revenues to boost the president's image. It was all changing too fast for the IOC's most senior member, the Grand-Duc Jean de Luxembourg. 'This huge, rather sophisticated, costly, sponsor and media-supported machine is in constant danger of leaving the rails,' he warned at the IOC convention. 'Are we not running the risk of one day seeing Olympism obscured by the concern for material gain?'

Samaranch had other worries. He'd got Mario Vazquez Raña onto the committee in Birmingham. Now track and field boss Primo Nebiolo was agitating even more to join them. But there was no vacancy for a new Italian member. And he couldn't risk a repeat of the embarrassment over Raña's election, when the majority of the IOC membership had abstained. Privately members were warned that if a way wasn't found to admit Nebiolo, he would do his best to damage the committee. He was demanding a bigger share of Olympic revenues for the summer sports federations and threatening to make his athletics world championships a bigger event than the Games.

One executive board member said off the record in Birmingham, 'Our President will not do the duel at dawn. Samaranch is afraid that Nebiolo will walk away from the Olympics. Personally I think we should challenge him.'

Instead Samaranch arm-twisted his membership into giving him the right to appoint two members to the Olympic committee solely on 'their ability or appointments they hold'. His members weren't prepared to duel with him either and a month later, Nebiolo joined the committee. To balance the appointment the leader of the winter sports federations, Olav Poulsen from Norway, was also admitted. He left two years later – Nebiolo stays and plots.

Having manipulated the Olympics to Spain, Samaranch wasn't passing up any chances to demonstrate the power and wealth of his organisation back home. It wasn't his money so it could be thrown at anything that might impress his countrymen. Seville, in southern Spain, had chosen 1992 to stage a grand Exposition and Samaranch wanted his Olympic movement lavishly promoted. Never mind the money being poured into the Games in Barcelona at the other end of the country, all Spaniards must see how well he'd done. The Olympic committee must have its own glass and marble pavilion at the Expo, even if it had to be torn down seven months later.

He persuaded his colleagues it would be $2 million well spent. Two years later the real costs began to emerge. In June 1990 the executive board learned the bill would now be $5 million. Three months later the construction costs had soared to $10 million. Fitting it out would cost $2 million and the operating budget for just seven months another $2 million – all to promote the old man in Spain. At the end of 1990 Samaranch backed down and agreed that the pavilion's design would be simplified: the total cost must not exceed $5 million.

Then he went on the road to promote himself internationally. Part of the package was a new biography from David Miller, chief sports writer of the London *Times*. It was a close collaboration and Miller did not examine Samaranch's political history in any detail, preferring the accounts of Mrs Samaranch and the old man's closest Barcelona associates. There were no pictures of Samaranch in his fascist uniform; only the intriguing statement that 'He has, by the catholicity of his public and private behaviour, been able to rise above any criticism of his involvement in administration during Franco's time.'

This was news to many Catalans who remembered the circumstances in which Samaranch left his home city after the death of Franco in 1975. On their national day,

23 April 1977, when freedom of speech had been re-established, an estimated 100,000 demonstrators assembled outside the Catalan regional council building in Barcelona. Behind locked doors was the man Franco had appointed to run his rubber-stamp regional government. When Samaranch declined to confront them, they shouted abuse which, for more delicate readers, can only be translated as 'Samaranch, Get Out!' This was another memory the Olympic leader had neglected to tell his biographer about.

By the time Samaranch arrived in London for the official launch of Miller's *Olympic Revolution*, the first edition of *The Lords of the Rings*, which took a markedly different view of the Olympic president from Miller's, had already been published around the world. What should have been a self-indulgent self-promotion was upset by jeers from the British press. '*Olympic Revolution*,' said the *Daily Telegraph*, 'paints an altogether more flattering picture of a man many believe has sold his organisation's birthright.'

Miller's colleagues at the *Times* were even less flattering about Samaranch. 'He seems to be a man with a charisma bypass,' wrote Simon Barnes who also derided the claim that Samaranch had no choice but to co-operate with Franco. Samaranch went on breakfast television and faced corruption allegations about his committee. 'I trust all the IOC members and they are doing a very good job for sport and for the Olympic movement,' he insisted.

That wasn't the view of *Time* magazine. Samaranch might have supposed that one of his main sponsors – the *Time/Sports Illustrated* group pay $40 million a time to produce the official programme for the Games – would give him an easy ride. He was wrong. *Time* devastated him. On the eve of the Games senior correspondent Paul Witteman observed in a special Olympic supplement that Samaranch's IOC was a 'well-endowed empire, but one that is shamed by scandal'. Then came, 'For decades detailed reports have surfaced about attempts by IOC officials to solicit bribes from city officials mounting bids for the Games.' If that wasn't bad enough, Witteman didn't seem to think that the Olympic president had any interest in reform. 'Unfortunately, Samaranch seems to prefer the comfortable status quo to the house-cleaning necessary to restore the movement's soundness and integrity. As a result, the Games run the dangerous risk of becoming merely another event cluttering the athletic calendar.'

Lausanne was stunned, but there was little they could do. They knew the allegations were true and anyway, it wouldn't look good using Switzerland's criminal libel laws against one of their bigger sponsors. It fell to the Munich-based sports newsletter *Sport Intern*, widely seen as a mouthpiece for Samaranch, to reassure the Olympic family. 'The IOC hopes that correct research will in future prevent such unjustified abuse,' wrote Karl-Heinz Huba, weakly. Richard Atkinson, associate general manager for *Time* in Europe was more candid, 'There's been a bit of a bust-up,' he admitted, 'but we aren't going to have our arms twisted. I'm glad we had the balls to do it.'

I went to Barcelona in the week before the Games with Vyv Simson, co-author of the first *Lords of the Rings*. Denied press accreditation, we lingered outside the IOC's base, the opulently refurbished Hotel Princesa Sofia. To one side were parked one hundred limousines and their chauffeurs, awaiting a call from Olympic committee members or their hangers-on. Smack in front of the main door was a news kiosk. The proprietor had made his own decision about the likely reading tastes of the members.

The most prominent display included *Climax, Busty,*

*Lesbian Love, Schoolgirls, Sweet Little Sixteen, Hard Core, Anal Sex* and for the more jaded palates – *New Cunts*. What he did not stock, and we know because we asked him, was *Time*'s Olympic Supplement. He may have guessed there was no market at the Princesa Sofia for hard truths.

\*

'By the time you arrive, all the essential props of an Olympic spectacle will be in place and nobody will bother even to ask whether the spectacle itself is necessary,' wrote Catalan novelist Manuel Vazquez Montalbán on the eve of the Games. 'But what comes after? Debts and a set of buildings of dubious usefulness.'

Montalbán, a life-long opponent of Franco, offered visitors to the Olympics his own guided tour of the city he loved but had seen almost destroyed by Generalissimo Franco and his supporters, few more prominent than Samaranch. The novelist was proud of Barcelona's unique reputation: the rebellious citizens had frequently risen up against oppression, held the world record for barricade construction and fondly renamed their city 'La Rosa de Foc' – 'The Rose of Fire' – because the flames of rebellion were constantly rekindled.

He pointed foreigners to the central police station on the Via Laietana where Franco's opponents were tortured by the secret police, suffering 'years of waiting and death sentences dragged out over nights of terror and sadism,' and the Camp de la Bota and the Fossar de la Pedrera where the corpses were dumped.

Most of the foreign media, reporting happy laughing Catalans revelling in Olympic glory, hadn't a clue about the tensions behind the marketing hype. Their dispatches showed little awareness of the Taboo. There are two topics the Spanish press are wary of: the private life of King Juan Carlos, and the compromises that had to be made to restore democracy after Franco's death in 1975. The price of reform had been no retribution against the fascist functionaries, the torturers, the executioners and wearers of the Blueshirt. They can all be seen today, walking the streets of Barcelona.

One beneficiary of this collective amnesia was Olympic president Samaranch, behaving as if he was again the powerful politician of yesteryear. 'If you attack Samaranch, you are attacking the transition and thus the modern political system in Spain, so it's taboo,' an historian at the city's autonomous university told me. Then he added an insight into Samaranch's beleaguered personality. 'In Spain, because he's a Catalan – he's an enemy. But because he was a keen collaborator, Samaranch is seen in Catalonia as a traitor.'

At one Olympic press conference a Catalan journalist wound Samaranch up, asking him why he uses the Spanish spelling of his name, rather than the Catalan – and did he feel any embarrassment having once served Franco, suppressing the Catalan culture and language? Samaranch fell into the trap, replying 'I am very proud of my past, you can be sure.'

The radical press in Catalonia didn't share the inhibitions of the establishment media. The weekly news magazine *El Triangle* reproduced the suspicions of many Catalans about the heavily commercialised Games. It ran a cartoon strip in which Barcelona's Olympic mascot Cobi, the rat-like bear with the silly smile, was transformed into a foxy *femme fatale* with high heels, fishnets, suspenders and uplift bra. From a snowstorm of dollars emerged Donald Duck. What they did next, explained my translator, reflected a popular Catalan view that their city had been screwed every which way by the Olympics and the sponsors. The pictures made this very clear.

The week before the Games *El Triangle* ran a front cover cartoon reminding readers how the man they ejected in 1977 had come back to dominate the city – and the country. There was Samaranch in his fascist white jacket and Blueshirt with right arm high in the vile old salute, driving a chariot pulled by Spain's prime minister, the mayor of Barcelona and the president of Catalonia. The salute and the uniform were important to Catalans, if ignored by the tourists with notebooks: that was how the locals remembered him and they were damned if they'd forget – ever.

The opening speeches at the Olympics are invariably bland and aimed at a world audience. But Mayor Pascal Maragall began his brief words with three sentences that electrified Catalans and mystified most foreigners. 'Fifty-six years ago, the People's Olympiad should have taken place here. The name of the President of the People's Olympiad is engraved on the old marathon door. He was called Luis Companys and he was the president of the Catalan Government.'

This was Catalan code to most reporters and went mostly unreported. But in those three sentences Maragall, a socialist politician, brought back all the anger against the dictatorship – and the joy that it had died with Franco. The People's Olympiad of 1936, the anti-Hitler Olympics, the anti-fascist games staged by the international workers' sports movement, was cancelled when Franco led his revolt against the Spanish government. Luis Companys was the lasted elected leader of autonomous Catalonia before it and democracy were crushed by Franco. Companys fled to France after the defeat of the Republic but was returned by the Gestapo to face a summary military trial.

Maragall did not have to tell the story of Luis Companys' execution on 15 October 1940. Every Catalan knows it. When the firing squad came for him Companys' last request was to be shot barefoot, so that his feet could feel the precious soil of Catalonia. As the soldiers took aim Companys shouted, 'Long live free Catalonia!' His death certificate states that he died in the fortress of Montjuic castle of a traumatic internal haemorrhage. Samaranch was then aged twenty and already climbing his way up the Blueshirt promotion ladder.

The Olympic stadium and many of the facilities for 1992 were built high up on Montjuic mountain, overlooking the city. From the stadium you can see the fortress higher up the mountain where Franco's – and effectively Samaranch's – enemies were gunned down like dogs. Any top-class runner competing in the stadium could have reached the fortress within a minute. On the way they would have passed the burial grounds, the unmarked last resting places of thousands whose crime was to resist fascism. 'Twenty years on,' recalls art historian Robert Hughes, 'if the ground of this mass grave was wet from rain, one could still smell the very faint but persistent odour of their decay in the air.'

Maragall's choice of words would have sparked other memories for Catalans. Franco, the man Samaranch still says he was proud to serve, had a fondness for garrotting his opponents. The very last one to die this way in Barcelona was Salvador Puig Antich whose throat was slowly crushed by the tightening metal collar in the central yard of the Model prison on 2 March 1974, eighteen years before the Barcelona Olympics and while Samaranch was the Franco-imposed president of Catalonia. Would a word then from the present Olympic president have stopped this repellent, slow-motion, body-thrashing, eye-bulging, last-breath-gasping execution? The victim's body is a little further up Montjuic in the public graveyard, to be found at plot number 2,737.

What a contrast on that Olympic podium in July 1992! The old Blueshirt in charge (financed and supported by the world's multi-nationals – the Cokes, the Kodaks, the Visas and the Panasonics – and by the world's broadcast networks, the BBCs, the NBCs and all their non-political sports reporters) burbling about Pierre de Coubertin and 'the dignitaries from twenty-seven states who are with us here today, a sign of the importance the world now attaches to the Olympic movement'. Next to him, the elected socialist mayor of the city whose brothers were arrested and sister Monica jailed for printing anti-Franco literature. As he mentioned the revered name of Luis Companys, Maragall would have known, as all Catalans knew, that Samaranch was a beneficiary of the volley that cut Companys down.

This wasn't Catalonia's only grievance against Samaranch. They resented their athletes competing under foreign colours, Spanish colours. Catalonia's national Olympic committee, formed in 1920, was crushed by Franco, but reformed in 1988, backed by the Catalan Parliament. Eighty per cent of Catalans, while delighted to host the Olympics in their own national capital, were unhappy that they couldn't compete as Catalans, only as Spaniards. They lobbied the Birmingham convention in 1991 for recognition but were rebuffed by the Catalan Samaranch who knew that King Juan Carlos and the government in Madrid would be opposed.

Despite the intense security at the stadium the secretary of the Catalan Olympic committee, Xavier Vinyals, smuggled himself in with the Lithuanian team and jogged round the track at the opening ceremony waving the Catalan flag. The local media reported his ingenuity – but none of the international sports experts even noticed it.

*

'The Olympic village for the athletes is undoubtedly the finest so far,' enthused Finnish Olympic committee member Peter Tallberg, a fifty-five-year-old former yachtsman appointed by Samaranch to speak for the competitors. Mr Tallberg of course qualified to reside at the five-star Hotel Princesa Sofia where the air conditioning protected the IOC from one of Barcelona's hotter summers. Such luxury was deemed unnecessary for the athletes and so the British Olympic association, followed by the Australians, went shopping for electric fans. The sharp contrast between the IOC's accommodation and the sweltering athletes, sometimes three to a room, provided stories for many of the television news crews in town.

America's millionaire basketball Dream Team took care to avoid the village. 'We don't intend to make a whole lot of friends here,' said John Stockton. 'The Olympic spirit is beating people, not living with them.' Even less friendly was Charles Barkley who had his own version of Olympic idealism; 'I couldn't care less. I'm here to kill them and let God sort them out later.'

To the credit of most of the American media, it attacked the Dream Team for their arrogance and bullying ways against opponents. If America had drafted its best amateur, college players, it would still have stood a good chance of winning gold, but the National Basketball Association had seen the opportunity to make a fortune. 'We're sitting on a goldmine,' said NBA salesman Rob Levine. Clothing deals, selling rights to screen their American league abroad: Barcelona was all about making money. At the end of the games Samaranch said, 'The most important aspect of the Games has been the resounding success of the basketball tournament.'

At the other end of the money scale were the athletes

from the CIS, the temporary unified team from the former Soviet republics, competing as one nation for the last time. Among their sponsors was Smirnoff vodka. Among my souvenirs from Barcelona is a Smirnoff T-shirt with the company logo on the front and the five rings on the back. The IOC's rule on hard liquor is quite clear: competing teams must not advertise alcohol. Russian reporters tell me that Samaranch twice patronised the Smirnoff hospitality suite during the games.

Other sponsors failed to use the seats allocated to them in their VIP packages and caused huge offence to fans queuing to see the sport. They would have missed all that was good in Barcelona: Linford Christie destroying a younger generation of sprinters; the emotional aftermath to the women's 10,000 metres, when the winner Derartu Tulu from Ethiopia lapped the track arm in arm with the silver medallist Elana Meyer, a member of the first South African team in the games since the demise of apartheid.

And when the Olympians finally left town, they left behind them a bill for the taxpayers of Spain – $2.34 billion.

No sooner had the long summer of sport come to an end than party time began. Primo Nebiolo spent an estimated $600,000 in his home city of Turin celebrating the end of the athletics Grand Prix season. More lorry loads of champagne were ordered for his next party, this time in Stockholm in late November. It was the seventh annual Gala of Nebiolo's International Athletics Foundation, set up with the $20 million he extracted from the Seoul Olympic organisers. Entertaining 800 guests cost around $500,000.

Nebiolo made a brief trip to Seoul to preside over the world junior athletics championships. His suite in the Sheraton hotel cost around $3,000 a night. The total bill for his entourage was $72,000. The championship was a financial disaster. So few spectators turned up that primary school pupils were drafted in to fill the seats.

Hardened Olympic party goers turned up in Monaco in mid-October for Mickey Kim's General Assembly of International Sports Federations convention. Meetings ran for a week and officials bravely coped with life in the $420 a night Loews Hotel. The official business included excellent seminars on the design of sports facilities. Most delegates, one official confided to me, found more interesting things to do.

After all this hard work on the French Riviera the sports leaders jetted off to Acapulco for another tough week. Seven hundred delegates turned up in the luxury resort for the convention of Mario Vazquez Raña's Association of National Olympic Committees. Adding to the party atmosphere, the IOC stopped by with their executive board. Mario dug deep to pay for air fares and partying for sixty IOC members.

Nebiolo also called a meeting of his Association of Summer Olympic International Federations to change the rules so he could remain as their leader, again without an election. Mexican president Carlos Salinas dropped by to collect an award from Mario, to add to the Olympic Order he already had from Samaranch. Since he left office Senor Salinas has had to deny he knew anything about his family's alleged involvement in political murder and narcotic money laundering.

It had been a busy year and members needed a rest. Next year, 1993, some would be almost permanently on the road, sampling the cities bidding for the games of 2000.

# CHAPTER 15

## Serial Freeloaders Stop Off In Berlin

Her first engagement was the show *Anything Goes* and Berlin danced to the merry tune throughout one senior IOC member's visit. Mrs Flor Isava-Fonseca, in town to check out the city's plans to host the Olympics, guzzled her way through its finest restaurants for a week, provoking a local MP to ask, 'Did Flor Isava come to Berlin as a representative of the IOC or the Guide Michelin?'

After the excesses which won Barcelona the Games the IOC claimed they'd tightened up their rules. Long, leisurely, repeated visits to bid cities were outlawed and expensive gifts banned from the campaigns for the Olympics that would herald the twenty-first century.

These decrees were handed down by the IOC's executive board – Venezuela's Mrs Isava was a member – and then ignored. More than half the Olympic committee mocked the new regulations as they jaunted from one beseeching city to another, vying for the title of the world's greatest serial freeloaders. It was shake-down time again and, as ever, Samaranch turned a blind eye.

Tashkent and Milan dropped out early in the race for the millennium Games. Brasilia followed later. That left

Istanbul and Manchester as outsiders and Beijing and
Sydney as the bidders to watch. One other bid floun-
dered alongside for three years, bleeding scandal as fast
as it soaked up unbelievable amounts of money. Berlin's
campaign consumed an astonishing DM 86 million of
taxpayers' money. It was public welfare subsidising the
private business sector and the IOC – but nobody's sure
where the money's all gone. Allegations of sleaze and
misappropriation mounted and early in 1995 Berlin's
state parliament launched an inquiry. MPs requested
all the bid teams' files, but most had disappeared.
At public hearings witnesses seemed unable to recol-
lect key events. Berliners watched the recriminations,
admissions and disclosures with increasing horror.

'Berlin's bid had nothing to do with a festival of
youth, peace, or sports,' said one critic. 'It was simply
small interest groups – politicians, sports officials, big
companies and the IOC trying to get their hands on
public funds.'

The Olympic bid was the dream road to gold – for
the lucky few. Colossal profits could be extracted from
constructing Olympic venues; land values would soar
as the city was rebuilt. And there would be jobs: jobs in
sports administration, jobs running the bid, jobs creating
the money machine to drive the Games.

The plans were hatched without involving athletes
and as always today, big business was the catalyst. Berlin's bid was brewed up at a Mercedes 'Olympic party'
thrown by the Daimler-Benz company in their home
town of Stuttgart in December 1990. Samaranch rubbed
shoulders with leading German businessmen and Berlin's Christian Democrat mayor Eberhard Diepgen. Also
invited was Lutz Grüttke, former chief German spin
doctor for IBM. Grüttke was highly recommended by
Daimler boss Edzard Reuter; three months later he was
appointed director of the Berlin 2000 bid.

Grüttke didn't last long – and neither did his budget. He took lessons from Lausanne: bills for first class flights, top class hotels and sumptuous meals fluttered in his wake as he squandered generous hand-outs from public funds. Within six months the budget was over-spent by DM 1.6 million. Auditors couldn't find receipts and political scandal loomed. Quietly, the mayor's office chipped in more taxes, Daimler provided the rest. The bills were paid.

The auditors discovered that Grüttke had hired a public relations firm to hype the bid. It was a water-tight contract, worth DM 13 million, which threatened to bankrupt the whole enterprise. And there was worse: Grüttke turned out to have been a director of another company which had a stake in the expensive PR firm. As the state attorney began investigating possible conflicts of interest, the PR firm departed taking DM 3.8 million for just eight months work.

Grüttke signed his own death warrant, modelling suits in *Der Spiegel* magazine. The advertisement dis-played a cluster of Olympic flags, breaching the rules against 'ambush marketing' – when companies that don't sponsor the Games try to make it look as if they do. Despite the embarrassment, Grüttke insisted on a pay-off to quit.

Berlin's was the most expensive bid and management consultant Nicholas Fuchs was hired to raise the money. He too was a friend of Daimler. Fuchs brought in Lufthansa, Bertelsmann – one of the world's largest media conglomerates – and a cluster of banks, engi-neering firms, the monopoly telephone company and of course Daimler, to sponsor the bid. They closed the door behind them and set up a private business, Berlin 2000 Marketing Ltd. As Fuchs said later, 'You have to be free of any sort of public scrutiny.'

But Fuchs didn't want to be free of public money. His Bossard company was paid DM 590,000 – for just four months – to manage the marketing business. Another tranche of public funds went to rent high-class offices. This was all very hush-hush and the public were led to believe that the big sponsors were bringing in private sector cash. The reverse happened – they took from the public purse. What's left of the files are still being checked by auditors but it looks as if they handed over more cash to the sponsors than they raised for the bid committee. The bottom line may be that the marketing company became an Olympic washeteria, laundering public funds into private corporate pockets.

These big-hearted Olympic sponsors claimed to be putting up cash for an ideal – but what seemed to happen was that many enjoyed a profitable relation-ship with the bid. They supplied a range of services and nobody argued with their invoices. There was no competitive public tendering to disturb this cosy world.

Bertelsmann was one of the bigger winners. They donated DM 1.5 million to the marketing company – on condition they were kicked back at least DM 250,000 worth of business. Eventually Bertelsmann was paid DM 2.3 million for making the bid committee's promotional video, and there were other profitable contracts for group companies.

Bertelsmann were joined in the marketing operation by Germany's other major media group, the Springer empire, and both supplied directors for the bid com-mittee. Both had sought to acquire lucrative television rights to the Olympics. Bertelsmann had outbid the European Broadcasting Union for the rights to Atlanta but were denied the contract because they couldn't deliver pictures everywhere on the continent. Back on the trail for 2000, and pandering to Samaranch, they produced a theme video for his Olympic congress in Paris in 1994. Oddly enough, it was all about the importance of sponsors.

The two state channels were also competing for Olympic rights. They too became sponsors – and were paid to promote the bid on their networks. They could help sort out problems too. A comedian who pilloried Samaranch as a retired fascist was yanked off the air. Another state broadcaster wanted to run a clip of the incident, but its request was refused.

And then there was Daimler, playing its version of Olympic squash rackets. Like Bertelsmann, they knocked the money in - and it came bouncing back. Better than Bertelsmann, Daimler had its own men in control, putting a senior executive into the bid committee and later the marketing company, where his salary ate up ten per cent of Daimler's cash contribution. Daimler boss Edzard Reuter chaired the bid committee trustees and his deputy, Matthias Kleinert, was a director of the marketing company. Why was the motor firm so Olympian-minded? Berlin's bid offered Daimler 'unbelievable economic opportunities', explained Kleinert. The company was already investing in property in the city and trying to sell the politicians an expensive traffic management scheme.

In public, Daimler were benefactors; they were the biggest single sponsors, handing over DM 6.5 million. Less than half was cash – the rest would be in services. Daimler stipulated that they alone could assess the value. Their money too came bouncing back: Berlin Olympic bid slogans were plastered on Daimler cars competing in the German touring car championships. The bill was DM 1.7 million.

To keep such shenanigans private, they had to massage the media. Nobody inside the new Berlin Olympic industry wanted independent scrutiny of their activities. With a few exceptions, the media was bound into the bid machinery – or bought off. Berlin's principal radio stations and most daily papers became sponsors, through Fuchs' private marketing company. The boss of the local state television and radio network in Berlin joined the bid's support group and some of his journalists were paid to write sympathetic articles.

'Friendship' was the keynote of the bid committee's relationship with the press. In a secret strategy document its chief media manager said journalists should be wined and dined and the friendship lubricated with small gifts. It seemed to work. Independent reporters were paid to contribute articles to the bid's magazine. The sports editor of one daily paper, combining his duties with membership of the German national Olympic committee, was paid to help write the formal bid book for the IOC. A senior reporter with a sports news service was paid DM 5,000 a month to advise the bid.

But the media's heroic attempts to sell the bid to Berlin failed. MPs, academics, the church, and labour unions were unimpressed. Opponents formed the NOlympic movement protesting that public money, needed to rebuild the city's housing and social services in the wake of reunification, was being diverted into the Olympic campaign. Anti-Olympic slogans and banners were plastered across the city, dwarfing the efforts of the official campaign.

Every kind of opposition was mobilised, from peaceful demonstrations to sabotage. Sponsors were the main target; cars and lorries were torched, windows smashed and locks super-glued. Activists took wire cutters to the cables that carried one big sponsors' television service and protesters took their fight all the way to Lausanne, spray-painting Olympic House and lobbing eggs at Samaranch during his museum opening ceremony.

The spin doctors went to work on the foreign press. The support of international Olympic pundits was essential because they were read by IOC members and the barons of the sports federations. More money was cranked into another 'friendship' campaign. Flights, hotels and entertainment were provided for at least twenty foreign reporters. The bid placed their greatest hopes on one British cheerleader. David Miller of the London *Times* wrote warmly about Samaranch. His positive, auth-orised biography of the Chief Guardian of Olympic Idealism – with no mentions of Blueshirts or stiff right arms – was translated into German by Bertelsmann; it couldn't harm their strategy to obtain television rights from the IOC.

Support for the Olympic campaign was slumping when Miller arrived in the city. Local polls showed just over forty per cent of Berliners were for the bid. In the country as a whole, between half and two-thirds of the people were opposed. But Miller seemed to have been given a set of statistics dating from before the disclosure by German TV of an explosive secret dossier on IOC members; he reported sixty per cent welcoming the Games. Opponents were dismissed as 'a left-minded young West Berlin popu-lation accustomed to hand-outs from the rest of Western Germany' and he seemed unaware of criticisms by leading public figures. 'Idealistic' was Miller's description of the bid chief executive who later shredded most of the files. The bid committee was delighted and reprinted his *Times* article in the bid magazine.

*

Only seven IOC members are incorruptible. The rest

can be venal, dishonest, depraved and degenerate, their votes available to unscrupulous bid cities offering cash, expenses fiddles, intriguing sexual activities, drugs, alcohol or excessive hospitality. Fact or fantasy, that's what the dossier hidden in Nicholas Fuchs' office said.

'We can only win the Olympics,' the marketing company boss once claimed, 'if we play by the real rules.' That meant digging out dirt on the Olympic committee and using it to win votes.

He got what he was looking for at the second attempt. Fuchs wanted previous bid cities' dossiers on IOC members – they all have them and they all deny it – and had flown first to Atlanta where he claims he was told, Sorry, you're too late, they've already been sold to a rival bidder. So he sent a special agent – codenamed Astrid – to Athens, to find out what they learned in their unsuccessful bid for the Games of 1996.

Astrid's report painted a bleak picture of the Olympic committee. Potentially open to bribes were members from Eastern Europe, Latin America, Africa and Asia: he named the five best prospects. Who was the biggest fraudster on the committee? Astrid named him too, claiming he overcharged bid cities for the costs of air tickets for inspection visits. And then there was the travelling salesman, the member who promised his vote to Athens – if the contract to extend their metro system went to his country.

Fuchs' dossier was a tightly kept secret – until the night in June 1992 when it appeared on the investigative TV programme *Monitor*, produced by journalists Mathias Werth and Philip Siegel. They'd obtained copies of Astrid's notes on the fallibilities of the moral guardians of sport. The shock waves effectively ended Berlin's hopes – and undermined the IOC's image world-wide.

Three weeks before the Barcelona Games *Monitor*

revealed a second report, again compiled by Astrid. The source this time was a German sports official, codenamed Augustinus but revealed as August Kirsch, then vice-president of the German national Olympic committee. There was more on the sexual preferences of IOC members and yet another supposed bribe-taker was named.

So who was Astrid? In 1995 *Spiegel* magazine unveiled him as Dr Manfred Lämmer, a professor at the Sports University in Cologne and a leading light in awarding Europe's Fair Play sporting honours.

The Berlin bid leaders went a deeper shade of red after the television exposés and offered grovelling apologies to the IOC. It must have been hard: Astrid's reports may have exaggerated IOC foibles but many of the allegations are believed accurate by Olympic insiders. Fuchs' Olympic career was over and he was shown the door. Then the bid leaders set about wasting millions more of the taxpayers' money. They went to the Barcelona Games to work but managed to have a good time.

Berlin's team rented an annex of the Cap Salou hotel. Nobody looked at the map until just before the Olympics. Then they discovered their 'handy-for-the-Games' hotel was 130 kilometres from Barcelona, to the west of Tarragona. Its only advantage was that they wouldn't be bothered by the Olympic crowds. They cancelled and went looking for new rooms. By this stage Barcelona's hoteliers could name their price. The Berliners paid whatever was asked, running up a final bill of DM 660,000.

It wasn't just the bid committee who were freeloading off the charitable taxpayers back home, watching the sport on TV. Mayor Eberhard Diepgen was accompanied by directors of the marketing company, the sponsors who were supposed to be putting their own money into the bid, not whacking the public purse.

Alongside them, no doubt with notebook at the ready, was Professor 'Astrid' Lämmer.

Ever generous with other people's money, the bid team splashed out on expensive dinners for IOC members and their wives. Public funds bought them tickets to the events, some from black market scalpers. Was it all worth it? The manager of the bid team, assured the parliament's investigators, 'We had a fantastic time!'

So too did the IOC leadership when they travelled to Berlin. The politicians wanted to hurl extravagance at them. The weary taxpayers might have got restless, so they were told that the German national Olympic committee were footing the bill for a meeting of the IOC executive board. What does it cost to arrange a three-day meeting for these dozen Olympians? More than DM 1 million. What did it buy for Berlin? 'A unique chance to show our best qualities as a bidding city,' said the bid team.

The city's Grand Hotel presented a grand bill. Those three nights cost more than DM 300,000, including Samaranch's exclusive suite. The IOC graciously contributed one third of the bill – public welfare covered the rest. The IOC leadership must have been starving when they hit town. The tally for one official dinner with the Berlin bid team came to – wait for it – DM 100,000. What upset Berliners even more was the location. Samaranch and his crew were entertained – to their great pleasure – at exactly the same spot, the Pergamon altar, where the Nazis had wined and dined another IOC leadership in 1936.

And then there were their wives to be paid for. Olympic business is never done without spouses coming along for the shopping. Their German hosts took them to tour Berlin's historic Royal porcelain factory where they ended up in the salesroom with Mrs Samaranch lingering in front of the goodies. Eventually a sports official produced a credit card and she went away happy. One version has it that she acquired a fine coffee service – but German IOC member Walther Tröger insisted the gift was a vase.

Germany's taxpayers had always been a soft touch for the IOC. Six years earlier in 1986, members had ripped into the budget of Berchtesgaden (sidelined with Falun and Anchorage in the swindle that gave victory to Albertville and Barcelona for 1992) prompting a scathing report from the Federal Audit Office. Among the rip-offs was the bill run up by Peru's Ivan Dibos who brought his wife and three children to enjoy the town's best hotel.

Berlin's bid organisers did their hurried best to evade a similar scandal. As the threat of outside investigations loomed, mounds of documents detailing the visits of more than sixty IOC members were shredded. What remains still reveals colossal waste and self-indulgence.

Mrs Flor Isava arrived in Berlin in April 1993 from her home, the Shangri-La country club near Caracas, Venezuela, accompanied by her daughter Anabella. Mrs Isava helped make the new rules preventing IOC members exploiting bidding cities. They were clear: visits to inspect the facilities were limited to three days and the value of gifts should not exceed $200. When that was greeted with hilarity the IOC hastily announced that gifts were now prohibited. 'No $100 gifts, no $50 gifts, no gifts,' insisted director general François Carrard. A columnist in the London *Times* described the gift ban as coming 'from the if-you-believe-this-you'll-believe-anything-department'.

Flor Isava whiled away six nights in the exclusive Bristol Hotel Kempinski. Her daytime schedule was not arduous. She rested the first day, had no official engagements on the second and then it was a good dinner and off to the theatre for *Anything Goes*. On the third day Mrs Isava toured potential Olympic sites in the morning, had another fine lunch and then watched a riding tournament. More gourmandising followed with dinner at the Restaurant Chalet Corniche.

Day Four started mid-morning with an excursion to meet the bid organisers. Lunch was at the TV observation tower, she attended the launch of a yacht and devoted the evening to a ritzy dinner with Mayor Diepgen.

Day Five began, again mid-morning, at the Hitler Olympic stadium and lunch was at the Radio observation tower. Dinner at the plush Café Einstein was followed by a concert.

Day Six took Mrs Isava to Potsdam outside Berlin to see the site for the equestrian centre, followed by yet another good lunch. In the evening she dropped in at a tennis club and then dined at a Michelin one-star restaurant.

The morning of Day Seven was free and then she was chauffeured to the airport. Over those six days – twice the permitted number – she spent no more than ten hours inspecting the facilities. As she departed Mrs Isava told Berlin journalists, 'The city must show that it wants the Games.' As her restaurant bills were up to DM 600 a time, you have to wonder what more she expected.

Sixty-two IOC members visited Berlin and most violated the bidding rules. Only twelve of them stayed three days or less and many lingered up to seven. Some made a second visit. Many ran up unexpected bills, others left town with personal bills unpaid. The community chest picked up the bill for their forgetful guests.

When the wife of Argentina's Antonio Rodriguez

wanted to take some photographs, the committee bought her a camera. Her husband had dental treatment paid for by Berlin's taxpayers. Russia's Vitaly Smirnov left a tobacconist's bill behind and another member had his dog vaccinated – again at Berlin's expense.

Lamine Keita from Mali stayed four days; his hotel bill was DM 1,600 but his phone bill – thirty-five calls – totalled another DM 2,500. Mongolia's Shagdarjav Magvan brought his daughter along for a four-day stay. He enjoyed the delights of the exclusive Ephraim Palais restaurant and in a party of a dozen, took dinner at one of the city's finest eateries, the Wirtshaus Schildhorn. His limousine bill alone came to DM 3,300.

Many visiting members asked the Berlin team to book them medical check-ups during their stay – then left without paying. 'It was something that occurred relatively often,' admitted Brigitte Schmitz, who was in charge of international relations for the bid. 'At least every other visit.' That suggests about thirty members played this trick. Many of these bills were paid by the private marketing company.

Then there were the forbidden gifts. Berlin offered – and the members grabbed them. Evidence in the few documents that escaped the shredder suggest at least DM 120,000 – and probably much more – may have gone on porcelain, coins and medallions. Other gifts, like two expensive raincoats for members, were described in the accounts as 'advertisements and souvenirs'.

The bid committee kept a special file on its dealings with IOC members – and every document has disappeared.

It was so much fun that the Berlin team – and the greedy Olympic committee members – resolved to do it all again. Six weeks before the vote in Monaco to select the host for 2000, Stuttgart – Daimler's home town –

staged the world track and field championships. The IOC bidding rules were quite clear: no second visits allowed to a country bidding for the Games at the expense of the bid city. Yet the Berlin committee paid for at least thirty-one members to travel to Stuttgart, again at public expense. With them came a gaggle of wives, children, friends and girlfriends. The rules were being flouted again – but Samaranch himself was there, with his wife, so who could criticise?

And it was all so tempting. Berlin stressed that rooms and 'all other extra costs arising' would be taken care of. Just in case any members couldn't see bonanza time coming, the invitation spelled it out with the seductive words, 'You will not be asked to present a credit card.'

The biggest freeloader was the Sudan's Zein Abdel Gadir who, with one of his two wives, helped himself to DM 3,115-worth of mini-bar, room service, laundry, telephone and restaurants. Libya's Bashir Attarbulsi absorbed another DM 2,534. Australia's Phil Coles, listed as sharing a room with Ms Patricia Rosenbrock, spent DM 670 in the bars. Paul Wallwork was back for a second trip, with his daughter Helena, and so was Mongolia's Shagdarjav Magvan, this time with his wife.

Ivan Dibos showed up – but it appeared he hadn't come for the track and field championships in the Daimler stadium. He was on a non-Olympian mission. He was seeking exclusive rights to sell Volkswagen cars in his homeland, Peru.

The company's representative in Latin America didn't want to deal with him so in July 1993 Dibos wrote to his fellow IOC member Carlos Ferrer – a director of the Volkswagen-Seat company in Spain – asking him to fix a meeting with VW's boss, Ferdinand Piech, at the company's headquarters in Wolfsburg. A day later

Dibos called Brigitte Schmitz in Berlin, also asking her to help lobby the important Mr Piech.

Dibos faxed Schmitz a copy of his letter to Ferrer, scribbling on it that either German IOC members Berthold Bietz and Willi Daume, or Axel Nawrocki, director of the Berlin bid, should be able to help. Dibos also mentioned that his father – a former IOC member – had been mayor of Lima, he himself was now deputy mayor and involved in a local TV and radio station.

Ferrer found no problem with this Olympic lobbying and duly wrote to Piech at VW on behalf of his entre-preneurial IOC colleague. Dibos, he wrote 'might be of valuable assistance to promote VW in Peru'. Berlin's bid team threw themselves behind Dibos's demands and Ms Schmitz wrote a memo saying that the Peruvian IOC member's visit to Stuttgart and Berlin depended on the appointment in Wolfsburg. Bid leader Nawrocki asked businessman Heinz Windfeder, a director of Ruhrgas AG and also of the Berlin 2000 marketing company, to help; and also arranged that yet another German IOC member, Thomas Bach, was told about the request.

Volkswagen have since confirmed that they agreed to a meeting between the company's boss and Ivan Dibos.

Dibos turned up in Stuttgart and ran up a bill for extras of DM 2,048. He bought with him his business partner, Vittorio De Ferrari who hoped to share the VW franchise. His bill included DM 1,416 for mini-bar, tele-phone and restaurant meals. Who paid for this business trip? The taxpayers of course.

Missing out on the Olympian good life in Stuttgart were the athletes; they were housed in an abandoned US army barracks on the edge of the city. Some moved out into hotel rooms – for which of course they paid themselves. Kenya's Charles Mukora, a member of track and field's ruling council and of the IOC – requested

$4,371 in cash from Berlin for upgrading his tickets. He claimed the difference between tourist and first class from Nairobi.

For members and their friends not interested in the championships, the organisers offered tennis and golf – all free, naturally – and a variety of twenty-seven different tours, all with chauffeurs and guides laid on, ranging from shopping to balloon trips to horse-riding. Daimler organised a special away-day, including test-driving rally cars – and charged the Berlin bid DM 100,000.

The final woe for taxpayers was the secret subsidy for the championships. They lost a small fortune and Stuttgart persuaded the bid team to contribute DM 750,000. Berlin's total bill for these summer follies was DM 1.5 million. When questioned by the Berlin parliamentary investigators German IOC member Walter Troger explained breezily, 'We thought this might help our image so we decided to ignore the rules.'

Berlin broke the rules to the very end of the campaign. After Stuttgart they sent delegations to see eleven African and Latin American members at their homes. All had already visited Berlin and eight of them were in Stuttgart. Defending this blatant breach of the regulations, Berlin's Brigitte Schmitz said that the bid team responded to demands from members who just couldn't bear not seeing their generous Berlin friends again.

The bid team's boss, Axel Nawrocki, who shredded the most sensitive files, is adamant that the IOC has never accused them of any violations of the bidding rules.

*

*The research for this chapter has been contributed by Matthew D. Rose.*

# CHAPTER 16

## *On Your Marks, Get Set, Lunch!*

Springtime 1993 in Beijing and an old man and his friend cycle slowly across the city's most famous square. They chat, they smile, the pursuing cameramen record each gesture. Tonight the sequence will be screened on every TV set in China; it's the picture-opportunity dreamed of by the butchers of democracy. Four years after they slaughtered 3,000 student protesters, the Guardian of All Things Moral is in town to create happy new images and expunge that other picture – the one that brought the world to tears – of the student who stood alone, defying the tanks in Tiananmen Square.

The state-controlled media will ram the message home: the outside world is indifferent, we don't care any more about the bloodshed, the trials, the jailings. Look, we've sent the Olympic movement's leader to signal that we back the party bosses in all their work.

His friend is Chen Xitong, mayor of Beijing, leader of the city's Olympic bid and the party boss who signed the order that sent the army to gun down the democracy demonstrators. The two cyclists will meet again in the autumn in the luxury of Monaco when the Olympic committee convenes to select the city to host the millennium games. Barring accidents, Beijing will triumph. It's all been arranged.

Samaranch was on a winning streak. He'd steered successive Olympics to Barcelona, Lillehammer, Atlanta and Nagano. Could he get his way over the choice of a host city for the year 2000? It would be a tough fight. His sponsors favoured Beijing: the Games could open up markets among a quarter of the world's population. But there was unease about honouring the old men who'd shown such contempt for human rights. And had they got any real interest in sport?

Sydney, the other front runner, making the third successive Australian bid for the Summer Games, was a sports-crazy city which promised an open society where athletes and fans would feel comfortable. So why did Samaranch go out of his way to back China?

'There's nothing earth-shattering about Sydney winning, so it must be Beijing,' the president of an international sports federation told me, early in the campaign. 'If Samaranch can swing it to them he can claim to have brought China back into the international fold. That might be enough to capture the Nobel Peace Prize.'

Capturing favourable headlines was the IOC's first victory. The candidates were spread across five continents and the media boosted the contest more than it ever had before. As pundits everywhere speculated about the final vote in Monaco in September 1993, the Olympic committee – and their sports event – enjoyed unlimited, free advertising.

'The IOC could not lose,' said Germany's Walther Tröger. 'It had five very good bids.' There had been a sixth – and surely that was a good one as well? Samaranch appeared to think so; as he toured the bidders he played his old Casanova trick. He kept all the cities panting by letting each of them believe they

Samaranch with fascist officials at a 1967 ceremony. *(Above)*

Samaranch presents Horst Dassler with the Olympic Order in 1984. *(Below)*

A smartly dressed Samaranch gives
General Franco the address of his
tailor. *(Above)*

Samaranch in the
Spanish fascist
dress uniform is
sworn in as a
national councillor
in 1967. General
Franco (second
from left) looks on.
*(Left)*

Samaranch presents Romanian dictator Nicolae Ceaucescu with the Olympic Order in 1985 and praises his support for Olympic idealism. *(Right)*

A cartoon from a Barcelona magazine on the eve of the 1992 Games. Pulling Samaranch's chariot are Spanish Prime Minister Felipe Gonzalez, Barcelona Mayor Pascal Maragall and Catalonia's President Jordi Pujol. *(Below)*

German hunter-killer submarines on the eve of World War II with the five rings on their conning towers.

First vice-president Mickey Kim and his leader with their wives. *(Above)*

Mario Vazquez Raña takes the oath to join the IOC. *(Below)*

Opening the Atlanta Olympics organizing committee offices. From left, Andrew Young, Anita DeFrantz, Billy Payne, Robert Helmick, Samaranch, Maynard Jackson. *(Above)*

The boss of world track and field, Primo Nebiolo. *(Below)*

Tonbandbericht IMB "Möwe" vom 29. 3. 1989

B e r i c h t
über Gespräche im Zusammenhang mit meiner Teilnahme
an der EC-Tagung der AIBA in Nairobi/Kenia

1. Einschätzung der wesentlichen Ergebnisse der EC-Tagung
in Nairobi/Kenia

In Nairobi/Kenia fand vom 13. bis 20. 3. 1989 eine Beratung
der Internationalen Boxföderation statt. Im Rahmen dieser
Beratung wurde eine intensive Auswertung der Vorkommnisse
bei den Olympischen Spielen vorgenommen und entsprechende
Schlußfolgerungen gezogen sowie Bestrafungen gegenüber
Kampfrichtern und koreanischen Funktionären ausgesprochen.

Bei der Beratung zum Strafmaß für eine Anzahl Kampfrichter
gab es im Vorfeld der Exekutivkomiteesitzung eine Reihe von
individuellen Beratungen, die sich im wesentlichen mit den
Vorkommnissen in Südkorea beschäftigten und die zu einer
Abstimmung hinsichtlich der Höhe der Strafe führten.

Das Büro der Vizepräsidenten hatte in Frankfurt/a.M. die
Empfehlung gegeben, die die im Finale tätigen Punktrichter,
die das Fehlurteil zustande brachten, auf Lebenszeit von
der Liste zu streichen. Diese Festlegung konnte aus folgen-
den Gründen nicht eingehalten werden.
(Über das, was ich jetzt berichte, gibt es in keinem offiziellen
Dokument eine Information, lediglich Vizepräsident Günter
Heinze vom DTSB wurde mündlich über folgendes in Kenntnis ge-
setzt):

Bei der Diskussion zum Strafmaß wurde bekannt, daß ▅▅▅▅
▅▅▅▅▅▅▅/▅▅▅▅▅▅▅ vom koreanischen Veranstalter
10 000 Dollar erhalten hat, von denen er je 300 Dollar an
drei afrikanische Kampfrichter auszahlte, mit der Bitte, auf
jeden Fall die Koreaner als Sieger zu bringen. ▅▅▅▅▅▅
▅▅▅▅▅▅/▅▅▅▅▅▅, ▅▅▅▅▅▅▅ des Kontinentalbüros Süd-
amerikas, hat 5 000 Dollar erhalten, davon an zwei Kampfrichter
jeweils 500 Dollar mit der Weisung ausgezahlt, auf alle
Fälle die koreanischen Boxer als Sieger zu bringen.

Der ▅▅▅▅▅▅▅ Vertreter im Exekutivkomitee, ▅▅▅▅▅▅▅ -
verwandt mit dem ▅▅▅▅▅▅▅ ,weil sein Sohn die Tochter des
▅▅▅▅▅▅▅ geheiratet hat - war bereit, diese Angelegenheit auf
den Tisch des Hauses zu packen, weil er über eidesstattliche
Erklärungen seines Kampfrichters verfügte, der ausgesagt hat,
daß er 300 Dollar mit der genannten Weisung von ▅▅▅▅▅▅ erhalten hatte.

The first page of Karl-Heinz Wehr's secret report listing the bribes paid to win gold medals in Seoul. Censors have blanked out the names - but not the amounts in dollars. *(Above)*

Karl Heinz-Wehr together with Professor Anwar Chowdhry. *(Above)*

Samaranch tours Beijing on a bicycle in the company of Chen Xitong president of the 2000 Olympic Bid Committee. *(Below)*

were in with a chance. Being jilted in Monaco seemed unthinkable.

He was at it in Latin America: 'The city is surprising and splendidly prepared to host an event of this type,' Samaranch assured Brasilia after his visit. He'd gone too far this time – his evaluation committee, sent to inspect Brasilia's plans, couldn't but report that the bid had virtually no facilities, its leaders had failed to involve local sports bodies and, worst of all, there was no five-star hotel suitable for the IOC. The city's last hopes evaporated when Brazil's president warned, 'I hope the government will not be drawn into such a madness' – and then there were only five cities left.

Another first-time bidder was Istanbul. In a slavish attempt to impress, the Turkish parliament pushed through a law that committed taxpayers to under-writing the cost of preparations and gave draconian legal powers to the organisers. In effect, they'd written a blank cheque from the Turkish people to the IOC. These Games would bridge east and west, claimed the bid team and, with an eye to Samaranch's Nobel ambitions, they added that their city was 'an island of peace in a region of the world torn by conflict'.

At least one of the visiting moral guardians got up to the old tricks. He tried to seduce an Istanbul hostesses, offering a cheap IOC scarf for her company. The Turkish team worked hard all the way to Monaco but were never seen as likely winners by those in the know.

Humiliated in the battle for the Games of 1996 – eleven votes in the first round of voting and only five in the second – Manchester immediately tried again. Britain's media shamelessly bumped up the city's slim chance, encouraged by Samaranch during his visit. 'You gave us a unique and wonderful lesson in how to present an Olympic bid,' said the Olympic Casanova. 'I think the chances here are very, very high.'

The *Times* translated that into 'Britain's Games bid wins high praise.' It was all flim-flam but Mancunians badly wanted to believe it. On the eve of the vote in Monaco Manchester's bid team claimed they were among the front runners. That wasn't how the rest of the world saw their chances.

Manchester's leader, lofty Bob Scott, annoyed many on the Olympic circuit when his charm deteriorated, under pressure, into bombast. The Sydney team thought he 'came on strong at times' when lobbying IOC members. Critics often found Scott's large index finger jabbed in the direction of their chests. Manchester's canny Labour leadership extracted large sums from the government to improve facilities and brighten up their city and Prime Minister John Major did his ineffectual best, but when he hosted a cocktail party in Barcelona for Olympic committee members, only nine out of ninety showed up. The IOC's inspection team approved the plans for the Games but, as ever, the chief priority was their own comfort. The city, if successful, was advised to build a new hotel especially for them.

While most British reporters hyped Manchester's frail odds, Steve Bell, cartoonist for the London *Guardian*, spotted what was really going on. He drew Samaranch in the starting blocks, grinning, and watched by suppliants from the bidding cities. The caption read, 'Juan Antonio Samaranch, on your marks, get set, lunch!'

More than seventy IOC stalwarts heroically endured pampered, first class flights to Sydney. Australian members Kevan Gosper and Phil Coles instructed their bid team that the Lords of the Rings should be 'well looked after'. And they were. The first to arrive in government-provided limousines in October 1991 included Mickey Kim and his chum from the executive board, America's Anita DeFrantz. She had a super time. 'Sydney is a wonderful place for sports,' she told reporters. 'Already I have played tennis, been windsurfing, rowing and I am going sailing this afternoon.' Their host, bid leader Rod McGeoch remembered, 'It was fun to sail with these kind of people in world class 12-metre yachts.'

McGeoch insists that he never experienced any improper requests from IOC members, there was no freeloading or extortion. He published his recollections after Sydney won and it seemed he'd met an entirely different Olympic committee from the one that almost made Germany their second home during the campaign. Perhaps they were sated by Berlin's hospitality. He was not troubled by the member in Stuttgart who slipped him a note requesting two bottles of scotch, six cartons of Kent cigarettes and medicine for a diabetic child. Flor Isava showed up in Sydney, bringing another relative along for the ride, this time her grand-daughter Alexandra.

McGeoch went on the road to hype Sydney's bid and learned his first lesson in deference while visiting Havana to lobby a clutch of members free-loading at the Pan-American Games. The Castro government allocated him a beat-up but serviceable ancient Mercedes with a driver to get around in. It turned out to be the best transport in town and that irritated the Olympians. 'I don't think it's a good idea for a bid city to have a chauffeur-driven car,' warned the Olympic committee's François Carrard, 'while IOC people are being driven around in old taxis.'

McGeoch got his come-uppance in Saudi. He sat around Riyadh for a few days while the IOC's Prince Faisal was too busy to meet him and then he went home. McGeoch insists this affront was the fault of courtiers, and couldn't possibly have been capriciousness by the Prince.

Unlike some of the more cynical bid leaders, McGeoch appears to have fallen under the Lausanne spell. The first edition of *The Lords of the Rings* in 1992 disturbed Rod, not because it disclosed the Chief Guardian's fascist record but because the book was 'very personally offensive to President Samaranch', and this from a man who claims to have a 'more acute sensitivity about human rights than some others'. At the Barcelona Games McGeoch was suckered by the propaganda, announcing that track and field was now 'drug free'. The IOC couldn't but like him.

The Sydney team traipsed off to Lausanne for the opening of the Olympic museum, thrilled that their new uniforms and ties made Manchester's men look dowdy. The smiles froze when reporter Ross Coulthart of Australia's ABC TV, had the temerity to ask Samaranch about rumours of sleaze in the IOC, to which he breathtakingly replied, 'It is clean and it was.' Sydney's politicians, along for the jollies, were infuriated and there was almost a punch-up when they confronted the disloyal television crew. Back in Sydney there were threats to cut state funds to the network.

Most of Sydney's brave journos reported Samaranch's visit to Sydney from the prone position. The Europe-based Olympic family laughed behind their well-manicured hands. Samaranch was accompanied by Karl-Heinz Huba, proprietor of *Sport Intern* the slavishly loyal journal, who noted that the Australian press pack was 'as quiet as a lamb'.

Samaranch was playing Casanova again, wooing a rapt Sydney audience: 'After the start some will be faster than others and I think the Sydney bid could be very, very fast,' he cooed. The Sydney press erupted with the headline, 'Olympic Chief hints at Sydney 2000 success' and when he followed up with 'You are one of the favourites', a government minister enthused that Samaranch's visit was a 'stunning success'.

The Australians genuinely felt theirs was the best bid

and were depressed that China, who had snubbed the IOC for decades and ran the largest police state in the world, might win for no other reason than they offered more than a billion potential shoppers for the Olympic bazaar. How could they undermine Beijing's bid?

McGeoch flew to London for secret talks with Australian-born spin doctor Sir Tim Bell, confidante of Margaret Thatcher. They planned to set up a London-based human rights group to highlight China's abuses. They also plotted a book *The So-called Suitable Candidate*, questioning China's ability to stage the Olympics. Bell would mastermind these projects from faraway London, at a cost of up to £250,000, and they would never be linked to Sydney. Their plans collapsed when the Australian government found out and feared for its trade relationship with Beijing.

While Samaranch made eyes at the other bidders, he seemed close to slipping a wedding band on Beijing's finger, going out of his way to encourage an Olympic bid and garlanding sports leaders with Olympic honours. Less than three months after the Tiananmen Square massacre the Olympic committee members elected He Zhenliang, a man tied closely to the Beijing regime, to be one of their vice-presidents. This was Samaranch's wish and the members complied.

Two years later he proposed awarding Olympic Orders to senior Chinese politicians, and again the members fell into line. At the 1991 IOC convention in Birmingham Chen Xitong, mayor of Beijing but, much more significantly, the leader of their bid for the 2000 Games, was honoured. The citation praised him as 'an ardent defender of sport for youth'. This was the man who had personally signed the order calling the Chinese army into the capital to gun down the 3,000 young people who were ardent defenders of liberty.

The same Olympic honour went to Zhang Baifa, the deputy mayor, who shared the IOC's view of history. 'The so-called Tiananmen Square incident is something of the past and the Chinese people have almost forgotten about it,' he murmured menacingly. Samaranch was sending a reassuring message to the murderers. He was also sending a signal to his members; we are going to do business with these people.

In secret, he already had. One Beijing-based source, close to the team bidding for 2000, told me that Samaranch had meetings with China's leader Deng Xiaoping in 1984 and 1985 when they discussed a future bid. Samaranch made several more visits that were not reported to the Chinese people. 'The question our leadership asked all the time was, how can we be sure we will win?' says the source. 'Going for the bid was a difficult political decision. Historically in China if decision makers are in doubt about the outcome, they don't do it. There were strong political and tactical arguments against it. Why take the risk, they say.' Samaranch must have given an assurance they would win.

But how was Samaranch to wash away the blood on the cobbles of Tiananmen Square? What could deflect the ceaseless stories about persecution of dissidents, labour activists and religious leaders? No problem; the IOC was a great force for social change, they'd done it before and would do it again. Taking the Games to China would overnight turn it into a model democracy with civil liberties guaranteed.

This fantasy came out of the Seoul Games. Despite the absence of evidence Samaranch frequently claims that Olympic influence brought an end to Korea's military dictatorships and helped establish democracy. Full human rights have still to come to Korea, the government is hugely influenced by big business and free trade unions are still a dream for most workers. Samaranch also overlooks his support for the junta that bought the 1988 Games from the IOC and his private opposition to free elections. When he awarded the Olympics to Seoul in 1981, there was no talk of overthrowing the dictatorship.

But when he went to China in the 1990s, it was as the Great Reformer. There was no sign of Casanova, no seductive praise to woo the locals. His messages were strictly for the ears of his far-flung Olympic committee. 'IOC Members may consider that the experience of involvement with the International Olympic Movement could help a country,' was an early Samaranch prompt to swing their votes to Beijing.

His message got louder: 'The Olympic Games in Korea helped to change this country,' Samaranch said in Shanghai. 'Today it is an economic power and a full democratic country.' His members may have believed this – but it didn't wash with the New York-based Human Rights Watch: 'This is a nonsensical comparison,' said a spokesman. 'Deep changes were already under way in South Korea long before the Games.'

In China the people were crying out for deep changes. More than a million people detained every year without trial, some incarcerated for decades. Public executions were a common sight, and the murderous occupation of Tibet went on and on. One small group could expect no encouragement from Samaranch. The Chinese authorities arrested the handful of protesters who dared voice warnings that their overheating economy could ill-afford to finance an enormous Olympic construction programme.

My Beijing source insists that controversy about human rights didn't worry the Beijing bid team. 'They sorted this out with Samaranch. It was part of the discussions and agreements before deciding to make the bid,' they tell me. 'One of the big questions for both China and Samaranch was how would the world use the human rights issue of Beijing's bid and how would China and the IOC respond. If either side had been unable to handle this, the bid would never have been made.'

Samaranch tailored his views on human rights to suit his audiences. In Shanghai he declared the IOC's decision would not be based on human rights. Two days later in Sydney he changed his mind. 'Human rights are important,' he insisted.

His best case for Beijing – and for the elusive Nobel – was echoed by the reporter closest to him. 'Samaranch considers the Olympic Games, a weapon of peace, could serve to bring together China and its ideological opponents,' wrote David Miller in the Times, 'in the same way that the Seoul Games assisted South Korea.' Many human rights organisations would consider this to be nourishing a myth.

Backing for Samaranch came from the man most anxious to succeed him. 'If you want to influence change in China and your objective is to improve human rights,' said Dick Pound, 'this is an opportunity to do it. It's a made in heaven opportunity.'

It was also a heavenly prospect for the IOC's partners. A twenty-page advertising supplement in Time magazine paid for by sponsors seemed to be softening up the world for a Beijing victory. 'It seems unfair that actions of a few elderly politicians should prevent China's youth from playing host,' wrote David Miller. And here again was the Korea card: 'Samaranch is thought to be among those who feel that, despite the differences between the two countries, the Olympic Movement could do for China what it did for South Korea.' Miller dismissed the rival bidders in one sentence.

\* \* \*

We can't expect Beijing's city council to follow Berlin's example and probe how much was spent on visiting IOC members. But all reports suggest the Olympians tackled the lavish hospitality vigorously; they had few problems accepting gifts from blood-stained hands, kind words from voices that have ordered public executions.

'No visiting king or president in the last two decades received a welcome as overwhelming as the one that Beijing bestowed this week,' reported the *New York Times*, 'on a group of obscure but, in certain ways, very powerful foreigners.' The Olympic committee was in town – and didn't the local people suffer. Heating was cut off to many neighbourhoods so as not to stain the sky with coal smoke. More than a quarter of a million children were mobilised to clean traffic signs.

My source in Beijing calculates that the Beijing bid team spent around $25,000 on each IOC member. 'Many came for more than one visit and brought their families with them. Everyone was given what they wanted. African members who wanted expensive American cigarettes found them in their rooms.'

Reports that members went shopping at Beijing's magnificent Friendship Store and were encouraged to leave without paying weren't denied by the IOC. For those more interested in posterity than shopping, Beijing promised that if they won the Games, all IOC members would have their names inscribed on China's Great Wall. Their most ardent admirer was bloody-handed Chen Xitong who simpered, 'We look upon the IOC as Gods – their wish is our command.'

Nothing was too much: Beijing tossed $1 million into Samaranch's museum fund and overawed their rivals with loans to its art gallery. Each bid city sent respectable offerings; China's devastating contribution included ceramic art, jade and gold imperial robes and two terracotta statues of warriors from a royal grave. These were art treasures that temporarily put the new and derided Olympic museum on the map. The members had to be grateful.

The Chinese stunts culminated with 50,000 students deployed on the Great Wall shouting cheery support for the bid. Was that not enough? Samaranch should be awarded the Nobel, urged a Chinese sports leader, for 'his contribution to world peace'. But the Beijing–Samaranch love affair was under threat, thanks to international pressure and the US Congress's opposition. Sixty senators wrote to Olympic committee members warning their image would suffer if they 'worked with an authoritarian government to stage an event televised around the world'. The European parliament joined in and suddenly, China's bid had the aroma of stale haddock.

Beijing peaked just before the Monaco climax. They had remembered that it was all supposed to be about sport! Their national championships were deliberately delayed until the eve of Monaco and then their women runners produced stunning successes in middle and long distance events. World records were destroyed again and again – but all this achieved was more worries that Chinese sport was dope-fuelled.

Back home some political prisoners were released but the few favourable headlines world-wide were swamped by the horrors of pictures of female babies left to die in Chinese orphanages – a story thoughtfully released by the Australian media. And then it was time for everybody to pack their bags and head for the seaside.

'The European lobster-guzzling record is under threat,' warned one London columnist as the Olympic committee arrived in Monaco. Most had trained in Berlin and Stuttgart as well as Beijing, Sydney and Istanbul for this final, week-long blow-out of the year. Look at the fine restaurants! The shopping! The casinos and cabarets advertising Girls, Girls, Girls! Their only obligations were accepting more gifts and spending a couple of hours selecting a host for 2000 – and then getting out of town fast before the losers they'd flirted with caught up with them for the only candid chats of the long campaign.

The week-long party was sponsored by Mercedes, Coca-Cola and Rank Xerox and the committee pretended they were as royal as their hosts, Prince Rainier and his family. Here, at one soirée, was the new Olympic protocol: 'Mrs J.A. Samaranch will receive her guests in the presence of Princess Caroline,' warbled the pompous invitation. Then they were off 'to visit the most prestigious yachts in the world . . . with cocktails aboard'. There was the usual wives and hangers-on programme while the mostly male committee took the decisions. There was a boat trip to Villefranche and a tour of the Fragonard perfume factory on the Côte D'Azure.

In these dying days of the long campaign the five rival cities played their last cards. Berlin's team took the daughters of Mario Vazquez Raña, Ivan Dibos and India's Ashwini Kumar to dinner at the Cantinella restaurant and then stung taxpayers another DM 200,000 giving each member a white leather hand-bound book with photographs of German athletes and a short message explaining why they should vote for Berlin.

The British team, boosted by a demented domestic media insisting Manchester had a real chance, flooded the principality with cheerleaders. Soccer legend Bobby Charlton and Barcelona gold medallist Linford Christie were joined by a handful of little-known British politicians.

China's international image slipped another peg or

two when their own muscular security guards, supported by local police, attacked non-violent Tibetan demonstrators. American TV crews filmed it all and the Beijing team flared up, hinting they might boycott Atlanta – then hastily denied they'd said any such thing.

The Australians kept up their spirits, cheekily renaming the Olympic committee's residence, the Hotel de Paris, the Brothel de Paris because they had to prostitute themselves in the lobbies and the bars. They had to apologise when found out. Sydney gave away Drizabone raincoats to committee members, offered sports scholarships for third world athletes and New South Wales premier John Fahey, hastily adopting the language that Samaranch wanted to hear, said that a Sydney Olympics would 'deliver a message of peace' to the world. But they were haunted by the private knowledge that Samaranch's personal lawyer believed Beijing would be hard to beat.

The first clue that Beijing was on the skids came from the London *Times*. 'The notion that the weight of Samaranch's opinion favours Peking, widely reported in the Western press,' announced David Miller, 'is wholly unsubstantiated.' There was more from the same source. 'Beijing is a high risk choice . . . the IOC's intention may be shifting.'

But even as Samaranch appeared to hesitate, his loyal *apparatchiks* were plunging on down the road to defeat. A last-ditch battle was launched by the unashamedly pro-Beijing faction. Jean-Claude Ganga from the Congo, the young Kuwaiti Sheikh Ahmad who fears China may oust him from the Olympic Council of Asia, Mario Vazquez Raña and soccer's João Havelange all kept up their support and track and field's Primo Nebiolo predicted Beijing would win forty-eight votes and victory in the first round.

Throughout 23 September 1993 the bidders showed off their wares to the committee. The prime ministers of Australia, Turkey and Britain grovelled in turn and then the committee moved to the vote. Istanbul went on the first round with seven votes. Berlin followed them out with nine in the second round. Bob Scott's bombast collapsed when Manchester won only eleven votes – the same as their 1990 total – and then it was Sydney and Beijing.

But something odd had happened inside the polling room. Eighty-nine members had started voting – and now there were only eight-eight! Swaziland's David Sibandze had gone! He couldn't find a good enough reason to complete the only positive function committee members are ever asked to perform. He claimed he was needed for local elections back home. If he knew this in advance, why did he waste Olympic money on air fares and the good life in the Brothel de Paris?

McGeoch and his team pulled it off at the line, beating Beijing by forty-five to forty-three. Samaranch's apologists parroted that the vote was a 'victory for sport', ignoring the fact that virtually half the IOC members had turned their back on the best and most sport-oriented bid.

An hour after their defeat Beijing was behaving badly again, warning that they might not wait until 1997 to take control of Hong Kong. That was bluster, but their threat to resume nuclear weapons testing was carried out ten days later.

Both of the ageing plotters who cycled across Tiananmen Square for the cameras had been damaged. Samaranch survived but his infatuation with the Beijing dictatorship has permanently damaged his image. Chen Xitong, the party boss who got the Olympic order for his commitment to slaughtering young people was forced from office in 1995, accused of corruption.

# CHAPTER 17

# *Knickers Off Girls,*
# *the Olympians Are Coming*

We're in the Atlanta Olympic stadium, and as the athletes parade, the commentators crank up the idealistic clichés. They're not telling us the truth; there's a vile secret they all know but it's the Big Taboo so they won't breathe a word. We can. Let's shout out loud: thirty-five per cent of the competitors have been sexually abused on their way to the Games. Who did it? The IOC.

Men just turn up and compete. Not so easy for women; they must submit to a degrading gender 'test' before being declared fit to compete. For thirty years female athletes have been forced into a humiliating, scientifically discredited charade to prove they're not men. The IOC can't think of a justification for this because there isn't one. So let's have a guess: they tried to keep women out of the Games and failed. Their mandatory sex test is a display of their power over the interlopers.

'The most crude and degrading experience I have ever known in my life,' is how pentathlon gold medallist Mary Peters remembers her sex test. She was ordered to lie on a couch and pull her knees up. 'The doctors then proceeded to undertake an examination which, in modern parlance, amounted to a grope. Presumably they were searching for hidden testes. They found none and I left.'

Peters was an early victim of the male backlash in the 1960s against a new generation of successful women athletes – or 'girls' as they are still known to so many sports administrators and reporters. The boys, sorry, men who then controlled international sport – and in their old age still do – held lunatic ideas about female success. *Sport: Physical Training and Womanhood*, a typical textbook published in 1939, stated baldly that too much activity caused female genital organs to decay. This kind of assumption, that if you're good at sport you can't be a real woman, dominated the thinking of that generation. It still does, but protected by the Taboo, the male officials never have to admit it.

When women began demonstrating they could be as committed and professional as men, there should have been celebrations. Instead, the officials panicked. These women were getting out of line – they must be put in their place. It didn't help that most of the new female stars were from the Eastern Bloc and benefited from intense new coaching and dietary regimes unavailable in the West. So prejudiced were the old men that they failed to see that some of the 'suspect' women, with their deep voices and muscular build, were no more than victims of compulsory anabolic steroid regimes.

Rather than recognise these superb athletes, the whispers began; to win the Cold War on the sports field, the Reds must be synthesising genetic monsters. The response: this new breed of women stars should prove they really were women. All female athletes must be tested for 'femininity'.

And as degradingly as possible: in the first 'test', at the European track and field championships in Budapest in 1966, an amazing total of 243 female competitors were compelled to parade virtually naked before a panel of doctors. Later that year, at the Commonwealth Games in Jamaica, all the women athletes had to unveil their external genitalia to a gynaecologist. Similar inspections were imposed at the Pan-Am Games in Winnipeg and the European track and field cup in Kiev.

The IOC couldn't wait to get in on the fun. In 1968, at the Mexico Games, their new medical commission began testing. The naked modelling had so angered the athletes that a more 'scientific' test was required. It all seemed so simple to the Olympic committee. Men most often have an X and Y chromosome; women usually have two X chromosomes. A quick check should weed out the monsters.

But millions don't fit this convenient pattern. Men can have two X chromosomes – and still be real men. In any case, the tests are laughable. Geneticists have demonstrated that the IOC's tests can categorise testosterone-soaked men as eligible for female events in the Olympics.

But the IOC medics just wouldn't leave those girls alone. In Mexico the white smocks were scraping the inside of women's mouths for chromosome testing. At the Munich Games they tweaked hair samples. By the time they got to Barcelona they had yet another trial for women athletes and the only merit was that it had an even longer name than all the previous ones. But it still wasn't any good. The polymerase chain reaction test – PCR for short – was rejected by just about every expert – but it was good enough for the Lords of the Rings.

The world's leading geneticists don't trust it, it's not a common procedure. When inexperienced technicians get to work they can produce false positives – and a lifetime of misery for the victims.

'The story of gender verification is an absolute disaster,' says Professor Malcolm Ferguson-Smith of

Cambridge University. 'The [IOC] medical commission have taken the view that women who show signs of masculinisation however slight must have an advantage. I challenge that view because it's never been shown that the sort of women we're talking about with slight masculinisation due to genetic problems have an advantage over XX women of the same height.'

Scientists like Ferguson-Smith have refused to get involved in the testing. He was joined by Canadians in Calgary in 1988. Four years later French doctors in Albertville declined to do the test and in Barcelona a prominent Spanish geneticist joined the boycott because he 'had no clear idea what the results actually mean'.

The chairman of the IOC medical commission, the medically unqualified Prince de Merode, says 'In my opinion, it's a great success.'

Merode's 'success' can mean psychological trauma and career disaster for women deemed to have 'failed' the test. In theory they can request further investigations but as Dr Elizabeth Ferris, a former British Olympic diver puts it, 'Few women have ever wanted to go beyond the initial screening test. Affected women are usually advised by usually male team officials to retire immediately, feigning illness or injury, to avoid humiliating publicity. Yet they would probably have passed the remaining tests.' At least a dozen women are thought to have quietly quit the Olympics since testing began, six of them in Los Angeles in 1984.

Despite the hazards, a few fight back. American swimmer Kirsten Wengler 'failed' the test in the 1980s and was banned from women's sport. Oh, and by the way, they said, you can't bear children. Her parents paid for additional tests which showed the laboratory had simply got it wrong. Wengler recalled the horror of her predicament; 'You can't talk about it with your friends. You can't go back to school and say I just feel so weird and horrible because I'm not sure I'm really a female. It is so humiliating and embarrassing.' And she was one of the lucky ones.

Maria Patino is the only other woman known to have challenged this spurious science. She failed the test at the World Student Games in 1985, because she has so-called male XY chromosomes, and was ejected from the Spanish team and from university. 'Not only did I lose my scholarship. The most important thing is that I lost my self esteem,' says Maria. 'I lost the confidence of my friends, I lost all my records and I lost the best years of my life.' After a long battle the international track federation backed down and reinstated her.

There wasn't even delayed justice for Polish sprinter Ewa Klobukowska. At the Tokyo games she won bronze in the 100 metres and a gold in the women's relay. Later chromosome analysis revealed she was XXY; Ms Klobukowska was banned from competition. Her condition is found in one in every 1,000 women and today there is no way she would be banned. No-one has said sorry.

If women refuse to be tested before travelling to Atlanta the IOC could have problems. Both the American Medical Association and the American College of Obstetrics and Gynaecology have called for this farcical ordeal to be abandoned. There is surely an American law the women could deploy to prove harassment and, in these days of professional athletes, restraint of trade.

Not before time, the IOC is becoming isolated within world sport. Even the old men of track and field, the biggest international federation, have abandoned them. Track and field put together its own study group in 1990, daringly included some women and decided to drop the tests. Mumbo-jumbo science is out and their new policy is simple: individuals who are reared as women are eligible to compete as women. Any obvious discrepancies would be picked up on a compulsory health check for all athletes – men and women.

The IOC turns its back on scientific evidence and ignores the pain it deals out gratuitously to women. It doesn't have a formal policy on gender and instead relies on the opinions of octagenarian Dr Eduardo Hay, an IOC member for Mexico since 1974, and until very recently, vice-chairman of their medical commission. Hay insisted that gender testing must stay.

In the spring of 1994 Samaranch invited a group of scholars to Lausanne to debate Olympic issues. Inevitably, the sex test came up. What was the current view of the IOC, asked Professor John MacAloon from Chicago. Director general François Carrard promised to 'check and report back'. A few minutes later he popped back and reported that 'those concerned seemed to be satisfied with the tests currently practised at the Games.'

The seven token women in the IOC club have never seemed remotely concerned by the indignities their sisters in sport endure. Just one courageous woman champion on the Atlanta podium refusing her medal from an IOC member would bust the taboo on public discussion. A boycott threat to the sponsors might do the trick; with their female markets at risk, they'd soon tell the Lords to take their grubby hands off female competitors. If nothing changes, watch out for the two classes of athletes in Atlanta; the men and the humiliated.

Fingers and feet tapped as 'Sisters Are Doing it for Themselves' boomed out of the speakers and the conference got under way. Outside, a damp breeze blew off the English Channel but in Brighton's Grand Hotel hundreds of women from around the world – and a few men – were settling into four days of debating women's sport and the challenge of change. Whatever that conference title meant, the atmosphere was lively, open and constructive, a sharp contrast to the pre-programmed Olympic centennial congress in Paris three months later.

The sisters talked coaching, sports science, sexism and networking. There was lots of good news away from Samaranch's Olympic world and one messenger was Sarah Springman from triathlon. Triathlon is a new sport with new attitudes and most importantly new structures. The triathlon federation set up a women's commission in 1990 with a brief to establish gender equality by 2000. By 1992 two out of the six members of their executive board were female. Free air tickets offered by race organisers are shared between male and female athletes: that's equality of opportunity at the start line. They lobby the media for balanced reporting of male and female event's and fight for the same prize money.

The emancipation of triathlon athletes is a world away from the brotherhood. So what are *they* doing for fifty per cent of the world's population? In late 1995 the IOC, after years of deliberations, announced that there might, possibly, be a new policy to empower women just a little – but it wasn't for sure.

With the usual pomp and puffery the brotherhood announced that 'it was necessary to intensify without delay the promotion of the presence of women within sport and its technical and administrative structures.' That got the headlines. The small print said the opposite. Their proposals, examined carefully, promised not much for the girls, and definitely, absolutely, without a doubt, not in our lifetime.

The old boys, had a goal – 'the strict enforcement

of the principle of equality'. Fine words, no change. National Olympic committees might be ordered to meet a ten per cent target of women members on their ruling committees – by the end of the century!

Was this a commandment from Mount Olympus? Certainly not. The IOC's executive, which consistently takes major decisions without reference to its members, was having an unusual rush of democratic zeal; only its full convention, meeting in Atlanta the following year on the eve of the Games, could approve this extreme reform.

There was more tough stuff in the pipeline. The members would also be invited to impose a target of twenty per cent for national Olympic committees by as soon as 2005. As these committees do little and have no input into the activities of the Lords, the earth was not shaking. But hold on: moving with all speed the IOC promised it might well come up with a new strategy for still more female representation in sport early in the next century – but only when Samaranch and most of his elderly cronies have retired.

The IOC was so tickled with this dramatic proclamation that it completely forgot to include itself in the reforms. Enlarging its own female membership to double figures – still barely ten per cent of their ninety-nine male members – wasn't mentioned. Samaranch had to busk his way out of trouble when questioned by reporters. 'The IOC will have to act very rapidly,' he said hastily, which was true. Then he pushed disbelief to new heights, adding 'we will fight for the rights to which women are entitled.'

What about the big sports federations: Would they be thrown out of the Olympics if they didn't drag themselves into the twentieth century before the dawning of the twenty-first? Not likely. They were only being 'strongly invited' to meet the same targets as the national Olympic committees. The IOC imposes myriad petty-rules on federations at the games, but on this fundamental principle of human rights, it has ducked the issue – making only a wishy-washy recommendation.

Samaranch's bold new steps were praised by American member Anita DeFrantz. 'It's additional viewpoints, additional ways of viewing the world, of viewing opportunity, of thinking, of ideas,' she waffled. 'It's been missing. Now we have an opportunity to start the process of inclusion.' With the likes of Anita on their side, the suffragettes might still be clamouring for the vote.

# CHAPTER 18

# *Too Few Tears For the Disabled*

Another opening ceremony, another flag raising. Traditionally, the same flag is handed on from one Games to the next. But this flag would never be seen again. The emblem that flew over the Paralympic Games in Lillehammer in March 1994 was being forced into early retirement after only three appearances; at Seoul, Albertville and Barcelona. For the last time, the disabled competitors saluted their flag with its five tear drops, arranged in two rows like the Olympic rings. When they re-assemble in Nagano in 1998 they will have just three teardrops on their flag.

This change wasn't the choice of the Paralympics organisers. It was forced on them by the IOC. Drop your emblem, they demanded, or we cut off your funding. It's hurting our profits. Disabled sportsmen and women around the world resisted as long as they could. But as one of their leaders told me, 'We are a little weak organisation.' Eventually, they had to comply.

The IOC's attitude to disabled sport undermines its claim that the Olympic Games are universal and open to everyone. The Olympic Charter claims to respect 'universal fundamental principles', and that sport should be 'practised without any discrimination of any kind'. To which might be added 'as long as you have four limbs and all your faculties'.

Suggestions that the disabled should have parity at the Games are resisted by the Olympic committee and so half a billion human beings – more than the combined populations of America and Russia – are excluded. The moral guardians of sport are leaving the Atlanta stadium empty for the first week of the Games; what a missed opportunity to stage exciting competitions for athletes who have overcome greater odds than any able-bodied competitors.

World War Two left millions of disabled veterans whose plight spurred new techniques for treatment. One innovator was Ludwig Guttman of the Stoke Mandeville hospital in England. Guttman believed sport could help rehabilitation and his first open competition, with fourteen male and two female competitors, coincided with the Olympic Games in London in July 1948.

Guttman forecast that 'the Stoke Mandeville Games would achieve world fame as the disabled men and women's equivalent of the Olympic Games.' He was right, and they grew in step with the Olympic four-year cycle. In 1960 twenty-three nations took teams to Rome and by 1976, when they were hosted in Canada, the 'Torontolympiad' attracted double that number.

Dr Jens Bromann, who competed for Denmark in events for the blind remembers, 'Guttman told the IOC that as long as he was living he would call these games "Olympic" and that he would never give up that term because sport for the disabled was as ideal as the spirit of the Olympic Games for the able-bodied.' Guttman died in 1980, the year of the 'Olympics for the Disabled' in Holland. The title would never be used again.

The accession of Samaranch, stage-managed by Horst Dassler with his to plans to auction off both the word

'Olympic' and the five rings, brought with it a new attitude. The committee could only sell what it owned: the
new partners would only hand over billions of dollars
in return for exclusivity. Unfortunately disabled sport
had also laid claim to the symbols. According to the new
régime in Lausanne, this was 'misuse' and had to stop.

'I think the first time we had direct discussions with
the IOC was in Lausanne in the late spring of 1983,' says
Dr Bromann. 'There were three major topics Samaranch
wanted us to accept. We should never again use the
name the "Olympic Games For The Disabled", and
he wanted us never to use any of the symbols linked
to the IOC or close to the five rings. That was a
heavy discussion. Third, he wanted us never to ask for
representation on the official IOC sports programme.

'It was difficult to discuss with Samaranch. At a
meeting with him you have one hour and when you
express something he just looks at you and continues
his talk. When he was finished, the meeting was finished
and there was nothing we could do.

'I have said to Samaranch that they could do a lot
more to help sport for the disabled. What they have
done, I find, is very, very limited, very little. The
financial aid that we got was pocket money, peanuts.'

Bromann does however stress that the IOC president
has been supportive in other ways. 'Samaranch has been
present at many of our games, he forced organisers in
Seoul and Barcelona to put more energy and money
into the Paralympic games, he has done a lot of good
things for sport for the disabled, no doubt about that.
But I think that in some circles within the IOC, they are
a little bit afraid of what this sports for the disabled can
develop into.'

Samaranch's priorities became clear early on in his
reign; things that promoted him personally would

benefit from the flood of new money. Resources that could have gone back into sport – for able-bodied or disabled athletes – were diverted to his hobby: stamp collecting. His favourites became a personal portrait gallery.

In 1981 the Philippines issued a stamp displaying the heads of the deeply corrupt President Ferdinand Marcos and President Samaranch, tastefully linked by the Olympic rings. Samaranch was so taken with this recognition that he ordered IOC staff to set up an international federation for Olympic stamp collecting – FIPO – and an exhibition in Rome the following year.

More of the new funds flowing in from the partners were redirected to creating an Olympic stamp collection. What date should we go back to, asked the Lausanne palace staff? Only to 1980, replied Samaranch, choosing the year he came to Olympic power.

The initiative of President Marcos was soon followed by San Mariño, Korea, São Tomé and Bolivia. The Swiss government produced a first day cover entitled 'Lausanne, Ville Olympique'. Gold, silver and bronze medals were struck to be awarded for the best stamp collection at the Los Angeles Games.

This all cost money, far more than could be spared for the disabled. In 1984 the IOC spent $20,000 on disabled sport, $24,000 on making an instantly forgotten film 'Lausanne Ville Olympique' and $40,000 on FIPO. Only one IOC member, Kenya's Reggie Alexander, asked why they were spending so much on philately. The next year, 1985, there was more money to spend: disabled sport's grant trebled to $60,000. FIPO's increased five times to $200,000.

The next Olympics were in America, and Samaranch is credited with pushing for two wheelchair races in Los Angeles. There should have been a wheelchair Games in

Illinois but this was abandoned after funding problems and transferred successfully to Stoke Mandeville. An Olympic Games for the Disabled was organised in New York, but according to Bromann, Samaranch said at the Lausanne meeting 'that he had asked the US Olympic Committee to do their utmost to stop us using that name.' He was successful and they were changed, to the World Games for the Disabled, and the profitable sponsorship revenues of the Los Angeles Games were safeguarded.

The disabled sports movement made a fresh start in Seoul. They had a new name for their event – the Paralympics – and for the first time their own flag with their own emblem, created by the Korean organisers. This was the five teardrops, in the colours of the Olympic rings, and similarly arranged in rows of three and two.

Disabled athletes felt the new emblem gave their movement a distinct identity. But still Lausanne would not leave them in peace. The rumblings began between Seoul and Barcelona: a handful of national Olympic committees were concerned that the five teardrops might be confused with the five rings and harm their marketing programmes. The teardrops had to change. Disabled sport wouldn't give way. Their next contact with the IOC was in the muscular form of its lawyer, Mr Howard Stupp. This five-times Canadian wrestling champion was now the IOC's director of legal affairs, overseeing the growing number of lucrative commercial contracts and protecting their revenues.

The International Paralympic Committee – the IPC – was summoned to Lausanne in January 1991. They were still getting only a mere $40,000 a year and could spend it only on projects approved by Lausanne. According to the minutes of the meeting, Stupp arrived midway through it to lay down the law on the emblem. If it wasn't so tragic, it would be funny. The five rings was one of the world's best-known logos, visible on consumer products in every store. The five teardrops were virtually unknown outside disabled sport. Stupp told the meeting of the IOC's 'serious concern at the teardrop logo used by the IPC for the Paralympics'. If they had plans to license it to sponsors, they 'could face legal problems'.

In November that year IPC president Robert Steadward reported to their General Assembly in Budapest: 'We have been informed by the IOC's Director of legal affairs that "unless this matter is resolved to the satisfaction of the IOC, a recommendation will be made to the next IOC Executive Board meeting regarding the sanctions to be taken by the IOC against the IPC."'

'Sanctions' against the disabled? What would they do? Shoot a few guide dogs? Smash up some wheel-chairs? The leadership of the IPC bowed and presented their assembly with another emblem: six teardrops in a single ring. The delegates were unhappy. The assembly rejected the new design and voted to stay with their five teardrops. 'A huge majority decided not to accept dicta-tion from the IOC and I think that was when the attitude towards them changed very much within disabled sport,' remembers Dr Bromann. 'Most of the delegates were sick and tired of the IOC and what they stood for.'

The athletes had spoken but the IOC wasn't listening. In May 1992 the IPC went back to Lausanne and the IOC wheeled out its big gun: executive board member Richard Pound. He issued a direct threat. 'Continued use of this logo,' announced Pound, 'could only adversely affect any future relations between the IOC and the IPC.' The meeting was scheduled to move on to discuss disabled sport and the modest funds the IOC had budgeted. But there was a condition. The min-utes record Pound saying, 'Only when this matter was

solved to the satisfaction of the IOC could further discussions concerning assistance and advice take place.'

IPC President Steadward then asked about funds which
the IOC had agreed to forward to IPC in 1992. Pound
'reiterated that the issue of further assistance depended
solely on the resolution of the logo problem; this had
been a unanimous decision of the IOC Executive Board.
The funds were in the IOC budget and would be released
when the matter was satisfactorily concluded.'

But Lausanne hadn't reckoned with the Norwegians.
Early in their preparations the Lillehammer organisers
merged the marketing of the Winter Games and the
Paralympics. Even as the IOC was threatening the
IPC, Lillehammer was promoting the Paralympics with
the unacceptable five teardrops. Lausanne objected
but Lillehammer's chief organiser Gerhard Heiberg
resisted; the IOC withdrew, but with poor grace. Legal
director Howard Stupp penned a brusque letter to
Heiberg in June 1993 in which he conceded the use
of the five teardrops one more time 'because it will not
be used for other competitions'.

Stupp recognised that although the IOC had lost the
battle, it had won the war. The IPC leadership agreed to
reduce their emblem to three teardrops after Lillehammer.
'I wish we could show more strength but it is difficult
because what we always run into is a lack of money,'
says Dr Bromann. 'Unfortunately, we are a little weak
organisation and sometimes we are trapped.' André Raes,
the IPC's general secretary, confirms, 'We compromised on
five teardrops because we did not want to jeopardise our
relationship with IOC. Yes, we were under pressure.'

Atlanta's impressive bid documents predicting what
a great Games they'd stage had one major omission:
there were no plans for a Paralympics. The IOC didn't
require it. A year after they were awarded the Olympics,

the organisers offered a handful of exhibition events for disabled competitors. Andy Fleming, of Paralysed Veterans of America, responded, 'Glory for a handful of people at the expense of closing off the wonderful opportunity for thousands of other people.'

Inexplicably, Atlanta seemed reluctant to stage a disabled sports event. 'The cost seems prohibitive unless someone provides the funding,' grumbled a spokesman. But early in 1992 the Atlanta organising committee was embarrassed into offering $15 million in cash and services towards the cost of a paralympics. Eight months later Andy Fleming was appointed to lead the Atlanta Paralympics organising committee.

There was one huge catch. Fleming's team had to go out and raise at least $60 million from sponsors – but they couldn't play the market. They could only approach sponsors already signed up by the Atlanta Olympic committee – and certainly not their competitors. Fortunately Coke signed up first and then the Paralympics moved into the less competitive area of medical sponsors.

But more trouble followed. The US Olympic committee, which boasts of raising a million dollars a day from its sponsors, demanded a share of the royalties raised by the Paralympics' mascot, a lively bird named Blaze. They didn't just want them *during* the Games – they wanted a cut long after the event was over. The Paralympic committee rejected the demand, saying it would hobble their future budgets. When negotiations failed they took the USOC to court. Eight months later a truce was declared with the USOC complaining the settlement would cost them 'in the six figures' in marketing and licensing revenue.

When Samaranch had told the disabled sports movement that they could forget about being equal competitors in his Olympics, he demanded a pledge the officials couldn't give. 'We said to Samaranch and the IOC, we could not give up this right for disabled people. We could not in 1983 say for disabled people in the future that they should never have the right to be at the Olympic Games,' says Dr Bromann. 'For many athletes the utmost you can achieve is to be at the Olympics.'

Samaranch's obduracy has divided the disabled sports movement. 'Some people say "we don't want to be mixed up with that organisation, we want to stay clean." Some others think the IOC has been too dictatorial and that we should maybe go in totally another direction, find ourselves another name and stay away from the city and the country where the Olympics are held,' says Bromann.

That's one opinion: others are still determined to find a way for more disabled athletes to enter the Olympics. They note that the Olympic Charter claims 'the activity of the Olympic movement . . . reaches its peak with the bringing together of the athletes of the world.' But not yet: when disabled sport told the IOC in May 1992 that they had set up a committee to examine ways in which disabled athletes could be further included in the Games, Richard Pound replied this was impossible for 1996 as the programme was already fixed.

According to the minutes Pound declared, 'The IPC faced a dual problem – it had to convince the IOC to include further disabled events in the programme, and on the other hand it would have to convince the international federations to reduce participation in able to accommodate more disabled athletes.'

Pound's response reflects the IOC's position on many moral issues. They could lead a wide public debate about the relationship between their Games, disabled athletes and the Paralympics. As long as they delay, the Olympics remain untrue to their Charter.

# CHAPTER 19

# Keep Taking the Medicine, But Don't Let Us Catch You

'Chinese sport is very clean,' declared Samaranch in October 1994, on the eve of the Hiroshima Asian Games. He makes this kind of implausible claim routinely – that the Olympic movement is winning a war against doping – so it's unlikely he reflected on the wisdom of his remark during the next few weeks.

The Chief Guardian spoke – and immediately all the Olympic guardians were at it: poor old China was getting a raw deal. The hard-to-take-seriously Olympic Council of Asia (proprietors: the ruling Al-Sabah family of Kuwait) rebuked 'racism and the western media for untrue doping slurs against Chinese athletes'. Billionaire Bob Hasan from Indonesia, newly-recruited to the IOC, blustered, 'We have been too quiet, too nice. We have to be on the offensive. We have to tell the world the allegations are not true.'

The Olympic choir was in full voice. Senior Lord of the Rings, India's Ashwini Kumar, chimed in: 'It's become the custom that the excellence of Asian athletes is denigrated by sports administrators in the West. We must stop this pernicious habit.' Never a man to miss a headline opportunity, track and field's Primo Nebiolo praised the Chinese for their 'better organisation, better strategy, better philosophy, better ideology'.

The Asian Games ended, the labs were silent and a confident Samaranch insisted once more, 'all the tests were negative.' A week later in Lisbon he claimed, 'We think doping is really declining and there are very few problems in the main competitions.'

Six weeks after Samaranch's bold claims for China's clean sport the truth leaked. On 16 November 1994, the *Chicago Tribune* claimed a Chinese swimmer who had won gold in the Asian games had been caught on the dope. Why hadn't the result been announced? There were 'political reasons'. That's code for not embarrassing Samaranch. The *Tribune* claimed the offender was women's world 400-metre freestyle champion Yang Aihua. Could this be the same Yang Aihua who earlier in the year had insisted, 'We have an anti-doping policy which forbids drugs and punishes those who break the law. The reasons for the success of our team are our very good coaches and our training methods, which are the best in the world'?

She was backed by a Chinese foreign ministry spokesman who reassured the world of sport: 'Chinese athletes have been subjected to many tests on many occasions. The results of these tests show none of these athletes have taken illegal drugs.' It was all lies.

And the news got worse, much worse. It wasn't just Yang Aihua who was doping. Another ten Chinese athletes had tested positive. Five women and six men, seven of them swimmers, plus a hurdler, a cyclist and two canoeists had all been taking the same steroid; dihydrotestosterone, believed by many athletes to be undetectable. Ben Johnson thought he was on it in Seoul – he'd been conned by his handlers – and according to the underground dopers' network, it was the drug of choice at the 1988 Games. But now the steroid could be identified and Professor Manfred Donike, who had supervised the Hiroshima testing, said there was no doubt that China was systematically doping its competitors.

Facts? Who cares about facts? Chinese IOC executive board member He Zhenliang denied systematic doping. The Olympic Council of Asia insisted these were 'purely individual cases which cannot be generalised for other athletes'. This time there was no comment from IOC headquarters and Samaranch kept his head down for three months before surfacing in Rome in February 1995 to assert, yet again, that the war against doping was being won. 'We've been fighting it for a long time and have had good results,' he said.

Trust me, everything is being taken care of, promised Samaranch again a couple of weeks later in Monte Carlo, insisting that 'The Olympic movement continues its relentless struggle against doping.' His director general, François Carrard, tried to close the controversy down with his odd opinion that 'the Chinese sports authorities are doing their utmost to control the doping problem.' Ten months later Samaranch, back in Japan, announced, 'We are advancing a lot in the fight against doping.'

Since his accession in 1980 Samaranch's campaign to minimise the extent of doping in sport has become an art form. He dissembles, makes preposterous claims believed by few in sport – and gets away with it. He has to – to preserve Lausanne's luxury lifestyle. If the public ever catch on to how dirty élite sport has become, the sponsors and TV networks will pull the plug on the billions they pay the IOC for a clean, moral event.

Strange things happen to the results of dope tests. Some go missing and even when the evidence is clear and damning, somehow nobody gets to hear about it.

Instead the rent-a-quotes trundle out again; doping is under control, don't worry, be happy.

A Colonel from the KGB may have saved the Moscow Games. Not one positive dope test was recorded in 1980 – although he claims there were several. And he should know; the colonel was obeying the edicts of the old men in the Kremlin and fulfilling the hopes of the IOC's new boss. The old fascist and the grim party leaders needed a pure Olympics.

Great sport in the Lenin stadium was a must. A smooth-running, scandal-free Olympics would become a model for the world – and provide a focus for morale-boosting in Lausanne. A record-breaking Olympics would suit the marketing men. Since a dope-free, record-breaking Olympics was only possible in Samaranch's dreams, they would have to cheat.

Positive tests should have engulfed the Moscow Games. Doping was growing exponentially and although Montreal four years earlier had escaped with only eleven positives, the syringes were ankle-deep on the road to the Olympics. So well done the colonel and his KGB colleagues. They were heroes in the struggle for socialism and the Olympic ideal. Retired now and living in Moscow he insists, 'No names, I don't want to let down my former colleagues or the athletes.'

Then he explains: the KGB was ordered to infiltrate the anti-doping operation and posing as interpreters and assistants, brought special skills to the testing. Some of the athletes came over all shy when asked to give urine samples. The good comrades turned discreetly away while the cheats quickly pumped clean urine from concealed bags into the sample bottles. The colonel also alleges that some athletes used the technique, relatively easy for women, horrifyingly painful for men, of pumping clean urine into their bladders via a catheter. Both these techniques have surfaced over the years in other countries.

The colonel claims that some dopers were caught in Moscow. Who were they? 'One from Sweden, our friends from East Germany, and our shooters turned out to be positive,' he says. 'The Soviets were rescued with tremendous efforts.' The colonel has no regrets about his Olympic endeavours. 'Why should one see dark clouds on the clear Moscow horizon? And the Olympics were such a tremendous success.'

And of course they were; scant attention was paid to the subsequent re-analysis of the urine samples by Germany's Professor Manfred Donike. As he did after every Olympics, the professor took them back to his lab for further scrutiny. He found evidence of a large number of athletes using testosterone, the human hormone that anabolic steroids mimic. Although this was banned by the IOC, the scientists couldn't agree on how to measure whether an athlete was doping or merely excreting a higher level of natural hormone. While the argument continued for the next four years, athletes continued to use it without fear of sanctions.

Russian journalists weren't fooled. 'Doping control in Moscow?' laughed one track and field reporter to me years later. 'There was no doping control!' Look at how many retired Soviet athletes are now suffering health problems, he pointed out, from the large doses they had been forced to take.

The IOC made much of these 'dope-free' Games. Afterwards the chairman of their medical commission, the Prince de Merode, claimed that many nations had tested their athletes in advance and withdrew those who failed. He also praised the Moscow dope lab as 'a good example for future organisers'.

Merode changed his tune later, admitting privately that some of the testing equipment in Moscow was flawed. But that wasn't what the rest of the world was told. Samaranch's *Olympic Review* published an article about the Moscow Games which stated, quite baldly; 'Prince de Merode stressed that the Olympic Games in Moscow had been the most "pure". Proof of this is the fact that not one case of doping was registered.'

That was the IOC's plan for Los Angeles; the 1984 Olympics must appear 'pure', without too many embarrassing dope results. Sports lovers, athletes, TV networks and sponsors were misled by Samaranch and his IOC leadership; as they publicly proclaimed victory in their 'war' against doping, they ought to have known the figures they published about the Los Angeles Games were false. The inside story of doping control at the 1984 Olympics is at odds with the published facts.

At the end of the Games the IOC could have revealed that many more athletes had tested positive than the twelve it admitted to. Vital documents identifying the cheats were mysteriously shredded. Why, if the IOC is so keen on good clean sport, didn't they tell us? Could it, by any chance, be because they didn't want to spoil the salesmen's pitch?

Montreal had left a financial hangover and Moscow suffered the American-led boycott. This had to be third time lucky. Absolutely nothing must blemish the idealistic event Horst Dassler's salesmen were busy touting to new sponsors. Doping was the spectre at the festival: if the IOC had to report any substantial increase on the Montreal eleven, the networks and the sponsors would turn away and Dassler's cash well would dry up.

Plans for doping control got off to a bad start; the Los Angeles organisers refused to test for testosterone, claiming it was a natural body substance. Had they prevailed then LA would truly have been a doper's delight. The athletes had learned that if there was no out-of-competition random testing, it was easy to beat the dope cops at the Games: just stop taking steroids several weeks before the event, but carry on injecting testosterone.

The Los Angelenos also declined to test for caffeine. What was the point, everybody drank it. The row between them and de Merode simmered for two years and he told a Soviet sports magazine. 'I can't help recalling the ease with which the IOC tackled all the problems with the organisers of the Moscow Olympics. Things stand differently with the Americans.'

Eventually the Americans gave in, but their chief organiser Peter Ueberroth was irritated by press stories about doping and told the IOC that he deplored coverage which made the public think 'all athletes were doped.' He urged them to stress the very few positive results to deflect suspicions that all athletes were 'drug addicts'.

America's athletes were among the best prepared for whatever dangers the LA dope testing might pose. The US Olympic committee invited their élite competitors to use the facilities – to learn how to urinate into a bottle, they explained. What the cheats among them learned was the clearance times of whatever drugs they were ingesting. Perhaps it was coincidence that not one American athlete was caught in 1984.

In the first week of the Games a few volleyball players and weightlifters were caught doping but there were no stars; the sponsors' favourites were clean. Then the testers caught up with Finnish distance runner Martti Vainio, who had taken silver in the 10,000 metres. He was called before the medical commission and agreed that his Games were over. But before the positive result was announced he turned up for the first heat of the 5,000 metres. He knew he shouldn't have been there, so who told him to run? Was it whispered in the Olympic corridors that his problem would be taken care of, don't worry, just run, we'll sort it out?

Whatever promises were made to Vainio, they couldn't be delivered. 'There was only twenty minutes to go when I was told Vainio had failed a test,' says Fred Holder who was a trackside judge for the 5,000 metres. 'Something had to be done. Vainio accepted my decision to exclude him without argument but later in the afternoon I encountered Nebiolo.' The boss of track and field was livid. 'He insisted that it was his decision to take and that the result should have gone to his executive council – which wasn't due to meet again until after the Olympics.' Holder ignored him, assuming that Nebiolo's notorious vanity made him want to be seen to take a big decision. Holder also told me that he suspected Samaranch wanted any decision to be taken less publicly.

Vainio commented later, 'I think there are others. I am the only one who was found guilty. It is right that I am punished, but how many other athletes should be in the same boat?' Later it was disclosed that Vainio had tested positive at the Rotterdam marathon two months earlier. These two offences should have brought a life ban. He was faced only with the offence at the Olympics and suspended for eighteen months.

The next secret row came when Italy's shot putter Gian Paolo Urlando was caught. Again, before the result could be announced, the back-stairs meetings fizzed. According to a report discovered in the East German Stasi files, Italian and world track president Primo Nebiolo sought out Professor Donike of the IOC's medical commission. Apparently there was a quarrel when Nebiolo asked if anything could be done for Urlando, and why it was necessary to have quite so many positives?

The bad news was piling up. What could be done? Easy. If the lab was finding too many positives – close the lab. Dr Arnold Beckett, a member of the testing team, says that three or four days before the end of the Games lab director Dr Don Catlin told him they had orders to shut down operations. 'Much to my surprise Catlin said very clearly that he'd got information from on high that there should be no continuing of the testing,' Beckett said. 'He was very annoyed.'

Beckett adds, 'We were not alarmed; we had already experienced many problems with doping control and much obstruction in our work, but assumed it would be completed after most of the IOC members had departed.' Catlin's integrity has never been challenged over the disputed total of positive tests in Los Angeles and he says he has no recollection of such an instruction.

At the midway stage in the Olympic fortnight, Samaranch must have felt he was staring over the lip of the abyss. The drip, drip of positive dope tests was becoming a trickle and with finals looming in many of the events known to shelter dopers, he had to fear disaster. Worse still, the biggest stars were competing; commercial suicide loomed if any of them were disqualified for cheating. On the track Carl Lewis was about to equal Jesse Owen's four golds, Seb Coe retain his 1,500 metres title and Evelyn Ashford and Valerie Brisco-Hooks outrun their rivals. Future Olympic stars Ben Johnson, Merlene Ottey and Florence Griffith-Joyner would win lesser medals.

Many positive results from unidentified athletes were passed on to the IOC medical committee, recalls Craig Kammerer, assistant director of the laboratory. The testers waited for the suspect athletes to come and witness a second test of their sample. Says Kammerer, 'At the end of the Games we had a whole slew of positives, but no competitor ever showed up for a

B sample. Some of these were testosterones, some steroids, and some ephedrines. We were never given an explanation of why nothing was done. It wasn't our job to hand down sanctions, so we didn't spend a lot of time thinking about these missing positives, but it did make one wonder what was happening.' The record books show twelve positive tests and disqualifications at the Los Angeles Games. The IOC could live with that. But there was no public disclosure that many more athletes were guilty.

The LA Olympics were declared a great success. But the scientists from the doping lab expected further action on the remaining positive tests. The IOC's executive board met in November 1984 but failed even to mention them. Half a year after the Games ended, several of the scientists met in Cologne. There was Donike, Beckett, Dr Robert Dugal from Montreal and medical commission chairman the Prince de Merode.

When challenged about the lack of action over the nine tests, de Merode had a remarkable tale to tell. He explained that during the Games he kept the list of athletes tested – and the code numbers fixed to their samples to maintain confidentially – in a locked cabinet in a room at the Biltmore hotel. The day after the Games ended he had gone to his office and discovered it had been emptied and the vital documents removed. The LA organisers explained the room rent had ended that day and all the documents had been removed and shredded. The identities of the athletes who had tested positive would never be known.

'It was a scandal and you may say "Why did some of us not take action?"' says Beckett. 'Very simply, from what de Merode said, he seemed to us to be a completely innocent victim and therefore nothing could be done.

'We decided that I would take responsibility,' Beckett

added. 'I wrote a letter, which was signed by Donike and Dugal, which in effect said that we had studied the situation, acknowledged that de Merode was an innocent victim and realised that we could not proceed further.'

The suspect athletes escaped, and so did whoever gave the order to force open de Merode's locked cabinets and shred the documents. But the scientific data on the positive tests remained, even if it could not be tied to individual athletes without de Merode's list of the code numbers.

Two years later Catlin and Kammerer sent the draft of an article about the Los Angeles dope testing, intended for a medical journal, to de Merode. 'He sent a letter back telling us that we couldn't publish this data,' says Kammerer. 'He claimed it was the property of the IOC. Catlin told the prince we could publish the data, it was in our contract that we had a right to publish.'

They compromised: 'We agreed not to publish the day-by-day account of the lab results. This would have shown clearly on what days the positives occurred and what the substance was. From that people could have matched the list of positives declared to those that had not been acted upon.'

Catlin denies there was pressure to limit the disclosures. 'I was convinced that the issue of what happened to the missing positives was not going to disappear,' he says. 'But I would not still be a member of the IOC medical commission if I had published a report without the co-operation of the prince.'

Athletes and sports reporters weren't fooled. They muttered for years about the ones that got away. A decade later BBC TV's investigate sports programme *On the Line* began digging. Beckett and Kammerer confirmed the secret positives and the mystery of the document shredding. The revelations were screened in late August 1994. What did the IOC have to say? 'We have no comment on the specific allegations,' said IOC communications director Andrew Napier. 'But we would point out that until 1988, the IOC and its medical commission were almost alone in the fight against drugs in sport.' De Merode admitted the shredding had been 'a mistake'.

Was there a conspiracy in LA? Did Olympic leaders order the shredding – or did the penny-pinching organisers screw up? It didn't matter to the Guardians; sports fans were hoaxed but the Olympics remained a good investment for sponsors. The same old men who deceived us over LA did the same at the next two Summer Olympics and will be controlling what we're told in Atlanta.

Ben Johnson had beaten nineteen dope tests in the two years before the Seoul Games. Would he get away with it again? With his enormous muscles he looked like a steroid freak and most track and field insiders reckoned he'd got the biggest drugs cabinet in the business.

Johnson duly roared to success in the 100 metres; he was confident, he was sure he was taking an undetectable steroid, the same as so many of his rivals. Then came the knock on the door. Would he please come and see the medical commission? His lazy dope doctor had given him horse medicine and the lab had found him out.

Korean journalists got hold of the story first. Perhaps they got a leak from lab technicians fearing a cover-up or maybe they spotted Johnson and Canadian team officials being roused from their hotel. Whatever, the story was out of the IOC's control. Western reporters were tipped off that it would be the next morning's front page in Seoul and chased after the Prince de Merode. 'You'd be on to a good thing if you ran this story,' he confirmed. 'A report will come from the Medical Commission in the morning recommending that Johnson is banned and his medal taken from him.'

Ritual denials poured out of the Johnson camp. Canadian member Dick Pound defended him until the evidence became overwhelming. Samaranch appeared temporarily flabbergasted and then clung to the spin doctors' script. 'We have disqualified the fastest man in the world,' he said, claiming the IOC had proved its determination to stamp out doping. Not everyone was convinced, including a member of his medical commission. 'If the professors hadn't been there in Seoul,' says this IOC member in confidence, 'I think they would have swept the Johnson result under the carpet. There would have been a cover up.'

'The IOC is winning the war against doping,' repeated Samaranch two months after Seoul, and that seemed the end of the Johnson affair. Neither the IOC nor Primo Nebiolo's track federation investigated the scandal. Fortunately, the Canadian government did.

Judge Charles Dubin headed a judicial inquiry and eventually Johnson, his coach, his doctor and a string of other athletes admitted doping. Johnson's athletic drug dependency, it was revealed, was well known in Canadian sports circles. The cosy conspiracy of the Olympic family was demolished when Dubin reported. The Lausanne party line – that testing during the event deterred the cheats – didn't stand up to scrutiny by a smart lawyer. His inquiry heard reams of technical evidence about the time it took for traces of illegal drugs taken in training to clear from athletes' systems. The stars admitted under oath that they knew what to take and when to stop. Tests in the Olympics were just a necessary but unthreatening chore before collecting medals and more endorsements.

'Despite knowing the fallacy of in-competition testing, as they have for many years,' wrote Dubin, 'the medical commissions of sports organisations such as the IAAF and the IOC have taken no steps to make the fallacy more widely known. They have given the impression that their competitions are fair and that the laboratories cannot be fooled.' His verdict on the world's most moral sports organisation? 'This concern for appearance, not substance, has been a continuing theme in the evidence.'

And of course Johnson wasn't the only cheat in Seoul. 'The general public has long been led to assume that if only one athlete tested positive, the others were not also using drugs,' said the judge. 'We now know, as the IOC and the IAAF have known for many years, that this assumption is false. The athletes caught at Seoul were not the only drug users. They were the only detected ones.'

The Dubin report was of no great importance, said the IOC's Dick Pound. 'In carries no weight at all.'

Had Dubin known the full truth about the doping in Seoul his comments might be unprintable. The labs caught ten cheats, but a year later Professor Donike revealed he had, again, re-tested a number of the men's samples: at least fifty had been taking steroids. There was more: 'As many as twenty athletes tested positive and were not disqualified,' revealed the Seoul lab director. There will always be marginal and inconclusive tests but the IOC declines to publish the raw data. Until this happens, as one expert commented to me, 'It opens the door to drive a truck right through.'

Six years after Seoul the doping secrets of East Germany were revealed. Hidden in the Stasi files were the records of their 1988 swimming team, clean when they raced and steroid-choked in training. Kristin Otto, who had won six golds, had steroid levels three times the permitted maximum a year after the Games. Similar levels were discovered among her fellow stars. The reporter who dug out the truth joked, 'Otto had more testosterone in her than the entire starting team of the Dallas Cowboys.'

Olympic year 1992 opened with the IOC convention in Albertville where Samaranch praised 'the constant and stubborn fight the Olympic Movement is conducting against doping.' He hadn't read the editorial in a new academic journal *Drugs In Sport* which the same month commented, 'Today, the use of drugs in sport is so pervasive that most athletes must use them if they wish to remain competitive.'

The experts agreed. 'The danger is that if there are no doping scandals, the Olympic audience might interpret that as a sign that drugs are vanishing from the Games,' warned Dr Robert Voy, former chief medical officer of the US Olympic committee. 'A lack of positive tests will only indicate that the athletes who use drugs are more sophisticated than the doping control programme.'

Samaranch responded the same as before. 'The IOC Medical Commission has been at the front line for a quarter of a century . . . we have always fought against doping with concrete actions, not just with facile words.' One of his concrete actions was to permit Ben Johnson to compete in the Games again after his two-year suspension. Johnson came last in his semi-final and went away, only to be banned for life the next year after tests showed he was at it again.

The dope cops caught just five athletes in Barcelona, half the number in Seoul. The Prince de Merode enthused, 'I'm very optimistic that the fight against doping is progressing very well. The prospects for the future are very good.' Samaranch added, 'I do sincerely believe we are winning the battle against doping.'

Samaranch qualified for a new honour in Barcelona. He presided over the biggest drugs festival ever; worse than the Seoul and Los Angeles Games rolled up together. The now regular post-Olympics examination of the samples had disclosed a staggering one in ten of the competitors were serious steroid abusers – that's nearly a thousand dopers at those Games. It's become a regular refrain: a few athletes are caught and then, months after the Games, the scientists always come up with more positives. The sports administrators bury them.

In March 1993 Canadian sports reporter Mary Hynes taped an interview with Samaranch in Atlanta. She asked him about the latest figures. He replied, 'Never heard these comments. Never. I was the other day with the Prince de Merode. He is very happy [with] how the fight against doping is going on. He is very happy.' Ms Hynes persisted; 'So you haven't been aware of any report of that sort?' The answer was a brusque 'No.'

Respected academics wonder out loud if the IOC has a clue what it's doing. 'They've acted really quite differently from the rest of the scientific community,' says Professor Chuck Yesalis of Pennsylvania State University. 'They don't tell people how they do their work. One might speculate, and it's only speculation, that they fight it because perhaps there's some problems with the quality of their work.'

Can we even totally trust the labs? To survive financially, they must have the blessing of the IOC. Dr Arnold Beckett, removed from the medical commission after twenty-five years' service, underlines the predicament faced by each lab; 'Will it be independent, truly? Or will it toe the line when it shouldn't toe the line?'

The IOC funds drug research but hesitates when it comes to action. With a great fanfare it announced in

1989 plans for a 'flying laboratory' to carry out random testing in countries without facilities. Sponsors were offering $1 million to get it off the ground. Then the IOC discovered it was looking at another $1,500,000 a year in running costs. Dick Pound was unhappy: the committee should give a moral lead, he said, but should not get involved itself.

In early 1991, they backed off completely. Leave it to the sports federation barons and the existing labs, said Samaranch, adding his usual mantra, 'this is in no way a step back. For a long time we were alone in the fight against doping which we have pursued since the 1968 Games in Mexico.' His claimed commitment was unconvincing: the IOC didn't bother to appoint a medical director until the early 1990s. Coincidentally, as the committee decided the flying lab was too costly, it was running short of money to fund the construction of its museum in Lausanne.

Two classes of dopers can be expected in Atlanta. Rich athletes can afford the drugs that don't show up in tests: human growth hormone, erythropoetin – which increases the number of red blood cells and so provides more oxygen in competition – and other hormonal drugs taken in dosages so low they clear the body within hours. They'll stay ahead of the testers with new versions of steroids coming out of commercial and illicit labs. Poor athletes who rely on steroids that show up in tests and who don't come off them well before competition are the most likely to get caught.

The IOC will only catch the cheats if it is really determined to do so. You can see why its determination slips. The first dope-free Olympics would have to exclude many stars. It would be a less rewarding Games for the viewers – and for the money men. But real sports fans would know they were getting the genuine article.

And the world's young athletes wouldn't be tempted to risk their health in the hope of winning medals. Don't be confident the IOC will lead the campaign for real sport.

The saddest comment I ever heard about doping came from Britain's Peter Hildreth, a high hurdler in Melbourne and Rome. 'I hope my grandchildren enjoy their sport,' he told me, 'but I hope they are never good enough to join the élite where drugs will surely be urged on them.'

# CHAPTER 20

# *Gunning For the Peace Prize*

Battalions of guerrilla insurgents stand by, armed and poised to engage, eager for the order from Generalissimo Samaranch mulling over the maps in the Lausanne war room. Wait for it; stand by, load the fax machines; take aim, dial! Moments later newsrooms everywhere are strafed with declarations of war, disguised in the language of peace. Juan Antonio Samaranch is gunning for the Nobel Peace Prize.

Heads down for the opening battle of the 1996 campaign for the peace prize, one of the more secret wars in history. We can hear it, we can see it, but all the time we're assured, it's not actually happening. The IOC denies everything: they're not campaigning for the Nobel, they haven't used Madison Avenue strategists, they wouldn't dream of such crass behaviour and this isn't the biggest barrage of the committee's secret ten-year campaign for hearts and minds. It just happens to be Samaranch's last chance to acquire this foreign territory. After Atlanta he'll have lost the initiative, and risk being out-gunned by rivals who, damn them, didn't even manoeuvre, just worked for peace and were astonished to be plucked out for the world's greatest humanitarian honour.

\*　　\*　　\*

Zealously Dick Pound has directed the crusade for the Nobel since October 1986 when he whispered to his colleagues in Lausanne that some of New York's top public relations men – a crack team of spin-troopers – were planning a new image for the Olympic committee.

So on 22 April 1987, Samaranch authorised a special budget for Pound to start the long march on Oslo. The Nobel, he instructed, was the 'clear objective' of the offensive.

Pound donned his fatigues, blacked up and disappeared into the underworld of image-doctoring. In 1990 he returned with the strategy to win the Nobel. This is how we get it, he told Lausanne. In four years it'll be the hundredth anniversary of the founding of the IOC; one hundred years of bringing the youth of the world together in peaceful competition. By then we must have established a beach head at the United Nations; we must have their support. Then we'll make a great fuss about the power of the Olympics to bring world peace. And of course, we've already got our foot in Norway's door; awarding us the Nobel will be popular in 1994 – we've given the Winter Games to Lillehammer!

What if we don't get it, asked a colleague. Easy, said Pound. Treat 1994 as a dry run, re-group and fight again in 1996. We'll make a big fuss about it being the hundredth birthday of the first Games in Athens. The council of war broke up with Pound declaring that both centenaries should be looked at as a 'springboard to obtaining the Nobel Peace Prize'.

Samaranch has already been awarded one peace prize – the problem is that nobody's ever heard of it and it doesn't carry much credibility. Claiming that their 1988 Olympics had laid 'stepping stones to world peace' the Korean organisers created the Seoul Peace Prize. Every two years they award it to an individual or organisation they judge has made an outstanding contribution to international harmony. The lucky winner gets a certificate, a plaque and cheque for $300,000. The first winner, in 1990, was none other than Samaranch. It couldn't have hurt his chances that one of the judges was – Mickey Kim. Samaranch put the plaque on display in Lausanne, the cash in his Olympic museum account, and his press office flooded the media with the news that the old Blueshirt was now recognised as a man of peace.

The following year, at the IOC's convention in Birmingham, Samaranch introduced his new image consultants. The tenth-biggest advertising and public relations firm in America, with 200 offices world-wide, Grey International had set up a squad of 'sportscommunicators' based in Brussels and were ready to go into action. Leading them was New York-based Jack Bergin, a veteran of tough campaigns with the steely Hill and Knowlton agency. Bergin learned his communications craft as an aide to Casper Weinberger, the defence secretary famous for controlling America's biggest ever peace time armaments budget.

Bergin's special forces at Grey were just the boys for the battle. Members of New York's crack marketing agency, they'd done their service where it counts – in fast moving consumer goods. Their armoury included the killer line, 'For a skin almost as soft as a baby's behind' for Mennen Baby Soft. Their 'Whose underwear is under there?' had gone into action for Fruit of the Loom.

Why had they been recruited? Grey told the press they would assist the IOC 'in communicating its re-dedication to the Olympic values on the occasion of the centenary celebrations of the Olympic Movement in 1994 and the Olympic Games in 1996.' This was an echo of Dick Pound's 'springboard' for the Nobel. The Olympic committee should be seen as 'being a positive influence even beyond the sports arena,' suggested Grey.

Samaranch pumped up the hype in Albertville on the eve of the 1992 Winter Games. 'We are feeling the effects of the wind of freedom that is blowing across our planet, a phenomenon we often helped to create,' he claimed to the IOC convention. Exactly what the IOC had contributed to the demise of the Soviet bloc he didn't say. But he added, 'The Olympic Movement offers the world its ideal of peace and human brotherhood.'

As the athletes gathered in Barcelona Samaranch contrived an interview with himself in his monthly *Olympic Review*: 'The IOC is stronger than ever and more respected world-wide,' he bragged. 'This is one of our reasons for our leadership role in the world.' What were his objectives? 'To give the contemporary world a philosophy of peace, fraternity and comprehension of the youth of today and a model for the twenty-first century,' he responded. Samaranch had effectively written his own Nobel citation.

Meanwhile his briefers were at work. Surprisingly, the liberal London *Guardian* fell for the PR line: 'Many must have wondered amid all the dazzle and noise of the finale what sort of recognition might be accorded the man who had presided over the largest gathering of nations in Olympic history, and in a manner that enhanced the reputation of sport and the movement,' asked their Olympic correspondent at the close of the Barcelona Games. The *Guardian*'s answer? 'There cannot be much dispute that he should be nominated for the Nobel Peace Prize.'

Miller of the *Times* rammed home the message. 'The IOC, under the guiding force of Samaranch, is the most universal social instrument of peace in our time,' was the concluding sentence of his washes-blue-shirts-white biography of the Olympic president.

Miller did it again a few months later, in the sports newsletter *Sport Intern*. 'What above all distinguished this celebration of the Games by his home city was the demonstration of peacefulness,' he trumpeted. 'At a time of war, starvation and financial crisis elsewhere, the example of sport could not have been more conspicuous.' Then he switched to his megaphone: 'The sporting world gathered in unique harmony, presented a face of tranquillity that must have carried a legacy of hope for mankind. Therein lies Samaranch's contribution to contemporary society. The gratitude owing to a sporting leader, by many, is without previous parallel.'

Samaranch didn't trust his mercenaries to fight the battle alone; he ventured out of the war room to do his own campaigning. One target was Inge Eidsvag, rector of the humanistic Nansen Institute in Lillehammer. Eidsvag is an expert on the Olympic movement, the Peace Prize and knows the Nobel committee members well. When he pitched up in Lausanne on a private research trip Samaranch summoned him.

'Samaranch soon started to talk about the Nobel Peace Prize and the rest of the conversation, which lasted almost an hour, was entirely about it,' recalled Eidsvag. 'He said he thought that the IOC deserved this prize and was puzzled they had never received it.' Eidsvag told Samaranch he was being unrealistic – the IOC had little chance of winning it in the foreseeable future. 'I found Samaranch's question a rather naive and vain wish on his part,' he said dryly.

Samaranch disagreed. The IOC deserved a prize, he told Eidsvag; it had done a lot for peace. Then he asked the Norwegian what kind of things people had done in the past to win the prize.

'He stressed that it was not for himself that he wanted the Peace prize but on behalf of the IOC,' says Eidsvag. 'But he would be the one receiving it, regardless of the organisation. Samaranch's initiative shows how little knowledge he has of the political landscape in Norway.' This was a direct reference to Samaranch's political history.

Inge Eidsvag told his story to reporters Einar Odden and Frank Brandsas who'd covered the IOC since Lillehammer won the Games. They sensed an exclusive and set off to investigate. Was Samaranch really campaigning for the Nobel? Had Grey been enlisted as his soldiers of fortune? They called former IOC executive board member Robert Helmick in Des Moines. During a press interview on the eve of the Barcelona Games Helmick had mentioned, casually, that Samaranch, when signing up Grey, had said, 'Success will be measured on whether or not we win the Nobel Prize.'

That's right, said Helmick to the Norwegian reporters, and added, 'There was a lot of talk about the Peace Prize when I was on the executive board and there was never any doubt that we liked being considered a candidate.'

Samaranch later derided Helmick's claim as 'false', to which the American responded, 'His memory must be getting old.' Helmick felt the IOC leadership had forgotten their responsibility to young athletes striving to get to the Olympics. 'It seemed like there was a decision that now we're going to use sport as an instrument for other purposes.'

If Helmick was right, Grey had been given the job of masterminding the campaign for the Nobel. Would the IOC admit it? Odden and Brandsas lunched the IOC's press director, Michele Verdier, in Lausanne. Brandsas asked her, 'Is it right that Grey is working to help the

IOC to get the Nobel Peace Prize?' She replied, 'Yes they are. It's the most important part of their job for us to work for the Peace Prize.'

Even Grey admitted it. Their Oslo office told Brandsas, 'It is still unofficial.' Their target year was 1994, the first centenary, and the year of the Lillehammer Games. That was enough: Odden and Brandsas published their scoop in Norway in February 1993. Within hours it was running on the international wires and for the first time in ninety-nine years, the world hooted with laughter at the IOC.

The Norwegian press published cruel cartoons reviving Samaranch's forty-year fascist record, depicting him throwing off his jackboots and fascist Blueshirt for Olympian robes and olive branches. Another showed him as a supplicant gazing up at a statue of Alfred Nobel. The caption read, 'But I thought he was from Lillehammer.' The story touched a nerve in Norway; had they been given the Games as a bribe for the Peace Prize?

Grey protested the story, insisting the company would never have agreed to direct a campaign for the Peace Prize. 'The IOC categorically denies that it has asked Grey or any agency to campaign for the peace prize,' fumed Samaranch. He was supported by his chief of staff, François Carrard; 'As director general I can assure you that we have never had any intention of using Grey or any PR agency for such an assignment.' They should win gold for amnesia.

Samaranch tried to turn the disclosures to benefit his campaign. 'I am not qualified but the IOC might be considered, because it has fought for 100 years for youth, peace, sport and solidarity. It should not be for me but for the IOC.' So who would we see accepting the prize – his driver?

He continued denying the story – all the while

encouraging it. 'Never, never will the IOC lobby for the Nobel Prize,' he insisted in Atlanta. 'That's up to the jury and we have nothing to say – only to say that we are ninety-nine years old and I think we do something for peace.'

Dick Pound on the other hand seemed flustered. He couldn't quite say yes – and he didn't completely deny the allegations. Pound admitted that the Olympic committee's executive board had discussed the Peace Prize. 'After President Samaranch won a peace award in Seoul, someone wondered about the Nobel Prize. Anyone would like to win it. But a) we'd never campaign and b) we'd be embarrassed to be thought of doing it.'

Samaranch wasn't in the least embarrassed about his next stratagem. Two months after Odden and Brandsas's disclosures he contacted Norway's prime minister Mrs Gro Brundtland, begging her support. 'The IOC is very much concerned by the human suffering caused by the ongoing armed conflict around the world,' wrote the man who had once espoused the politics of the jackboot.

Would Norway care to back his latest manoeuvre? The backroom boffins had dreamed up a new weapon for his Olympic war: an Olympic Truce. They'd dug out the old truce that had operated during the ancient Greek games, allowing the athletes safe passage to Olympia. Generalissimo Samaranch wanted the United Nations to make it official. Would the Norwegian government back him? To lend weight to his appeal, the IOC leader signed off the letter to the socialist prime minister with his new title, Marqués de Samaranch.

Mrs Bruntland was so fired up it took her four months to reply. She politely restated what everyone knew; the Norwegian government supported peace initiatives. It was easy for her to keep Samaranch at arm's length.

She'd got the Games. Britain's prime minister John Major still wanted them and had to play along. He went to Lausanne for an audience with Samaranch, hoping to win support for Manchester's hopeless Olympic bid.

Samaranch rattled on about his truce and a bizarre new suggestion; his committee of freeloaders should be granted Observer Status at the UN. Thrashing around for a diplomatic escape from such madness, Major declared the idea 'excellent'. In Monaco in September 1993 for the Olympic committee vote on the Games of 2000, he was embarrassing Britain again: 'I am delighted to support the IOC in its bid for observer status at the United Nations and in its efforts to secure an Olympic Truce,' twittered Major. He needn't have bothered. Manchester lost.

Lausanne's delusions grew crazier by the day. Observer status was no longer enough: the IOC needed proper links with the UN Security Council, François Carrard told the boys from the press. 'We must have close bilateral contacts with the decision makers,' he insisted.

Next on the battle plan – love-bombing the United Nations. Samaranch chose a cunning route; he sent his envoys south and persuaded sports leaders to lobby the Organisation of African Unity. Never mind your famines and your own wars, chaps, just sign here. In June 1993 the OAU resolved that the youth of the world should be mobilised 'in the cause of peace'. Africa was now behind him, echoing the Olympic Charter; could Samaranch persuade the UN to follow Africa's lead and give him the world's endorsement? It would surely be noticed by the Nobel committee.

Ethiopian exile Fékrou Kidane was sent to New York to campaign on behalf of the IOC. He had good contacts among African politicians which would help get a resolution backing the Olympic committee's peace campaign on the UN agenda. But he hadn't always been so convinced of Samaranch's commitment to peace. Back in the late 1980s Kidane had been one of the first to spot the IOC's low-key campaign. 'It's high time that international public opinion was made aware that all the talk of peace and understanding was only a cover for a lot of other things,' wrote Kidane in his short-lived newsletter *Continental Sports*.

Offended by the corruption around the awarding of the Games to Barcelona Kidane had trained his sights on the Olympic president. 'Patient and astute, Samaranch already had his plan worked out. Once he became IOC president he had to have the Games. Now that is an accomplished fact, he would like the Nobel Peace Prize for the IOC.'

Times change. *Continental Sports* folded, Kidane was out of work and Samaranch needed someone to be his 'Olympic Truce Bureau Co-ordinator'. Kidane got the job, and with it a first class ticket to New York. He watched over the African lobby as it proposed that 1994 should be declared the 'International Year of Sport and the Olympic Ideal' and that Samaranch's Olympic Truce should be supported. Without debate the UN general assembly agreed. No plans were made, no budgets agreed. The comic intermission over, the UN returned to the real world and the war against narcotics.

But the IOC had got the resolution it wanted and first to employ it was Mickey Kim, telling a sports meeting in Finland, 'We must all strive to ensure the success of these projects which are so important to the universal humanism that we all need so much.' David Miller followed him in the *Times* at the end of 1993, urging that the Olympic committee was a 'worthy candidate for the peace prize'.

\*　　　\*　　　\*

The Peace Prize war was just waiting to be won. It was centenary year, the Winter Games were in the Nobel's homeland and the UN was backing the Olympians. The brave boys and girls in the Lausanne press office switched to automatic fire, spewing out press releases to the world's media. No expense was spared on garish 'Truce' brochures, stickers and even a brand new logo for the offensive.

The allies piled in. On 24 January 1994 at the IOC's glass and marble palace in Lausanne the Olympic Truce was launched. A lot of not very important people with inflated titles used up dozens of first class air tickets to say silly things that went virtually unreported.

Guyana's Samuel Insanally, taking his turn as president of the UN general assembly, addressed the troops. 'The resounding support of this initiative is a tribute to the IOC which under the inspired leadership of President Samaranch continues to do much through the medium of sport to promote the call to world peace,' he said. Mickey Kim applauded.

Switzerland abandoned its tradition of neutrality. The Truce had support 'from the whole of the international community,' said the Swiss foreign minister. It 'underlines the sense of responsibility and the high ideals which motivate the leadership of the Olympic community.' Samaranch simpered, 'We are convinced that in associating yourselves with our initiative, you are making a significant contribution to the search for peace.'

The Truce began on 5 February; a day the people of Sarajevo will never forget. A mortar crashed into their market place and sixty-eight people were slaughtered. Much of Samaranch's peace farce centred around the plight of the city that a decade earlier had hosted the Winter Games; if his truce didn't impress in Bosnia, it was unlikely to have effect anywhere else.

That Samaranch's preposterous truce failed to stop a single shot didn't discourage the public relations people in the psychological warfare division. Their fax machines fired a fusillade of support from the Organisation of American States, the World Health Organisation, the British government – which did not suspend its war in Ulster – the Japanese government and France's President Mitterand. China's premier took time off from genocide in Tibet to praise the Truce as did Boris Yeltsin, soon to unleash his armies on Chechnia. The Norwegians, not deceived, gave the 1994 Nobel to Arafat, Peres and Rabin who had actually done something for peace.

The troops were given compassionate leave while the advisers regrouped. The peace convoy went back on the road for a victory in 1996, just as Dick Pound had predicted. In November 1995, Generalissimo Samaranch personally led his troops to the United Nations, driving his tanks across the lawn and up to the podium in the general assembly.

'Olympism is a school of democracy – there is a natural link between the ethics of the Olympic Games and the fundamental principles of the United Nations,' insisted the old Falangist, presumably with his right arm strapped down tightly to his side. What else had the back room boys put in his speech? The IOC supported the family, peace, and more peace. All its money went into sports development, and the Olympians would never trade their souls. Would that do?

It did – the UN called for an Olympic Truce for Atlanta. But this time the resolution had been cunningly re-worded. It didn't just call for another truce in 1996. It called on member states to 'reaffirm the observance of the Olympic Truce in advance of each Summer and Winter Olympic Games'. This implied there had been

a world-wide truce during the Lillehammer Games –
even though there hadn't.

Fighting for the Olympic peace has been a dirty war.
When Ruben Acosta, president of world volleyball,
proposed an Olympic declaration for peace and international friendship Samaranch rejected the idea, claiming
it was 'practically impossible' to achieve. There was
only room for one on the Sports for Peace bandwagon.

The cycling federation suggested the IOC encourage
the Olympic movement to stop sending each other
Christmas cards and instead donate money saved to
disabled sport. Samaranch rejected that idea too; he
wasn't passing up the chance to send IOC cards to
world leaders and influential figures.

IOC member Nikos Filaretos suggested that the ninth
decade of the IOC's existence – the 1990s – should be
declared 'The Decade of the Woman'. It was already
well overdue but it was dismissed. Samaranch blundered. Egalitarian Norway would have liked the gesture. A plea from the hockey federation to stage its
Fair Play Trophy ceremony prior to the final match of
the Seoul Tournament was, of course, trashed.

The Mayor of Athens came up with another version
of the Olympic Truce in 1988. Why not an appeal to
all warring factions to suspend hostilities during the
Olympics? The mayor and his idea were dispatched.
Thanks – but no thanks.

The peace barrage will continue over the Georgia
skies. Expect to see Atlanta's chief organiser Billy Payne,
former civil rights activist turned Olympic booster
Andrew Young, and maybe President Clinton mouth-
ing empty 'peace' platitudes. Watch the opening and
closing speeches.

Does anybody apart from Samaranch and his cronies
think the IOC could possibly qualify for the world's

ultimate accolade? 'I think the international sports movement has a potential for peace but at present it is a rich, undemocratic social élite,' says Inge Eidsvag of the Nansen Institute. He even questions whether Olympic sport is conducive to peace. 'It can be argued that élite sport trains individuals to fight, to be individualists, to be good soldiers,' he says.

Vegard Ulvang, the Norwegian super-skier, has no doubts about Samaranch's long war for peace. 'The suggestion that the IOC receive the Peace Prize is completely wrong,' he says. 'I think the IOC has often represented the opposite of what is required to receive such a prize.'

# CHAPTER 21

# *Death In Paris*

Bringing together the IOC, the international federations and the national Olympic committees for a great summit meeting sounds worthwhile but the small print in the Charter underlines how pointless it all is. The IOC president presides, he alone sets the agenda and the congress is only consultative. No voting is permitted and the final report is written in Lausanne. Speakers are picked carefully, few dissident voices are heard and the keynote speeches address everything except the real issues.

The Olympic Charter calls for a congress to be held in principle every eight years. Samaranch had avoided calling a congress since the rubber-stamp convention of 1981 when sports officials from around the world travelled to Baden-Baden to be told the Olympics were being handed over to the multi-national sponsors.

There had been plans for a congress in 1990. By the mid-1980s committees and commissions, all with their own budgets, had been set up to plan a convention in Tokyo. The IOC persuaded China to delay the opening of the Asian Games scheduled for that year and agreed that the congress motto should include the word peace. That decision was taken the same day they resolved that their 'clear objective' in appointing American spin doctors was to procure the Nobel Peace Prize. But

Samaranch became unhappy; he'd discovered that this celebration of himself and his committee was to be staged without subsidies from Japanese taxpayers. Instructions were sent to Tokyo; the Leader would be there in two months time and he expected handouts.

The Japanese government caved in and guaranteed a chunk of the $8 million budget, and the IOC graciously pledged $100,000 of its own money. But as the Nobel campaign grew, Samaranch's enthusiasm declined. A congress in 1990 ruled out another one in 1994 when the combination of their centenary, the Lillehammer Games and the Olympic Truce provided a triple whammy with which to clobber the Norwegians. So Tokyo was abandoned, the money already spent was written off and a 'Congress of the Century' planned for Paris 1994. Samaranch told his closest colleagues it would be 'very prestigious'.

But there were good reasons to convene in 1994. There was the committee's hundredth birthday to celebrate in Paris where the movement began. Grandiose speeches could be made about the Olympics' contribution to world peace and delegates could talk until they were exhausted about the future of the Games in the next century. The low-ranking sports officials from around the world would surely feel that Samaranch was listening: lately he had made vague noises about the long-overdue democratising of the Olympic movement.

It was a disaster. Nelson Mandela said he was sorry but really too busy to make the trip to Paris; French President François Mitterand stayed home in the Elysée Palace and Placido Domingo cried off. The guest list at Samaranch's most important ever Olympic event was beginning to look a bit thin. Then the UN general secretary, the boss of UNESCO and the prime minister of Norway all sent their regrets. The front row of the VIP box at the centenary congress of the Olympic movement was going to be full of empty seats. This was Samaranch's last big public push of 1994 for the Nobel, the bill was already at $16 million and rising and now he had nobody to make world headlines.

The absence of his star names focused attention on the agenda, little more than a celebration of the longevity of the Olympic committee, and media coverage was universally hostile. The delegates found themselves and their contributions sidelined in debates which never questioned the commercial exploitation of the Olympics, the increasing power of television and what the IOC does with all its money. At the end of a week of hot air, the movement had no idea how it was going to progress into the twenty-first century. But Samaranch wouldn't be around then so it didn't matter.

The centenary was milked for all its worth. Paris wasn't hit once, but twice. Pierre de Coubertin and his aristocratic friends had announced the revival of the Olympics on 23 June 1894, and so a century later Samaranch and his Olympic club turned up at the ornate Great Amphitheatre of Paris's Sorbonne university to make self-congratulatory speeches. But there was a problem: their credibility with the media had diminished since the manipulations nine months earlier that had nearly given the games to Beijing. The sulky hacks kept asking how the IOC reconciled their open-to-professionals Olympics with Coubertin's amateurs-only Games. 'This is a very superficial approach,' said chief Olympic bureaucrat François Carrard, reassuringly. 'A man with his vision would understand what is being done.'

Two months later in August they returned to Paris for the money-no-object congress. The IOC announced that 'two thousand people from all parts of the international Olympic movement will meet to consider the future of the Olympic Games.' It was as much a class-ridden occasion as the one a hundred years earlier. The IOC and its important friends enjoyed the best functions 'by invitation only', as the schedule revealed. For the rank and file there were public spectacles. Oxford and Cambridge university rowing teams raced on the Seine, sky-divers with parachutes in the blue, yellow, black, green and red colours of the five rings dropped in at the Eiffel Tower with the Olympic flame.

Samaranch's original plan was for a grand centennial dinner at the Palais de Versailles (by invitation only) but this was later altered to a less ostentatious ceremony at the Sorbonne (again, by invitation only).

Without his big stars, Samaranch seemed confused. 'I leave the stand to President . . . er . . . Prime Minister Balladur,' he mumbled at the opening ceremony. The Olympic visitors promptly took a back seat as Balladur made his pitch for the forthcoming French presidential elections. 'I am personally keen for France to host large-scale and top level sporting events,' said Balladur, adding that he hoped to see the Olympics in France early in the next century. Rival presidential hopeful Jacques Chirac followed up with 'The people of Paris are deeply moved by the IOC's decision to choose this city to celebrate solemnly the anniversary,' a coded repetition of the Parisian politicians' desire to stage the Games.

Samaranch then set out his agenda. 'Our duty is to be at the service of the athlete,' he said. He then completely contradicted himself: 'The IOC must listen to all opinions . . . it will then be up to the IOC Session to analyse the consequences and take the necessary decisions.' In other words: you talk – we decide.

The congress was staged well away from central Paris, way beyond the Arc de Triomphe, beyond the end of Avenue Charles de Gaulle, across the Seine in the La

Défense business quarter. This ugly sprawl of tower blocks, the home of Esso, Citibank, Fiat, Hoechst and a host of other multi-national companies was entirely appropriate for Samaranch's new Olympic movement.

Riot police with clubs and guns guarded the entrance to the convention centre and its huge concrete dome. Once through the doors, delegates found themselves in what seemed like a hangar fit for a Zeppelin, faced by a carpeted walkway, striped in the Olympic colours, disappearing into the far distance. More security guards checked every accreditation and, denied admission, I sat for the next four days outside the Café de la Place, taking notes, watching the deal-makers muttering over their *café au lait*, and waiting for sympathetic reporters to bring me spare sets of documents.

Hundreds of volunteer hostesses in red waisted jackets over peek-a-boo blue mini-skirts ushered very important Olympic committee members to and from their limousines. Behind the fixed smiles, they weren't all happy. 'It's all about marketing but we're not being paid,' one of them told me. 'I'd rather be at the Olympics.'

Scattered around the dome were free-standing video monitors endlessly playing the IOC promotional film. Sponsor's logos were superimposed over shots of Olympic champions and the parade ended with Samaranch's tribute to his paymasters. 'Every act of support for the Olympic movement promotes peace, friendship and solidarity throughout the world,' he claimed. For those who hadn't got the message Samaranch concluded, 'For helping keep the flame alive, we thank the Olympic sponsors.'

The Olympic committee had stumped up $6 million from their reserves towards the $16 million bill. The city of Paris tossed another $5.4 million in the pot and the French government chipped in $4 million. A further

$600,000 came from sponsors Adidas, Hermes, Credit Lyonnais, Air France and Renault. All Samaranch could say when a reporter asked him to justify the cost was, 'I think it is worth it.'

Working the floor were father and son double act Artur and Goran Takac. I shook hands with Goran and congratulated him on his health. 'I look tanned because I have just been on holiday,' said the well-rewarded Olmpic bidding consultant. Mickey Kim and his entourage of sharply dressed black belt instructors wandered the huge hall looking like an ageing rock band: Dr Kim and the Limb Disjointers. They'd everything to smile about; at the end of the week Samaranch would confirm that taekwondo would be in the Sydney Games and their cash registers would overflow.

Many of them remained in the Café de la Place rather than attend the discussion on the Olympic Movement and International Understanding. Mickey's daughter was in town as usual; Kim Hae Jung is a pianist and frequently performs at Olympic functions. The previous year the Berlin 2000 committee had arranged a gig for her with the Berlin Philharmonic and she was now giving a recital in the Grand Amphitheatre of the Sorbonne for the greater pleasure of the guests of the congress, part of what they called the 'Cultural Programme for Accompanying Persons'.

I buttonholed one of the IOC's directors who immediately demanded anonymity, told me the IOC is much more democratic under Samaranch, insisted that Spaniards 'love' Samaranch, admitted he knew nothing about modern Spanish history and then gasped when he saw executive board member Dick Pound glaring at him. Information director Michele Verdier scampered around as usual with her bundles of files while her new boss Andrew Napier massaged the hacks during the day at the congress and at night in the bar of the Mercure hotel. Napier would have been unaware, as he pushed the party line, that within six months Samaranch would have ejected him from his job in Lausanne.

Around the big players ebbed and flowed the lowly sports administrators from around the world, many of whom had never seen the IOC at play before. These officials, the backbone of world sport who struggle to find the funds to organise sport and training for their young athletes, were looking forward to earnest and useful discussions and decisions. Instead, they discovered the agenda had been stitched up a year before to showcase the IOC leadership. Many looked quite poor in rayon suits and cheap shoes and most of them clutched the white plastic briefcases distributed to all delegates.

These folk are never on the sumptuous gift lists taken for granted by Olympic committee members. Inside their cheap goody bags were an Adidas tie, an XL size T-shirt with the congress logo, a zipper bag with pens, pencils, a portable hole puncher, sticky tape, glue, scissors, staple remover and a bottle of eraser fluid for blanking out residual Olympic idealism.

To cheer them up as they tried make their allowances stretch to cover the cost of meals delegates also got a declaration on fair play, a set of Paris postcards and the annual report of the Olympic museum. In case they still had daft ideas that there might be any voting at the congress there was a special brochure reminding them that Pierre de Coubertin had wanted the movement to be free of 'electoral uncertainty' – the IOC's standard defence for its lack of democracy.

These two thousand administrators were shipped in to make up the numbers, a few of them allowed to make supportive speeches about the Olympic committee. They were scattered in neighbourhood hotels.

Next up the pecking order were the rank and file Olympic committee members – and they weren't too happy either, despite staying in the Grand Hotel with its magnificent foyer decorated with chandeliers and paintings.

'The IOC footsoldiers were not having a good time. The public thinks they are at the centre of power – but they know they are cosmetic, just window dressing,' said a friend of mine who was also staying in the Grand. 'Stuck in a separate hotel, they couldn't even lobby their own leadership. Some of us complained to them that they were hogging the chance to speak, popping up at the podium four or five times. They rounded on us saying, "This is the only chance we get to speak!"'

The congress generated an estimated six million sheets of paper and more than four hundred speeches were delivered. How the time was shared out says all you need to know about the priorities of Samaranch's modern Olympic movement. His committee, then of ninety-odd members, the international sports federations and the national Olympic committees were each allowed ninety-two speeches, totalling six hours and thirty-five minutes per group; just over four minutes each. Out of the couple of thousand congress delegates, only one hundred and twenty were athletes and they got just forty-nine speaking spots, totalling two hours and thirty-nine minutes; a little over three minutes each. There was no open invitation to the world's competitors; they were hand-picked by Lausanne.

Just about everybody present – except for the IOC – thought it urgent to discuss the future of the Olympics, how to stop doping, getting control over commercialism and being given more money from the swollen accounts in Lausanne. Delegates who'd come half-way round the globe wanted to hear constructive criticism and visionary approaches to the problems besetting the movement.

What did they get? Four nebulous themes: The Olympic Movement's Contribution to Society, The Contemporary Athlete, Sport In Its Social Context, and Sport and the Mass Media. Not a lot for $16 million. The IOC's leaders claimed this would produce a blueprint for the Olympics in the coming century but many muttered that these were irrelevant debates. 'I think these meetings have much more value than you can perceive at the time,' insisted IOC director general François Carrard. 'We are expecting very precious results.'

The important speakers got more than three minutes. You could tell which ones they were because their oratory was printed on pink paper. Speeches from ordinary delegates were shovelled out in piles of white, mostly never listened to or read. One of the few pink contributors, on Sport in its Social Context, was Mr John Hunter. Does his name ring a bell? Did he win gold somewhere, sometime? No; he makes gold out of the games. Mr Hunter's an executive VP of Coca-Cola. Delegates had to put up with a sugar drink hustler taking centre stage in their Olympic discussions in Paris to tell everybody that 'To sponsor is to believe.'

Mr Hunter said that Coke 'cherish the same values, the same principles and the same beliefs as the Olympic Movement.' I understood that bit, even if it isn't true. He talked so much about belief that I half expected him to start baptising delegates in a font of the fizzy brown stuff – but then he got to his real message. 'Just as sponsors have the responsibility to preserve the integrity of the sport, enhance its image, help grow its prestige, and its attendance, so too, do you have responsibility and accountability to the sponsor.'

Another pink paper proselytiser wore what looked like the most expensive suit in Paris. Inside it was of course Professor Anwar Chowdhry, president of international amateur boxing, close chum of Stasi spook Karl-Heinz Wehr, at the congress to give a lecture on Olympic morality, a subject he knows more about than most. His impenetrable speech included references to 'historical dynamics', 'humanist personality formation' and 'ethical normatives'. I wondered for the sake of Mr Chowdhry's mental health whether he'd actually written this. The only words I'm confident were his own were 'Our movement reflects the present state of moral sense ... the decisions of the judges and juries are respected.' He said nothing about the Seoul boxing results.

The IOC's Judge Kéba Mbaye spoke on the same theme as Chowdhry, announcing that 'The Olympic movement remains the supreme moral authority in sport' and insisting, 'A long cherished dream has come true; the establishment of an Olympic Truce.' Fellow executive board member, China's Zhenliang He revealed, 'The Olympic movement is holding high the banner of international understanding, peace and progress' and the Congo's Jean-Claude Ganga said that few other organisations have such 'respect for democratic values and human rights'. He was speaking of the committee whose leader tried to give the Games to Beijing, and which is still accountable to no-one but the Coca-Cola company.

This was all good knockabout nonsense. Then it turned sinister. Former Adidas lawyer and Olympic committee member Thomas Bach suggested that the IOC should stop selling television rights and instead produce its own pictures and sell them. 'The production of television images as well as their transmission under the sole responsibility of the IOC,' said Bach, 'could be helpful for sponsors, for television stations but above all for sport and the Olympic Movement itself.' This would be Samaranch's ultimate: no troublesome journalists and television producers making their own decisions about what the world should be allowed to see.

Where Thomas Bach led, Mickey Kim was quick to follow. 'The evolution of sport and of television must remain under the control of institutional sports authorities,' he suggested. The IOC should 'co-ordinate and control media traffic', was another idea, straight out of the Korean spooks manual. It was backed by fellow IOC member, banker Richard Carrion from Puerto Rico. He also advocated the IOC keeping 'sole control of its own product'. Reuter commented that these proposals would restrict media coverage to the level permitted by totalitarian regimes. 'Fortunately for the media and for the Games,' said their reporter, 'few delegates seemed to take them seriously.'

Alternatively, there was Australia's Mr Clean from the executive board. Kevan Gosper's pink paper was littered with the word COURAGE, always in capital letters. Courage was needed to stop entertainment taking over the Games and élite athletes driving out competitors from the developing world, and to liberate a few more seats in the Olympic stadium currently owned by the corporate sponsors.

A flutter ran around the press corps; this was revolutionary stuff – for an IOC member! Was it his coded bid to displace Dick Pound in the Samaranch succession stakes? Wasn't he knocking the Leader's greatest achievements? Not in the opinion of the *Los Angeles Times*. 'Gosper, fearing he had been too blunt, went to the press room to inform reporters that he was merely tossing out some suggestions, that he was not sure when or even whether the IOC should act on them and that what really bothered him was "extravagant, unrelated" entertainment at sporting events. He was unable to describe what he was talking about but he presumably knows it when he sees it.'

One critic who did know what she was seeing and wasn't happy with it was French sports minister Michele Alliot-Marie. 'Let's not forget that the ancient Olympic Games died of these evils: money, corruption and cheating,' she said. 'I believe the abuses that one finds in sport are due in no uncertain measure to the relationship between sport and money.' Never before had a keynote speaker at an Olympic convention described the ancient Games as evil. And then, criticising Samaranch's greatest and only achievement, selling the Games for cash. That was her Olympic Order down the tubes.

There weren't many dissident voices in Paris and those there were spoke mostly to half-empty halls. Norwegian green campaigner Olav Myrholt said the IOC talked about protecting the environment but he felt its 'action seems to lag behind'. Professor Bruce Kidd from Toronto called for real gender equality in the games; not just in the events but also among the officials. Les McDonald of triathlon had been reading the official book of the congress, *For a Humanism in Sport*, and noticed it had only one reference to women. Former Olympic Hurdler Ed Moses pointed out that athletes have little or no say in most of the sports federations, the national Olympic committees or the choice of Olympic host cities.

The saddest conversation I had in Paris was with Norwegian skater Johann Olav Koss. 'I am here to suggest that you keep the flame alive for Olympic Aid. The torch should be handed over to the next organisers of the Olympics,' he pleaded with delegates. 'There should be an Atlanta Olympic Aid and a Nagano Olympic Aid. It should be a permanent feature of the

Olympic movement.' After his speech he told me, 'My appeal has had no immediate response from the IOC and Atlanta does not want to know. Nagano do appear interested. But, Nagano wants to pick up the mantle from Atlanta. When I spoke only twenty-five per cent of the chairs were occupied.'

A year later Atlanta did respond. Together with the UN they plan to raise $7 million to provide medicines, counselling and education for the estimated twelve million children who've lost their homes and often their parents in regional wars in the last decade. 'Because of its direct connection to the Olympics we saw not only a perfect but a beautiful fit,' said Billy Payne, citing the Olympic Truce.

Koss wasn't the only person speaking to empty chairs. Samaranch's soporific agenda had driven many delegates out into the autumnal sunshine of the La Défense plaza. At one session there were only sixty-three people in a room with five hundred chairs, reported one of my spies, and by the last day only one hundred out of two thousand delegates were still down in the basement, of whom many had fallen asleep.

A rising star of the Olympic committee, say its cheer-leaders in the press, is Belgian surgeon, Jacques Rogge. His test came in Paris. The congress had been prevented from doing anything positive, had avoided all the issues confronting the Olympics and couldn't even bring itself to review the creaking sports programme in the Games. How could the delegates who'd travelled such distances be fobbed off, rendered brain dead before being dispatched to the airport?

'When the IOC president announced in 1990 that a major change in the Olympic programme would be decided during the Paris session,' said Rogge, adopting the role of anaesthetist, 'the world of sport and the press reacted with emotion.'

Unlikely, but how could Rogge explain away the lack of action in Paris? 'As the games are a success, their programmes could not be bad,' said the man tipped for the top. As delegates slipped into a coma Rogge continued, 'it is recommended not to intervene on topics about which a decision was already taken by the IOC.' Which should have raised the issue of democracy in the Olympics – but that had also been promised and then reneged on.

Rocked by the earlier furore in Lillehammer about the lack of democracy and accountability within the IOC, Samaranch had improvised, 'We are going this way,' he claimed. 'The Congress in Paris may be a good way to modernise our organisation.' A mere eighteen days earlier he had been interviewed in Lausanne by one of America's big three television networks. Then he had taken a different view.

He was asked, 'Will the IOC come under pressure to democratise?' Samaranch replied, 'We think that a democratic system was invented by our founder Baron Pierre de Coubertin. For one hundred years we are applying the system and the results are not bad. We will follow the system in the future.' After the interview his press handlers put pressure on to stop the transmission – and succeeded. Whatever the reasons for cancelling a film the editor had passed for transmission, Samaranch managed to keep this indiscretion private. I worked on the programme and still have a transcript of the interview.

For many of the delegates, the Olympic congress in Paris was a throwback to a cruel history they had left behind. The South Africans, the East Europeans and other delegates from countries which had achieved free

ballot boxes in recent years discovered that the Olympic
movement had the hallmarks of the totalitarian societies
that had scarred their lives: no free votes or elections
and aloof, all-powerful leaders.

The Olympic committee tastelessly rubbed it in: on
the last day it announced that, retrospectively, the event
would be known as 'The Congress of Unity'. Were these
echoes of Brezhnev and Franco? Not at all. 'We are
very pleased by this decision. I think it shows that the
re-baptised "Congress of Unity" is not just a word in
the air,' burbled François Carrard. 'Samaranch declared
the theme of the Congress would be unity and then
gave no one a chance to disagree,' concluded the *Los
Angeles Times*.

The congress over, the Olympic committee staged
its own private, annual convention. Now the IOC
footsoldiers, who had seethed at their own impotence
through the week, took a mild revenge on Samaranch.
The control freak who thought he had the whole
Olympic movement buttoned down announced that
he wanted the unchallenged right in a year's time
to nominate ten new members to the committee, all
presidents of sports federations, without consulting his
members.

After what was said to be a stormy debate, more than
a quarter of the membership signed a petition demanding a secret ballot. Samaranch responded fast, to see off
the threat of an embarrassing defeat. The compromise
was that Samaranch could make the nominations but
members would have the right to vote on them.

Primo Nebiolo, who can expect to benefit from
the admission of some of his malleable fellow presidents crowed, 'I think it's a good decision which will
strengthen the unity of the Olympic movement.'

The committee had no stomach for further challenge
to Samaranch and meekly nodded through a dozen

new members, taking them up to the magic figure of one hundred members in their centenary year. After three years of stonewalling America, down to one member since the abrupt departure of Robert Helmick, Samaranch finally chose James Easton, president of international archery and also president of a $100-million-a-year family firm, making archery arrows and baseball bats.

Britain also got a new member: in came Craig Reedie, a financial advisor who'd been president of international badminton. His fellow member Princess Anne wasn't present to congratulate him; sensibly, she hadn't wasted time on Paris. Italian Olympic big shot Mario Pescante was admitted, with a caveat: Pescante – together with Nebiolo – was awaiting trial on corruption charges relating to the huge overspend on refurbishing the Rome Olympic stadium for the 1990 soccer world cup. It was agreed that if convicted, he would quit the committee. All defendants have since been cleared.

Alex Gilady, for long NBC's sports vice-president in London and New York became Israel's first member. NBC gave him the new title of International Olympics Liaison Officer. Gerhard Heiberg reaped the reward of organising the Lillehammer Games. Boris Yeltsin's tennis coach, former Russian Davis cup player Shamil Tarpischev, replaced an old Stalinist who had quietly been removed from the committee. Valery Borzov, winner of two golds in the Munich sprints and now Ukrainian sports minister gave Samaranch the opportunity to claim that 'Maybe in the near future more athletes can come in.'

There was also a vacancy for a new member from Indonesia. The last member had been deputy prime minister and defence minister under the cruel regime of president Suharto who has held power since the late 1960s. Would Samaranch make a gesture for peace and against the Jakarta dictatorship? Might he select the Indonesian writer Pramoedya Ananta Toer nominated for a Nobel prize but whose work is banned in his own country?

Not likely. Samaranch chose one of Suharto's close personal friends, Mohamad 'Bob' Hasan. Hasan heads the association of Indonesian timber growers, who log the rain forests. He is probably a billionaire, with around one hundred private companies ranging from forestry and construction to banking and insurance. Described as closer to Suharto than most of his cabinet ministers, Hasan plays golf with the dictator. He also heads the country's athletics and gymnastic federations and sponsors long distance road races with fabulous prize money.

Hasan coexists amiably with a regime under constant criticism from the UN. Suharto's annexation of East Timor in 1975 and subsequent murderous occupation has cost 200,000 lives in a population of only three-quarters of a million. Human rights group Amnesty International regularly highlights the abuses of the Suharto regime. The anti-subversion regulations, known as the 'rubber law' because they're flexible enough to trap anyone critical of the government, crushes attempts by the ill-paid workforce to create free trade unions and jails journalists seeking a free press. As 'Bob' Hasan set off for Paris and admission to the IOC, the regime cracked down on the media, closing publications critical of the government. The founders of a free journalists association, set up without government permission, have since been arrested. Hasan runs a weekly news magazine, *Gatra*, which has not fallen foul of the censors.

# CHAPTER 22

# *Keep Taking the Monkey Glands*

The dozen new members who joined in Paris were all male and reduced the average age of the committee by one year to a sprightly sixty-two. This was clearly too low and within a year Samaranch was campaigning to lift the retirement age beyond normal life expectancies.

It all stemmed from his determination to stay on forever at the head of the Olympic movement, perhaps even unto death. A marketing man who worked alongside the IOC for years, once predicted to me that Samaranch would never quit. 'He loves the power too much,' he said. 'They all do. Once they've lived that life of luxury and jetting around hob-nobbing with world leaders they can't retire back to mowing the lawn in their back gardens. They get too used to the power, it rejuvenates them, it's like monkey glands. Without it, they soon waste away.'

How long Samaranch had been planning his move we may never know. A couple of months before their 1995 convention in Budapest he wrote to his members suggesting they raise – or abolish – the committee's retirement age. He gave a copy to his faithful scribe Karl-Heinz Huba, who published it in his *Sport Intern* newsletter, and sat back to gauge the reactions.

\*    \*    \*

The committee first brought in a fixed retirement age in 1966, the year Samaranch joined, ruling that everybody then on the IOC could stay for life – but new members must quit at age seventy-two. By one year, Samaranch missed the automatic right to hold Olympic power until he dropped.

Retirement wasn't an issue for nearly two decades – until the money came flooding in and the new rich lifestyle of the committee became just too good to give up. The backlash began in Los Angeles in 1984 when Ecuador's Carlos Arroyo, then aged sixty-one, announced that the age limit of seventy-two was arbitrary and should be raised. He was backed by Algeria's Mohamed Zerguini, aged sixty-three, who got thirty more members to sign a petition calling for retirement at seventy-five. One of the few to oppose this was Judge Mbaye who feared mockery by the media. Samaranch over-ruled him and at their 1985 convention in Berlin pushed through the three-year age extension. Fifty-nine members voted for it with only fourteen against.

Within two years Mrs Flor Isava from Venezuela, now sixty-six, was agitating to abolish the age limit altogether. The executive board was tempted but decided that the IOC was already looked on as an old boys' club and rejected the idea. Samaranch's presidency rolled on: he declined to quit after the Barcelona Games, as predicted, and entered his fourth and final term which ends in 1997. He gave the appearance of being determined to retire. 'It is my obligation to respect the age limit for IOC members,' the seventy-four-year-old Samaranch told an Athens journalist in November 1994. 'I do not plan to be re-elected in 1997 as president and of course I will not be a candidate.' With the benefit of hindsight it looks like a smokescreen, to tempt ambitious rivals into the open.

He left it to the reliable Huba in *Sport Intern* to float his change of heart. The arguments were spurious and transparent. 'The IOC president is probably justified in his fear that the election of his successor in two years time could lead to a state of chaos,' wrote his devoted hack. 'A full blooded campaign to elect a president could cause a split in the Olympic family. Inevitably the IOC is being forced to consider how a catastrophe can be avoided.' A democratic handover of the leadership was being touted as dangerous; it all smacked of Generalissimo Franco's excuses for not relinquishing power. Sacred unity must be maintained and Samaranch was the only man to do it, was the heavy hint.

Samaranch offered his members three suggestions for change. They could raise the age limit to seventy-eight – allowing him to stand again as president in 1997 and rule into the next century; they could abolish the age limit – which again would guarantee him power unto the grave – or vote for no age limit for the president in office. Whatever option they chose, Samaranch would win what he wanted.

He soon got the replies he expected. His members were frightened of change: a new president might not turn a blind eye to serial freeloading, mild corruption and wandering hands among the hostesses. Samaranch had frequently flown the kite of cutting back visits to bidding cities but never taken action. Keep him in power for ever and let the good times roll on was the message. The Olympic committee would become even more geriatric – all the members would benefit from the change – but who cared? The world couldn't do anything; the IOC owned the Games.

Samaranch sent one more message via *Sport Intern*, on the eve of the convention in Budapest. He wasn't keen on a rule change which merely allowed him to say for four more years; he seemed to want an open-ended mandate.

The committee began arriving in Budapest in the second week of June 1995. 'Some feel the seventy-five age limit is discriminatory,' said America's Anita DeFrantz, in public a staunch supporter of the old Blueshirt. 'There are others who say it's important to be able to elect who you wish. He may simply believe that he has a few more things to accomplish as president.' A leading candidate for the succession in 1997, Dick Pound, seeing his hopes postponed, if not destroyed, spoke out strongly. 'I think we would all be complete laughing stocks if we removed the age limit,' he said.

Samaranch got off his plane in Budapest and told the waiting hacks, 'In principle, I am not a candidate at this moment, but that can change.' Belgium's Prince de Merode weighed in behind the plan. 'The IOC president has guided the Olympic movement very well these past years and if he is well, why shouldn't he be able to continue?' The executive board, meeting in advance of the convention agreed to put Samaranch's proposals to the vote. Challenged at a press conference that the manoeuvring showed their leader as a man who just wanted to cling to power, François Carrard replied dismissively, 'What the outside world may say will be said by the outside world.'

An insider at the committee was quoted anonymously, 'It's like asking turkeys whether or not they want the abolition of Christmas. Of course they'll say yes.' But when it came to the complex series of votes, the members made a complete hash of it. To change the Charter and its retirement rule Samaranch needed a two-thirds majority – fifty-nine of the eighty-eight votes available at the convention.

On the first ballot sixty-two voted to change the rule, without specifying how. Samaranch's hopes were looking up. But successive votes on different proposals left them utterly confused and after four perplexing eliminators, ended with only fifty-seven members backing the abolition of the limit altogether, two short of victory. Samaranch's plans to stay on were rejected and his potential successors were jubilant. So too were the hacks, fed up with his authoritarian ways.

'A crushing personal defeat,' said Reuter, 'his authority seriously challenged.' Another agency reported that members, 'baulked at making themselves objects of derision by completely removing an age limit which had been in force for almost thirty years.' Dick Pound was delighted. 'I'm satisfied. It was a wonderful afternoon of democracy in action. It's not a victory for me, it's not a defeat for Samaranch – he's a very good president, but rules of age limits are designed by organisations to protect themselves.'

Samaranch stayed out of sight – his fallback scheme would soon be revealed – and left Carrard to face the hacks. 'The president was quite satisfied with the outcome', Carrard insisted. 'It was not a vote of no-confidence'. The age issue might well come up again at their convention in Atlanta, the following year, he said. It was unlikely. Samaranch would have looked even more foolish, desperately trying again to change the rules – but now with only a year before the presidential elections. Samaranch's reign was over, a new era beckoned for the Olympic committee and the Olympic Games.

That was on the Thursday. The thugs went into action the next day. Samaranch quits over our dead bodies, they hissed to trembling IOC members, and yours as well, if necessary. The corridor lobbying was remarkable. Sign this letter demanding a new vote for an age limit of eighty, they insisted. Even Karl-Heinz Huba wrote that he was shocked. He had to. The hacks had seen it all. Huba denounced Brazil's João Havelange and

Mexico's Mario Vazquez Raña as 'not among the shining lights of world sport. How Vazquez Raña collected signatures confirmed once again all reservations held against the Mexican media mogul,' he tutted in *Sport Intern*. 'Several IOC members openly spoke of coercion; one South American member was threatened with neutralisation in the Pan-American sports organisation PASO if he didn't sign.' This makes clear who Huba *isn't* backing for the succession. I suspect his preferred candidate is Mickey Kim.

Then the trusted IOC chronicler exonerated the old Blueshirt from any part in the mayhem. Samaranch could easily have persuaded the convention to make a special case and let him stay on one more term but apparently he was 'tormented by his own scruples'.

The other corridor arm-twisters were reportedly Primo Nebiolo, Mrs Flor Isava and Jean-Claude Ganga from the Congo. They collected seventy signatures and presented their letter to Samaranch on the Saturday evening. One of the brave eighteen who didn't submit told a reporter: 'Changing the figure from seventy-eight, which we had already rejected, to eighty merely makes us look ridiculous.'

There was only one day of the convention left. For the campaign to succeed the executive board would have to approve the petition the next morning. One member, Marc Hodler, who seemed to have been left out of the conspiracy, said 'The board would have to submit a report to the session and I don't think we would have the time.'

It didn't need much time. Samaranch rammed the proposal through the board first thing Sunday morning and it was put straight before the convention. He refused calls for a secret ballot and eyeballed his quavering members. Hands up if you're against raising the age limit to eighty, he said. Ten brave souls signalled their dissent. Any abstentions? Two more bold spirits raised their hands. That was that: the silent seventy-four were assumed to be in favour and Samaranch declared the rule passed.

Carrard was wheeled out to deny that Samaranch had planned the coup. 'He was totally out of this,' said the chief bureaucrat. 'It's not the end of the world,' muttered Dick Pound. 'We'll get on with life.' Anita DeFrantz, who had sought a secret ballot, positioned herself delicately on the fence, explaining to reporters that she didn't vote for the age limit extension, but 'didn't vote against it'.

Samaranch's Olympic poodles were back on the leash. If no insurmountable scandals emerged in the next couple of years, he was on course to be Olympic president until 2001 when he would be eighty-one. And, of course, if he could change the rules once, he could change them twice. Avery Brundage had been president until he was eighty-five.

The Budapest convention saw another eleven members appointed to the committee, completing their line-up for the Stand of Honour in Atlanta. After a five year gap, another woman was admitted, former star Olympic gymnast Vera Caslavska from the Czech Republic. The rest were men: Sam Ramsamy, the veteran battler against apartheid who had spent 20 years in exile, became South Africa's new member and Mario Vazquez Raña's brother Olegario, president of international shooting since 1980, made the Olympic family the Raña family when he was sworn in. Former champion skier Jean-Claude Killy joined the club. Samaranch used his new powers to nominate other sports presidents, bringing in the barons from gymnastics, swimming and ice hockey.

The last decision in Budapest was to choose the winter

Olympics venue for 2002. What would sway them? As Dick Pound said, 'Choices can be based on friendship or where your wife wants to go shopping' and this time the choice was the boutiques of Salt Lake City. It had been inevitable since their defeat in Birmingham four years earlier. Out in their own cold yet again was the Swedish candidate, Östersund. As the biggest and most consistent losers in the Olympic stakes the Swedes would probably lodge an objection if they ever won. Their undeserved record of failure may continue until a new Olympic committee membership – in about fifty years time – forgets the horrors of Lillehammer and Norway's robust and free press and consents to return to Scandinavia.

*

[See Appendix A for list of IOC members, their occupations and retirement dates now the age limit is eighty, and ages in Atlanta.]

# CHAPTER 23

# Buy a Coke, Pay by Visa, Fund the Great Doping Cover-Up

'This isn't any charity. We've entered into a business transaction. We will make money,' says Mr Hugh McColl, the chairman of NationsBank, one of the Atlanta Olympics' biggest sponsors. 'That's what it's all about.' The candid Mr McColl celebrates the transformation of the Games during their one-hundred-year life. Founded by nineteenth-century European aristocrats to channel the restless energies and ideas of their masses, hijacked by Hitler – with the IOC's blessing – to glorify his new order, they enjoyed the briefest golden age in the 1950s. The Olympics in Helsinki and then Melbourne – memorable for the feats of the great long distance runners Emil Zatopek and Vladimir Kuts – were spartan, unprofitable, dope-free and enthralling, despite the bitter cold war dividing the world. 1960 in Rome was blemished by the death of a Danish cyclist from a drug overdose and Tokyo was the first of a series of Olympics staged more to honour governments and political systems than athletes.

The all-private, chain-link-fenced Atlanta event completes the metamorphosis of the Olympics into a vehicle for big business. Billy Payne, the Atlanta Olympic supremo, hails 'the incredible transforming power of the

Olympic spirit' but there's little sign that the centennial Games' brief visit will transform much for Atlanta's underclass. Billy's promise of a profit to plough into sports programmes in the inner city doesn't look as if it can be kept. When the Dunwoody suburbanites won the Games they predicted a surplus of around $160 million. Six years on and six months before the event, they say they're struggling to balance their books. Of course Billy may have a pot of gold that he daren't reveal – it might discourage the thousands of volunteers – but that doesn't look likely now. Without any distribution of Olympic wealth, the lives and hopes of the majority of the citizens won't be touched by Billy's Olympic spirit. Mr McColl's bank will.

Atlanta's struggle to find the money for the Games hasn't put off the raft of bidders for the Olympics in the next century. Cities around the world seem oblivious to the cost and grief borne by the failed candidates of the last decade and Samaranch is out there on the road, playing Casanova again. 'The IOC will be very pleased to come to Africa,' he told a press conference in Cape Town, and the South Africans beamed. No sooner had they assumed they were front runners for the summer games of 2004 than Samaranch was in a rival city announcing, 'Rome is the strongest bid there is.' In the Caribbean the leader of the San Juan bidding team revealed to reporters, 'The IOC says that Puerto Rico will be taken very seriously.'

As many as ten cities are expected to bid for the year 2004. They're getting ready to wine and dine the 'Holidays R Us' club of Lausanne. If Chicago University professor John MacAloon knows what he's talking about, they could be in for a rough time. 'It is a sad fact that every Olympic Organising Committee now must have a behind the scenes agency to prepare its female staff and volunteers for offensive acts against them by foreign visitors,' he told a meeting of Olympic scholars in 1994, 'not excluding, we are sorry to report, IOC, national Olympic committee and sports federation members and other leaders of the Olympic family.'

The hopeful cities will be lured into investing billions of dollars on a circus they say can improve the lives of their citizens. Accountants, entrepreneurs and politicians on the make will produce dazzling economic studies, predicting enormous financial benefits for cities and regions. Two recent television deals appear, superficially, to justify these claims. In August 1995 the American NBC network, with Seoul and Barcelona behind them and Atlanta to come, contracted to pay $1.25 billion for the American rights to Sydney in 2000 and the Salt Lake City Winter Games of 2002. Three months later NBC was back with an even bigger deal; $2.3 billion for the Summer Games of 2004 and 2008 and the Winter Games of 2006 – even though the host cities are yet to be selected. 'As long as the country is able to come forward with the appropriate infrastructure to stage the Games,' explained the IOC's marketing director Michael Payne, 'then for TV companies and sponsors it really makes no difference where the Games are held.' The Olympic committee hastened to explain that NBC's massive investment wouldn't affect the Games themselves.

That's not how NBC see it. If they're going to get their money back – and sell enough ads to make a profit – they want sports 'that bring women and entire families to the television sets,' said Peter Diamond, an NBC senior executive and also a member of the IOC's television commission, at a seminar in Lausanne in 1994. 'I'd like the IOC to find a way to have another day, or two, or three of artistic gymnastics.' Then he wanted more swimming in the Summer Games and more figure skating in the winter event. To hold women consumers during the second week of the Games, he wanted more events with female appeal. And most of all, he wanted more stars. The Olympic movement has discussed reducing the number of swimming events because in some years, particular swimmers can win serial gold in very similar events. Don't do it, said Mr Diamond.

In Munich in 1972 viewers saw Mark Spitz again and again mounting the podium, and Kirsten Otto take six golds in Seoul. 'Our public wants to see and experience the drama of the major athletes as often as possible,' insisted Mr Diamond, the voice of the paymasters. NBC had been happy with their Barcelona show – with one reservation. There wasn't an individual superstar. How unfortunate that hurdler Kevin Young had set a new world record 'but was gone from the Olympics the next day'.

It's chilling. The networks, whose ultimate aim is to sell more and more advertising time at higher and higher prices can't waste valuable space on ordinary athletes, unknown athletes, events that don't attract vast audiences. They'll either force the Olympic committee to drop sports that don't work well for their television viewers – or simply ignore them. NBC has a clear run until 2008 to revamp the Games. It's hard to believe the IOC will have the backbone to resist temptation in return for the $3 billion plus on offer.

But surely NBC's guarantee of big money for the next dozen years will make it easier to stage the Games? 'It clearly provides considerable financial security to the movement and to future cities bidding for the Games, knowing they already have the financing locked up.' said the IOC's Michael Payne. It's his bosses who've got the money locked up. In September 1995 the IOC announced that from 2004 the share of television rights given to host cities would drop – from sixty per cent to forty-nine per cent. Had this been the rule for 1996, Atlanta would have been denied just over $100 million, probably driving their Games into bankruptcy. Nonetheless Samaranch insisted, 'The IOC is very generous with the organising committees.'

On the contrary, countries that want the Games will have to be very generous to the IOC. When Atlanta's budget was looking particularly grim, Dick Pound announced, 'We will never again award the Games in future to a city which has no significant public sector commitment.' The IOC will take its profits, the sponsors and television networks will make theirs and the local taxpayers will foot the bill. In one sentence Pound confirmed that one result of the modern Olympics is to transfer wealth from the public to the private sector, providing welfare for already rich corporations. The IOC repeatedly insists that it is independent of politics and governments – at the same time as requiring handouts to subsidise it.

The IOC has needed reform for at least ninety of its hundred years. Even Pierre de Coubertin thought so. 'The modern Olympiad needed first of all to be created; now it needs purifying,' he wrote in 1906. 'It involves too many activities unrelated to sport, too many marginal ambitions. People help in the hope of a ribbon or a distinction, they use it for their own personal, political or other advantage.'

In the Stand of Honour in Atlanta will be the hundred or more members, hand-picked because they have no wish to challenge their authoritarian leader. They show no desire to expel Mr Wandering Hands and others like him. They are happy to award Olympic honours to mass murderers like Beijing's Chen Xitong and Korea's corrupt General Roh Tae Woo. They are glad to have Mickey Kim as their First Vice-President and we can't expect them to call for an independent inquiry into the Seoul boxing bribes. They sun themselves in

Samaranch's campaign for the Nobel and ignore claims that they connive in letting dopers off the hook.

Their unchecked, serial freeloading in Berlin and elsewhere during the campaign for 2000 sets a standard that bidders for 2004 will feel they have to emulate – whatever the rules. Members like Ivan Dibos from Peru, with the assistance of friends like Spain's Carlos Ferrer, will continue to seek business deals off the back of the Olympic movement. The message they sent from their 1994 Paris congress is that they have no plans to make themselves accountable to world sport and that athletes, who are denied any votes in the planning of their Olympics, will remain a commodity, refreshed with new blood every four years, to enrich the Olympic committee and their sponsors.

The IOC own the Games and believe that gives them the power to resist any criticism. In Atlanta we will rely on the media to scrutinise Olympic committee activities. 'Press conferences given by Samaranch are deliberately bland, so much so that they are generally excruciatingly dull to attend. This is his intention; he believes there is nothing to be gained on such occasions by appearing to be brilliant,' writes one of his greatest admirers, Dick Pound. 'Nor does he permit a series of questions from any single member of the media. He will always move on after each question to another person in the audience. He may, on occasion, deliberately answer a different question from the one that has been asked.'

Samaranch gets away with it because most of the reporters are sports specialists with little time or inclination to investigate the Olympic committee. Among most of the acknowledged experts in the media seems to be a reluctance to acquire confidential documents or stories that might destabilise the committee's benign image. Sports reporters frolic in a hacks' heaven, free from the rigour that's applied to other specialists. So we can't believe what we read in many of our newspapers. Television networks who've bought rights to screen the Games shrink from asking questions that might unsettle their Olympic friends.

Library shelves creak with weighty Olympic tomes by earnest professors. Few address the philosophical or moral quandaries arising from the sell-out of the Games. Olympic historians have failed to unearth the political backgrounds of Samaranch and Mickey Kim. For many, research begins and ends in the sanitised archives of Lausanne. Samaranch's favourites are rewarded with a preface, a personal endorsement from the president.

What little independent academic work there is tends to be buried in esoteric journals. Critical scholars don't get grants from Lausanne or free research trips, assistance publishing their books or sales-boosting reviews in IOC publications. Without thoughtful investigation and analysis by journalists and scholars, the barren clichés from Lausanne will be pumped out during the Atlanta Games, even though the evidence screams at us that something has gone terribly wrong with what should be one of the world's great movements.

The old Blueshirt from Barcelona will be on the podium in Atlanta, and again in Sydney, if he keeps his health. Ramming through another change in the IOC's retirement rules could see him presiding again in 2004. This last survivor of the evil era of the dictators in the mid-twentieth century, is a strange phenomenon at our most popular sports event. The world will see him on its television screens but never catch him submitting to in-depth interviews about his past and his personal agenda in the Olympic movement. Every political leader in the democratic world is frequently examined by the media, their histories dug out, their actions probed. But not the leader of this supposedly open festival of world sport. One investigative interview by a competent reporter would destroy him. Few sports reporters seem to find it odd that the Olympic boss cannot, dare not, give an unrestricted interview.

He seems bereft of ideas for the development of the Games. All the major changes occurred during the years of Horst Dassler. Since his death in 1987, the subsequent demise of his team of sports politics fixers and the near collapse and sale of the Adidas company to owners with clean hands, the Olympic movement has become paralysed, incapable of constructive thought or deed.

Samaranch seems to concern himself only with the pursuit of the Nobel and history's verdict on him. He has no reason to quit and the case for staying on is strong. His successor might well want to make his mark by ending the imperial farce in Lausanne which would do nothing but harm to what remains of Samaranch's reputation. Samaranch would be well advised to hold on to the key to the archives and financial records while he can.

In his own terms, he's been a brilliant success. Samaranch is as good as canonised by the international companies that sponsor the Olympics – with good reason. To associate themselves with the world's favourite sports event is for more complex reasons than just making bigger profits; it gives them an outpost in our heads. How can you hate an enterprise that brings you gold medal sport? Whose logo is entwined in the five rings? Their factory effluent might damage the environment, their products be over-priced or harmful to our health but the Olympic connection is protection.

This will be Samaranch's lasting achievement. The aristocrats who launched the Olympics were the supreme power in their age. Their dominance has passed to international capitalist enterprises, more powerful than many national governments. Acquiring the Olympics – and the spirit of passionate internationalism that comes with them – has been a sound move by big business.

The Paris congress could have discussed how to cut the cost of the Olympics, how to make it possible for countries in the developing world to stage them without distorting their economies. Such a debate is unwelcome in Lausanne or in the boardrooms. An artificially expensive sports festival needs the kind of money that only the corporate sugar-daddies can supply. That's why so many people now feel they're watching the Coca-Cola Games, even if there's no blatant advertising allowed inside the stadium.

It's hard to believe that any of the likely suspects to replace Samaranch is capable of cleaning out the Olympic stables. Front-runners Dick Pound, a former Adidas lawyer in Canada, Kevan Gosper and Judge Kéba Mbaye profess complete support for the way Samaranch has changed the movement.

Pound, who denied any conflict of interest when he represented Adidas, saying that he did not share his law firm's profit from the account, has forged what may be a winning image for himself. He's the hard man of money who berates the big networks and corporations into handing over billion-dollar fortunes. But his abrasiveness has cost him friends and he doesn't have an ethnic power bloc behind him.

Gosper, now retired from his high-flying position with the Shell oil company is also a former Olympic athlete, but again, has no power grouping behind him. Mbaye, who will be seventy-two in 1996, may not care for the full-time position. Anita DeFrantz, who makes a good living from running the foundation set up with the surplus from the Los Angeles Games, is said by those who know her to covet the Olympic presidency, but a committee which only occasionally elects women might find itself incapable of being led by one.

Mickey Kim would be the ideal successor to Samaranch's traditions. Votes from Asia and perhaps

Africa and certain malleable members could come his way. Mario Vazquez Raña is said to be ambitious but as he couldn't even get the committee members to vote him in, he'd have a struggle to win hearts, minds and pledges. Primo Nebiolo said recently, 'I don't have any intentions to be a candidate,' which means he's a certain contender. He will promise even more income than Pound has delivered but is detested much more than Raña. The younger generation of possible candidates, Belgium's Jacques Rogge, Germany's Thomas Bach and Norway's Gerhard Heiberg may have to wait decades for their chance. With a retirement age of eighty, they'd better be patient.

There's no need for the rest of the world to be so patient. Changing the way the Olympics are owned and controlled could be so easy. The multi-national sponsors sit comfortably in the best seats in Atlanta, but they're very vulnerable. It's their dollars that prop up the international jet-set lifestyle of the likes of Mr Wandering Hands; the boxing bribes cover-up; and, potentially most threatening, they let the IOC get away with suppressing positive dope tests.

Through 1995 many athletes and coaches, mostly from the sport of swimming, vigorously denounced Samaranch and the IOC for wanting two-year suspensions for dopers, rather than four-year bans or even life sentences. They've been angered by Samaranch's total support for China and his denials that there's a serious drugs problem coming out of Beijing. It's almost pointless for many of America and Australia's top swimmers to get on the plane to Atlanta unless the drugs issue is tackled seriously. One of the world's leading swim coaches announced at the end of 1995 that 'when I hear statements being made by Samaranch that the Chinese are okay . . . that's enough to make me puke.'

Samaranch is feeling the heat. In December 1995, speaking in Berlin, he asserted that 'In Atlanta, there will be very few cases of doping – or none.' That's what the sponsors want to hear but many athletes have had enough; they know doping is rampant and despise the Olympic committee for the cover-up.

If they banded together and followed the example of Norway's star skier Vegard Ulvang, who denounced Samaranch's fascism on the eve of the Lillehammer Games, the Olympic political picture would change overnight. There are other role models; the Black American sprinters in Mexico who signalled from the podium that they'd had enough of being exploited by sports officials won overwhelming international sympathy. One summer of athlete anger aimed at the IOC could trigger a simple act of public hygiene; the cleansing of the Olympic committee from the Olympics.

The multi-national corporations, whose open cheque-books enable the IOC to hold clean athletes in contempt, might well react swiftly. Our heroes and heroines of the track, the pool, the boxing ring and every other sports venue in Atlanta have great power. Declining to accept their medals from Olympic committee members and blaming the Cokes, the Visas, the NationsBanks, the Kodaks, the Panasonics and the rest of the big sponsors for funding a Games where clean athletes can't win would engage world attention, sympathy and perhaps bring decisive action. No sponsor would enjoy the accusation of propping up dirty sport.

A decade ago one of the most decent of sports leaders, the late Thomas Keller, president of international rowing, saw the trends and suggested, 'We must abolish the Olympic Games to protect sport.' How much better to have one last chance to reform them.

# CHAPTER 24

# *We Win the Samaranch Prize for Literature*

*After publication of the first edition of* The Lords of the Rings *Samaranch condemned the book as a stunt to put the Princess Royal, Princess Anne, in his place at the head of the Olympic movement. He also persuaded the Lausanne authorities to indict myself and my co-author Vyv Simson for criminal defamation – and there was a very odd phone call to a Barcelona office . . .*

'Hullo. This is Juan Antonio. I am ringing to see if you can do me a favour. I'm after those English journalists and they often call a number in Barcelona. Could you look and see whose it is?'

It was the Chief Guardian on the line. He thought he'd called one of Spain's highest-ranking state security officials. Instead, he'd got confused and phoned the target number he wanted checked out. That was a bad move. It belonged to the Barcelona weekly news magazine *El Triangle* and Samaranch found himself talking to the editor Jaume Reixach – who immediately recognised his voice. There was the briefest of conversations and then Samaranch hung up.

To have discovered that I and my co-author Vyv Simson had indeed been calling the magazine, he must have hired private detectives in Britain to obtain our phone records. Whatever else Samaranch found out about us, it's a fact that the security official he'd intended to call was given the Olympic Order for services to Olympic security. Reixach gleefully published the story under the headline 'Samaranch Plays at Spies'.

Then the real detectives came calling. 'Hullo, I'm from Scotland Yard's international and organised crime squad. It's about a book you've written.' The boys in blue were very courteous and I suspect not well pleased at the job they'd been given. The squad spends most of its time on the trail of international hoods, money launderers, illicit arms dealers – and now cheeky reporters.

What on earth were the Yard doing wasting British taxpayer's money pursing a vendetta for an unrepentant old Franco clone? They didn't have any choice. Samaranch's squad of expensive lawyers in Lausanne advised him to use Switzerland's Jurassic-age laws against defaming public figures and attacking their honour. They carry penalties of up to six months in jail and half a dozen Swiss hacks go behind bars most years for reporting truths unpalatable to the rich and powerful in their country.

Lausanne state prosecutor Mr Roland Chatelaine got in line and criminal charges were drafted. Samaranch didn't even try to claim we'd got our facts wrong; he just thought exposing his fascist history shouldn't be allowed.

The Swiss Ministry of Justice invoked the European convention on mutual assistance in criminal matters and the indictment was sent to the British Home Office who passed it on to the Yard to serve on us. I phoned the Home Office paper shuffler and asked them why they weren't defending the freedom of the press – and why they were helping impose repressive legislation, the like of which doesn't exist in Britain? They said they were only obeying orders.

We weren't surprised that Samaranch didn't sue in Britain or most other countries in the world where the book was distributed. If he'd tried it on in Britain Samaranch would have faced public cross-examination about his little right-arm secret, his favourite colour in shirts and where all the Olympic money really goes. In Lausanne, Olympic city, where the local politicians and newspaper proprietors take tea at the Olympic offices he would be spared such indignity.

It took more than two years to get the case to court. In the meantime Samaranch faced some embarrassment in the Swiss parliament. Geneva MP Professor Jean Ziegler asked the government to launch an investigation into 'the corrupt activities of Mr Samaranch as well as his dubious political past'. Out of the question, Ziegler was told. Why? One of Samaranch's smart moves after taking over the Olympic movement in 1980 was to persuade the government to grant the IOC legal immunity – similar to that enjoyed by the Red Cross. So Swiss investigators are barred from crossing the threshold of Olympic House.

State prosecutor Roland Chatelaine seemed oblivious to the irony: Samaranch could recruit him to use Swiss criminal law against disrespectful hacks – but he wasn't allowed to walk into Olympic offices and demand to examine the petty cash receipts.

The trial was set for the first week of December 1994 at the law courts in Lausanne's Palais de Montbenon. During the day it has a splendid view over Lac Leman. At night time the local hookers take over the surrounding park.

I was in America researching the spooky history of

Mickey Kim and my co-author saw little reason to leave Britain. Neither of us fancied turning up to fight a case against the Olympic committee in Olympic City, especially as prosecutor Chatelaine was quoted on the eve of the trial saying that we had shown 'a deep contempt towards the IOC, its president and its members, criticising their personalities, their behaviour and their management'. I would have pleaded guilty – except holding the contemptible in contempt shouldn't be an offence.

Judge Jean-Daniel Martin did all that was required of him. Those who were there came away with the impression that he listened in awe to the much more senior Judge Keba Mbaye of the Olympic committee. Mbaye was deeply distressed. He feared the book falling into the hands of his innocent grandchildren who would say 'but I thought the IOC was an honourable institution, not a bunch of crooks'.

Then the old Blueshirt took the stand. We'd got him entirely wrong. According to the reports he looked the judge in the eye and swore he had never exercised any political power in Franco's Spain. 'I was a high-ranking civil servant,' he told the court. This was the politician who boasted in the IOC's *Olympic Review* years back of twice being elected to Franco's rubber-stamp parliament. One of Samaranch's regular claims to the Spanish press, attempting to justify his years in the fascist Falange, is that he always used politics to benefit sport and not vice versa. The very day he was in court saying that, his office a mile or so away was preparing to ship out the 1995 edition of *Olympic Biographies*, the sanitised biographical details of the committee's members. On page eighteen Samaranch lists having been a Municipal councillor and also a 'Deputy'. He makes no claim to have been a civil servant.

When reported in Barcelona, Samaranch's claims

caused great mirth but Judge Jean-Daniel Martin wasn't laughing. He accepted Samaranch's word and gave us five days in jail, suspended for three years, with around $1,000 court costs to pay. If the Judge really believes that Samaranch was just a civil servant during the Franco dictatorship then he may also believe there are fairies at the bottom of his garden, the Moon is made of green cheese and the IOC are fighting a war against doping.

I hope he enjoys this new book. I hope you have.

# APPENDIX A

## International Olympic Committee Members

*Female members in italics*

| Name | Occupation | Date of joining | Date of retirement | Age in Atlanta | Possible number of years on IOC |
|---|---|---|---|---|---|
| 1. Grand-Duc Jean de (Luxembourg) | Monarch | 1946 | Life member | 75 | |
| 2. Alexandru Siperco (Romania) | Ex-communist bureaucrat | 1955 | Life member | 76 | |
| 3. Syed Wajid Ali (Pakistan) | Businessman | 1959 | Life member | 85 | |
| 4. Wlodzimierz Reczek (Poland) | Lawyer | 1961 | Life member | 85 | |
| 5. Hadj Mohammed Benjelloun (Morocco) | Businessman | 1961 | Life member | 84 | |
| 6. João Havelange (Brazil) | Businessman/boss of world soccer | 1963 | Life member | 80 | |
| 7. Marc Hodler (Switzerland) | Lawyer/president of world skiing | 1963 | Life member | 78 | |
| 8. Prince Alexandre de Merode (Belgium) | Businessman | 1964 | Life member | 62 | |

| Name<br>*Female members in*<br>*italics* | Occupation | Date of joining | Date of retirement | Age in Atlanta | Possible number of of years on IOC |
|---|---|---|---|---|---|
| 9. Major Silvio de Magalhaes Padilha (Brazil) | Retired military | 1964 | Life member | 87 | |
| 10. Gunnar Ericsson (Sweden) | Businessman | 1965 | Life member | 77 | |
| 11. Mohamed Mzali (Tunisia) | Retired politician | 1965 | Life member | 71 | |
| 12. Juan Antonio Samaranch (Spain) | Retired facist politician/businessman | 1966 | 2000 | 76 | 34 |
| 13. Jan Staubo (Norway) | Businessman | 1966 | 2000 | 76 | 34 |
| 14. Augustin Carlos Arroyo (Ecuador) | Businessman | 1968 | 2003 | 73 | 35 |
| 15. Louis Guirandou-N'Diaye (Ivory Coast) | Diplomat | 1969 | 2003 | 73 | 34 |
| 16. Vitaly Smirnov (Russia) | Former member, Moscow Soviet | 1971 | 2015 | 61 | 44 |
| 17. Roy Anthony Bridge (Jamaica) | Businessman | 1973 | 2001 | 75 | 28 |
| 18. Ashwini Kumar (India) | Retired military | 1973 | 2000 | 76 | 27 |

| Name (Country) | Profession | | | | |
|---|---|---|---|---|---|
| 19. Kéba Mbaye (Senegal) | Lawyer | 1973 | 2004 | 72 | 31 |
| 20. Colonel Mohamed Zerguini (Algeria) | Retired military | 1974 | 2002 | 74 | 28 |
| 21. Peter Tallberg (Finland) | Businessman | 1976 | 2017 | 59 | 41 |
| 22. José D. Vallarino Veracierto (Uruguay) | Estate owner | 1976 | 2000 | 76 | 24 |
| 23. Bashir Mohamed Attarabulsi (Libya) | Sports official | 1977 | 2017 | 59 | 40 |
| 24. Kevan Gosper (Australia) | Businessman | 1977 | 2013 | 63 | 36 |
| 25. Major-General Niels Holst-Sorensen (Denmark) | Retired military | 1977 | 2002 | 74 | 25 |
| 26. Lamina Keita (Mali) | Engineer | 1977 | 2013 | 63 | 36 |
| 27. Shagdarjav Magvan (Mongolia) | Businessman | 1977 | 2007 | 69 | 30 |
| 28. Philipp von Schoeller (Austria) | Businessman | 1977 | 2001 | 75 | 25 |
| 29. Prof. René Essomba (Cameroon) | Surgeon | 1978 | 2012 | 64 | 34 |
| 30. Datuk Seri Hamzah (Malaysia) | Retired government minister | 1978 | 2004 | 72 | 26 |
| 31. Richard W. Pound (Canada) | Lawyer/former Adidas attorney | 1978 | 2022 | 54 | 44 |

| Name<br>*Female members in italics* | Occupation | Date of joining | Date of retirement | Age in Atlanta | Possible number of of years on IOC |
|---|---|---|---|---|---|
| *Samaranch starts selecting Members* | | | | | |
| 32. Vladimir Cernusak (Slovakia) | Retired teacher | 1981 | 2001 | 75 | 20 |
| 33. Nikos Filaretos (Greece) | Business executive | 1981 | 2005 | 71 | 24 |
| 34. *Pirjo Haggman* (Finland) | Teacher | 1981 | 2031 | 45 | 50 |
| 35. Zhenliang He (China) | Politician | 1981 | 2009 | 67 | 28 |
| 36. *Flor Isava-Fonseca* (Venezuela) | Retired showjumper | 1981 | 2001 | 75 | 20 |
| 37. Franco Carraro (Italy) | Politician | 1982 | 2019 | 57 | 37 |
| 38. Phillip Walter Coles (Australia) | Sports official | 1982 | 2011 | 65 | 29 |
| 39. Ivan Dibos (Peru) | Businessman, politician | 1982 | 2019 | 57 | 37 |
| 40. Chiharu Igaya (Japan) | Businessman | 1982 | 2011 | 65 | 29 |

| | | | | | |
|---|---|---|---|---|---|
| 41. Prince Faisal Fahd Abdul Aziz (Saudi Arabia) | Government minister | 1983 | 2026 | 50 | 43 |
| 42. Anani Matthia (Togo) | Pharmacist | 1983 | 2007 | 69 | 27 |
| 43. R. Napoleon Munoz Pena (Dominican Republic) | Businessman | 1983 | 2008 | 68 | 25 |
| 44. Pal Schmitt (Hungary) | Diplomat | 1983 | 2022 | 54 | 39 |
| 45. *Princess Nora von Liechtenstein* | | 1984 | 2030 | 46 | 46 |
| 46. David Sibandze (Swaziland) | Businessman | 1984 | 2012 | 64 | 28 |
| 47. Major-General Henry Adefope (Nigeria) | Government minister | 1985 | 2006 | 70 | 21 |
| 48. Francisco Elizalde (Philippines) | Businessman | 1985 | 2012 | 64 | 27 |
| 49. Carlos Ferrer (Spain) | Businessman | 1985 | 2011 | 65 | 26 |
| 50. Prince Albert of Monaco | | 1985 | 2038 | 38 | 53 |
| 51. Dr Kim Un Yong (Korea) | not known, boss of Taekwondo | 1986 | 2011 | 65 | 25 |

| Name *Female members in italics* | Occupation | Date of joining | Date of retirement | Age in Atlanta | Possible number of years on IOC |
|---|---|---|---|---|---|
| 52. Lambis Nikolaou (Greece) | Civil engineer | 1986 | 2015 | 61 | 29 |
| 53. *Anita DeFrantz (USA)* | Sports administrator | 1986 | 2032 | 44 | 46 |
| 54. Jean-Claude Ganga (Congo) | Sports minister | 1986 | 2014 | 62 | 28 |
| *1987: Horst Dassler dies; no more advice for Samaranch* | | | | | |
| 55. Ivan Slavkov (Bulgaria) | Ex-communist bureaucrat | 1987 | 2020 | 56 | 33 |
| 56. Anton Geesink (Holland) | Sports official | 1987 | 2014 | 62 | 27 |
| 57. Paul Wallwork (Western Samoa) | Sports official | 1987 | 2022 | 54 | 35 |
| 58. *Princess Anne, The Princess Royal (UK)* | | 1988 | 2030 | 46 | 42 |
| 59. Fidel Mendoza Carrasquilla (Colombia) | Retired doctor | 1988 | 2005 | 71 | 17 |

| | | | | | |
|---|---|---|---|---|---|
| 60. Edward Wilson (New Zealand) | Businessman | 1988 | 2005 | 71 | 17 |
| 61. Ching Kuo-Wu (Taiwan) | Architect | 1988 | 2026 | 50 | 38 |
| 62. Rampaul Ruhee (Mauritius) | Sports official | 1988 | 2007 | 69 | 19 |
| 63. Sinan Erdem (Turkey) | Businessman | 1988 | 2007 | 69 | 19 |
| 64. Willi Kaltschmitt Lujan (Guatemala) | Businessman | 1988 | 2019 | 57 | 31 |
| 65. Major-General Francis Nyangweso (Uganda) | Retired military/ businessman | 1988 | 2019 | 67 | 31 |
| 66. Borislav Stankovic (Yugoslavia) | Sports official | 1988 | 2005 | 71 | 17 |
| 67. Fernando Ferreira Lima Bello (Portugal) | Businessman | 1989 | 2011 | 65 | 22 |
| 68. Walther Tröger (Germany) | Sports official | 1989 | 2009 | 67 | 20 |
| 69. Philippe Chatrier (France) | Sports official | 1990 | 2008 | 68 | 18 |
| 70. *Carol Anne Letheren* (Canada) | Marketing expert | 1990 | 2022 | 54 | 32 |

| Name<br>*Female members in*<br>*italics* | Occupation | Date of<br>joining | Date of<br>retirement | Age in<br>Atlanta | Possible<br>number of<br>of years<br>on IOC |
|---|---|---|---|---|---|
| 71. Shun-Ichiro Okano (Japan) | Businessman | 1990 | 2011 | 65 | 21 |
| 72. Richard Carrion (Puerto Rico) | Banker, Visa official | 1990 | 2032 | 44 | 42 |
| 73. General Zein El Abdin Gadir (Sudan) | Retired military | 1990 | 2020 | 56 | 30 |
| 74. Dr Nat Indrapana (Thailand) | Sports official | 1990 | 2019 | 57 | 29 |
| 75. Charles Mukora (Kenya) | Director, Coca-Cola Africa | 1990 | 2014 | 62 | 24 |
| 76. Colonel Antonio Rodriguez (Argentina) | Retired military | 1990 | 2006 | 70 | 16 |
| 77. Denis Oswald (Switzerland) | Lawyer | 1991 | 2027 | 49 | 36 |
| 78. Dr Jacques Rogge (Belgium) | Surgeon | 1991 | 2022 | 54 | 31 |
| 79. Mario Vazquez Raña (Mexico) | Businessman | 1991 | 2012 | 64 | 21 |
| 80. Thomas Bach (Germany) | Lawyer/former Adidas attorney | 1991 | 2033 | 43 | 42 |

| | | | | | |
|---|---|---|---|---|---|
| 81. Primo Nebiolo (Italy) | Businessman/boss of world track & field | 1992 | 2003 | 73 | 11 |
| 82. Sergio Santander Fantini (Chile) | Accountant | 1992 | 2006 | 69 | 14 |
| 83. Sheikh Ahmad Al-Sabah (Kuwait) | Member of ruling family | 1992 | 2041 | 35 | 49 |
| 84. James Easton (USA) | Businessman | 1994 | 2015 | 61 | 21 |
| 85. Craig Reedie (UK) | Businessman | 1994 | 2021 | 55 | 27 |
| 86. Mohamad (Bob) Hasan (Indonesia) | Businessman | 1994 | 2011 | 65 | 17 |
| 87. Mario Pescante (Italy) | Sports official | 1994 | 2018 | 58 | 24 |
| 88. Gerhard Heiberg (Norway) | Businessman | 1994 | 2018 | 57 | 24 |
| 89. Arne Ljungqvist (Sweden) | Doctor | 1994 | 2011 | 65 | 17 |
| 90. Austin Llewellyn Sealy (Barbados) | Diplomat | 1994 | 2019 | 57 | 25 |
| 91. Robin Mitchell (Fiji) | Doctor | 1994 | 2026 | 50 | 32 |
| 92. Alpha Ibrahima Diallo (Guinea) | Senior civil servant | 1994 | 2012 | 64 | 18 |
| 93. Alex Gilady (Israel) | NBC-TV executive | 1994 | 2022 | 54 | 28 |

| Name *Female members in italics* | Occupation | Date of joining | Date of retirement | Age in Atlanta | Possible number of of years on IOC |
|---|---|---|---|---|---|
| 94. Shamil Tarpischev (Russia) | Tennis coach | 1994 | 2028 | 48 | 34 |
| 95. Valery Borzov (Ukraine) | Sports minister | 1994 | 2029 | 47 | 35 |
| 96. René Fasel (Ice Hockey Federation) | Sports official | 1995 | | 46 | |
| 97. Jean-Claude Killy (France) | Director, Coca-Cola France | 1995 | 2023 | 53 | 28 |
| 98. Sam Ramsamy (South Africa) | Sports official | 1995 | 2018 | 58 | 23 |
| 99. Reynaldo Gonzales Lopez (Cuba) | Teacher | 1995 | 2028 | 48 | 33 |
| 100. Olegario Vazquez Raña (Mexico) | Businessman | 1995 | 2015 | 61 | 20 |
| 101. Antun Vrdoljak (Croatia) | TV executive | 1995 | 2011 | 65 | 16 |
| 102. Patrick Hickey (Ireland) | Businessman | 1995 | 2025 | 51 | 30 |
| 103. Toni Khouri (Lebanon) | Businessman | 1995 | 2015 | 61 | 20 |

| | Sports official | | | Age in 1996 | Years on IOC |
|---|---|---|---|---|---|
| 104. *Vera Caslavska* (Czech Republic) | Sports official | 1995 | 2022 | 44 | 27 |
| 105. Yuri Titov | (Gymnastics Federation) | 1995 | 1995 | 61 | |
| 106. Mustapha Larfaoui | (Swimming Federation) | 1995 | 1995 | 64 | |

Members number 96, 105 & 106 surrender IOC seat when they cease to head their sports federations.

*Honorary members*

| | Date of joining | Date of retirement | Age in 1996 | Years on IOC |
|---|---|---|---|---|
| Lord Killanin (Ireland) | 1952 | 1980 | 82 | 28 |
| Lord Luke (UK) | 1951 | 1988 | 91 | 37 |
| Count Jean de Beaumont (France) | 1951 | 1990 | 92 | 39 |
| Willi Daume (Germany) | 1956 | 1991 | 83 | 35 |
| Ahmed Eldemerdash Touny (Egypt) | 1960 | 1993 | 89 | 33 |
| King Constantine (Greece) | 1963 | 1974 | 56 | 11 |
| James Worrall (Canada) | 1967 | 1989 | 82 | 22 |
| Abdel Mohamed Halim (Sudan) | 1968 | 1982 | 86 | 14 |
| Raymond Gafner (Swiss) | 1969 | 1991 | 81 | 22 |
| Masaji Kiyokawa (Japan) | 1969 | 1989 | 83 | 20 |
| Virgilio de Leon (Panama) | 1969 | 1995 | 77 | 26 |
| Maurice Herzog (France) | 1970 | 1995 | 77 | 25 |
| Henry Hsu (Taiwan) | 1970 | 1988 | 84 | 18 |
| Berthold Beitz (Germany) | 1972 | 1988 | 83 | 16 |
| Pedro Ramirez Vazquez (Mexico) | 1972 | 1995 | 77 | 23 |

| | Date of joining | Date of retirement | Age in 1996 | Years on IOC |
|---|---|---|---|---|
| Manuel Gonzalez Guerra (Cuba) | 1973 | 1993 | 79 | 20 |
| Air Chief Marshall Dawee Chullasapya (Thailand) | 1974 | 1989 | 82 | 15 |
| Dr Eduardo Hay (Mexico) | 1974 | 1991 | 81 | 17 |
| Matts Wilhelm Carlgren (Sweden) | 1976 | 1993 | 79 | 17 |
| Dr Kevin Patrick O'Flanagan (Ireland) | 1976 | 1995 | 77 | 19 |
| Robert Guillermo Peper (Argentina) | 1977 | 1988 | 83 | 11 |
| German Rieckehoff (Puerto Rico) | 1977 | 1990 | 81 | 13 |
| Lt-General Dadong Suprayogi (Indonesia) | 1977 | 1989 | 82 | 12 |
| Gunther Heinze (East Germany) | 1981 | 1992 | 73 | 11 |
| Mary Glen-Haigh (UK) | 1982 | 1994 | 78 | 12 |

# APPENDIX B

# *Key Members of the Olympic 'Family'*

IOC      International Olympic Committee: Self-selecting, secretive, anti-democratic club of ninety-nine men and seven women who own the Olympics and take huge profits. Led by a career fascist whose deputy in 1996 was/is a senior Korean intelligence agent.

NOCs      National Olympic Committees: They collect money from the public and sponsors to send athletes to the games. Don't like to admit they have no power at the IOC. Usually defend the IOC and its leadership.

ANOC      Association of National Olympic Committees: Mario Vazquez Raña's powerless organisation. Gives him prestige – while his wallet can bear the strain. Plots with the IOC to distribute a share of Olympic revenues from sponsors. Irrelevant to Olympic movement.

OCA      Olympic Council for Asia: Regional branch of Raña's group. Run by the Kuwaiti ruling family. Accident prone.

EANOC      European Association of National Olympic Committees: Talking shop with a glossy magazine. In Raña's group.

ANOCA       Raña's chums in Africa.

GAISF       General Assembly of International Sports Federations: The sports barons at play. Rarely is an athlete seen – and most competitors have probably never heard of GAISF or are aware that it claims to speak for them. Controlled by Mickey Kim.

ASOIF       Association of Summer Olympic International Federations. The summer sports barons, led by Primo Nebiolo. Not an athlete in sight – but Nebiolo claims to be their voice. Carves up their share of the Olympic profits.

# APPENDIX C

# *The Olympic Games*

| Summer | Olympics | Winter | Olympics |
|--------|----------|--------|----------|
| 1896 | Athens | | |
| 1900 | Paris | | |
| 1904 | St Louis | | |
| 1908 | London | | |
| 1912 | Stockholm | | |
| 1920 | Antwerp | | |
| 1924 | Paris | 1924 | Chamonix |
| 1928 | Amsterdam | 1928 | St Moritz |
| 1932 | Los Angeles | 1932 | Lake Placid |
| 1936 | Berlin | 1936 | Garmisch-Partenkirchen |
| 1948 | London | 1948 | St Moritz |
| 1952 | Helsinki | 1952 | Oslo |
| 1956 | Melbourne | 1956 | Cortina |
| 1960 | Rome | 1960 | Squaw Valley |
| 1964 | Tokyo | 1964 | Innsbruck |
| 1968 | Mexico | 1968 | Grenoble |
| 1972 | Munich | 1972 | Sapporo |
| 1976 | Montreal | 1976 | Innsbruck |
| 1980 | Moscow | 1980 | Lake Placid |
| 1984 | Los Angeles | 1984 | Sarajevo |
| 1988 | Seoul | 1988 | Calgary |
| 1992 | Barcelona | 1992 | Albertville |

| 1996 | Atlanta | 1994 | Lillehammer |
| 2000 | Sydney | 1998 | Nagano |
| | | 2002 | Salt Lake City |

# NOTES

## 1: Our Games, Oh Really?

- &#35; Most of the issues summarised here are dealt with more fully in other chapters. At those points, appropriate citations and sources are given.
- &#35; All Olympic Oaths are taken from the 1994 edition of the Olympic Charter.
- 5. The producer of the opening ceremony is Don Mischer.
- 14. The quote that only 15 journalists in the world are capable of reporting on the IOC was made by director general François Carrard at a conference of academics in Lausanne in April 1994.

## 2: Norway Says No to Fascism, Greed and Fancy Coats

- 18. The VG poll was published on 3 February 1994 and carried out by Scan-Fact. 1,047 Norwegians over 15 were interviewed in their homes between 10–17 January 1994. They represented Norway in miniature with careful selection from urban and rural areas, social and economic class and gender.
- 18. Gerhard Heiberg's criticism of the IOC appeared in the Norwegian financial daily *Dagens Naerinsgliv*, reported by Reuter, 10 February 1994.
- 18. Mrs Brundtland quoted on Norway and egalitarian thinking: AP, 9 February 1994.
- 19. IOC Public Relations Director Andrew Napier reacting to Norwegian media criticism: AP, 6 February 1994.

19. Vegard Ulvang interview comments on Samaranch's fascist history: TV-2; transcript 8 February 1994.

19. Carrard's clumsy reaction to Ulvang: Reuter, 9 February 1994.

20. Olaf Poulsen attacking Ulvang: *Dagbladet* 10 February 1994.

20. *Dagbladet* poll on Ulvang: 11 February 1994.

20. Ulvang 'apology' quote: Reuter, 10 February 1994.

20. Heiberg 'IOC feel unwelcome in Norway' quote: AP, 9 February 1994.

20. The story of the Royal dinner to placate Samaranch is in *Et Eventyr Blir Til – Veien Til Lillehammer* (A Fairytale Comes True on the Road to Lillehammer) Gerhard Heiberg's account of the 1994 games, published by Cappelen, Oslo, 1995.

21. Jorunn Veiteberg interviewed during Lillehammer Games.

21. Interviews with IOC members Arroyo and O'Flanagan taped by Norwegian radio and transmitted twice in first week of Games.

23. Lillehammer mascot story – and the cost: part of a preliminary report from Professor Arne Martin Klausen of the Department of Social Anthropology, University of Oslo, of his study concerning the Mexican role in the making of the Lillehammer mascot, published in 1993.

24. The cancellation of the seminar on how the Nazi invaders hijacked ancient Nordic symbols is from Bente Erichsen's book *Culture Collision* published in Oslo, 1994.

24. Pound on Lillehammer revenues: AP, 9 February 1994.

26. Radovan Karadzic on peace: AP, 14 February 14 1994.

26. Carrard quoted on Sarajevo visit: Reuter, 17 February 1994.

26. *Dagbladet* editorial on the Sarajevo trip being a PR gimmick: 19 February 1994.

27. *Daily Telegraph* comment: 18 February 1994.

## 3: Looking After Old Friends and Good Nazis

28. Samaranch's elevation to the Spanish nobility was proclaimed on 31 December 1991.

 # The superb biography *Franco* by Paul Preston, Harper Collins, 1993, is the definitive biography of the dictator

and sets the scene for the corrupt society in which Samaranch prospered.

29. The desertion of the teenage Samaranch from the army of the Republic and more on his career as a property speculator: see *Arreu* magazine, published in Catalan in Barcelona, 21 February 1977.

29. Samaranch's membership of the Youth Fascists was referred to in *Solidaridad Nacional*: 13 July 1973.

29. Manuel Vázquez Montalbán: *Barcelonas*, translated by Andy Robinson, published by Verso, 1992. A wonderful book about the city, its food, its people and their centuries of struggle against repression.

– Montalbán, page 109; 'When Franco's troops entered the city, fourth on the list to be purged, after the Communists, the Anarchists and the Separatists, was Barcelona Football Club.'

29. In the archives of the Barcelona Civil Governor can be found a number of interesting documents concerning Samaranch's attempts in the early 1950s to get a toehold in fascist politics.

– 22 October 1951: Samaranch writes to the Civil Governor of Catalonia, begging for a seat on Barcelona council.

– Undated – but around 1951 – secret police report saying that because of his sexual philandering, he is not mature enough to hold public office.

– 6 November 1954: another secret police report on Samaranch. It states 'politically he identifies with the present regime' and notes that he owns a bachelor apartment for his sexual liaisons. Soon afterwards the fascist Falange gave him a seat on Barcelona council, Samaranch's first step on the political ladder.

– 12 November 1956: a letter from Samaranch to the Madrid government ending, 'I am always at your orders with my arm raised.'

– In January 1967 Samaranch was appointed National Delegate for Sport by the fascist Falange. This was the equivalent of sports minister.

# Two key publications that outline how the Franco dictatorship manipulated sport and Samaranch's role in imposing Falangist policy are:

– Doctoral thesis in the archive of the University of

London: *The Political Instrumentalisation of Professional Football in Francoist Spain*, 1939–77, by Duncan R. Shaw, Queen Mary College, March 1988.

- *The Politics of Futbol* by Duncan Shaw, *History Today*, August 1985.

30. Samaranch's message to Spanish Olympic team going to Mexico in 1968: Shaw thesis, page 94.

31. In the archives of *Vanguardia* of Barcelona, *Diario de Barcelona*, *Neuvo Diario*, *Correo Catalan* and *Mundo Diario* are large numbers of reports from the mid-1960s onwards about Samaranch's career in fascist politics.

31. In 1967 Franco introduced tightly controlled 'elections' for seventeen per cent of the seats in the Cortes. Only right-wing candidates were allowed to stand and the power and resources of the government were thrown behind 'official' candidates. Samaranch was one of them.

Result of first Cortes elections in September 1967.

| | | | |
|---|---|---|---|
| 'Official' | J.A. Samaranch | 526,367 | elected |
| 'Independent' | Eduardo Tarragona | 435,275 | elected |

53% turnout.

The authorities did everything possible to hamper Tarragona's campaign, refusing him permission to hold meetings in Barcelona until five days before the election. From 1967 to 1969 Tarragona denounced tax evasion and urged slum clearance, cheap housing and more schools. In 1969 he resigned – unheard of – from the Cortes because the Government rejected his request to set up a Civic Union of Catalonia to promote social, cultural and economic development and also housing, town planning, working conditions, medical services and schooling.

On the very same day the Franco government approved the setting up of the Club Siglo XXI 'to promote cultural welfare, and favour social harmony within order'. Sponsors included future Franco Premier Carlos Arias Navarro, future Franco Information Minister Pio Cabanillas and J.A. Samaranch.

Second elections to the Cortes: September 1971.

'Independent'    Eduardo Tarragona    389,159    elected
'Official'       J.A. Samaranch       273,495    elected
Samaranch's vote was halved and turnout dropped from 53% to 35%

31. Samaranch's correspondence with Avery Brundage is in the Brundage archive at the University of Illinois campus at Urbana-Champaign. The two letters quoted here were written in September 1960 and December 1966.

32. Mrs Brundage's holiday in Madrid and Barcelona and the Costa Brava was in 1961.

32. The IOC held its annual Session in Madrid in 1965.

32. Samaranch and illegal funds: letter and press cutting sent by IOC secretary Otto Mayer to Avery Brundage in 1959.

32. Samaranch was co-opted on to the IOC in Rome in 1966.

32. The last of a succession of career Nazi and fascist sympathisers from World War Two to leave the IOC was Karl Ritter von Halt, a Nazi party member and stormtrooper who was also Hitler's last *Reichssportführer*. He was a member of the Olympic committee from 1929 until 1964 and a member of its executive board from 1957 until 1963. Halt's record is cited in 'Toward a Theory of Olympic Internationalism' by John Hoberman, published in the *Journal of Sport History*, Vol. 22, No. 1, Spring 1995.

34. Geoffroy de Navacelle writing about Coubertin in *Olympic Review*, 1995.

34. For more on the ancient Greek Games – see *Five-Ring Circus*, editors Alan Tomlinson and Garry Whannel, Pluto Press, 1984. Essays by Jennifer Hargreaves and Bruce Kidd.

35. The Berlin Olympics: The Hitler quote that the Games were 'an invention of Jews and Freemasons' is from *Hitler's Games*, by Duff Hart-Davis, Harper & Row, New York, 1986, page 45.

35. Brundage's Masonic rank – he was a 32nd Degree mason – is from *The Games Must Go On: Avery Brundage and the Olympic Movement* by Allen Guttman, Columbia University Press, 1984, page 40.

35. Lord Aberdare's comment about Jews is from *Hitler's Games*, page 107.

36. Former IOC president Lord Killanin's memoirs, *My Olympic Years*, contains a photograph from 1961 showing a group of jovial IOC members: Crown Prince Francis Joseph [Liechtenstein]; Karl Ritter von Halt [Germany]; Lord Aberdare [GB]; the Duke of Mecklenberg-Schwerin [Germany]; Avery Brundage; Count Paolo Thaon di Revel [Italy, Mussolini's former Finance Minister]; Lord Killanin and J. Jewitt Garland [USA].

36. The friendship between American sprinter Jesse Owens and German athlete Lutz Long; see picture caption 'Olympic reality defeats totalitarian ideology' in *Olympic Revolution*, the Olympic biography of J.A. Samaranch, by David Miller, published by Pavilion Books, 1992, foreword by the King of Spain.

36. Gliding a demonstration sport in 1936; *The Nazi Olympics*, Richard Mandell, MacMillan, New York, 1971, page 155.

36. U-boats with the five rings. The story – and a photograph – are in *Olympic Review*, 1977: page 504 turning to 526.

36. Brundage's claim that the Berlin Games contributed to 'international peace and harmony'. From his official report to the American Olympic Committee, cited by Guttman in *The Games Must Go On*, page 78.

37. For more on the Workers' Games – see essay by James Riordan in *Five-Ring Circus*.

37. For more on General Walter von Reichenau see 'Toward a Theory of Olympic Internationalism' by John Hoberman, as above.

37. Complaints by the Italian Olympic committee against General Vaccaro, because of his past commitment to fascism, cited in Guttman, page 102.

38. Complaints against von Halt and the Duc de Mecklenberg-Schwerin cited in Guttman, page 101.

## 4: Sex, Death and Horst Pulls It Off

39. My thanks to Dr Eric Aldin for his memories from Tokyo in 1958.

40. What Bob Beamon did the night before his record-breaking

jump: From Dick Schaap's biography of Beamon, *The Perfect Jump*, cited in *The Complete Book of the Olympics* by David Wallechinsky, Little Brown, updated after every summer Olympics.

41. The Mexico Olympic massacre is described by James Coote in *Olympic Report* 1968, published by Robert Hale, page 23, and in Killanin's memoirs, page 49.

41. The slogan opening the Games in Mexico was 'Everything is possible with peace.' *The Olympic Games*, edited by Lord Killanin and John Rodda, published by Macdonald and Jane's, 1979, page 35.

41. Brundage's conferring with the Mexican authorities, quoted by Lord Killanin, page 50.

41. Mexican president's press secretary quoted; the massacre was a 'local affair', Coote, page 23.

41. General José de Jesus Clark quoted in Killanin's memoirs, page 50, that more people were killed in traffic accidents in Mexico every day than had been shot in the square that night.

42. John Carlos quoted; 'We are great American athletes for 19.8 seconds; then we are animals as far as our country is concerned.' Coote, page 28.

42. USOC report on the games of 1968, published by USOC, 1969.

42. Brundage quoted on the 'nasty' Black Power protest in *The Olympics* by Allen Guttman, University of Illinois Press, Urbana & Chicago, 1992.

42. British journalist quoted on 'joyous' Mexico closing ceremony: Coote, page 137.

43. Samaranch's instructions to athletes in Sapporo, 1972: see his message to chefs de mission in *Olympic Review*, 1972.

43. Samaranch's admission that his public, political and social life were finished in Spain after Franco died: *Independent*, 27 August 1988.

44. Interviews with Christian Janette: conducted in 1991 and 1992.

45. The *Times* report on Samaranch being 'all things to all men', 16 July 1980, by John Hennessy.

46. The Catalan magazine which dubbed Samaranch 'the Chameleon' was *Arreu*, 21 February 21 1977.

46.  The German scholar Arnd Kruger sums up Samaranch as having 'succeeded in laundering his Blueshirt white'.


## 5: Roll Up, Roll Up, Ideals for Sale

47.  Products endorsed by the Olympic Movement: Vodka is endorsed by the Russian Olympic committee; sugary drinks with caffeine – Coca-Cola, the biggest IOC sponsor; steroid-free beef steaks by the USOC; the remainder of the products are officially endorsed by the Atlanta Olympic Organising Committee.

48.  Dassler's astonishing article on commercialising the games was in *Olympic Review*, 1980, page 26.

49.  Quote from Stuart F. Cross of Coca-Cola can be found in *IOC Marketing Matters*, Issue 4, Spring 1994.

49.  Samaranch's ecstatic comments on Daimler-Benz: *Olympic Review*, December 1991, page 552.

50.  Pound quote on Baden-Baden's Brenner's Park Hotel in his book *Five Rings Over Korea*, Little Brown, 1994, page 40.

54.  Pound on increase in IOC income: *Olympic Review*, 1992, page 100.

54.  Killanin memoirs, page 9; 'In 1980 when my presidency terminated the IOC was on a sound financial footing, whereas when I took over in 1972 it was working on a very tight budget. In December 1972 the IOC had assets of $2,084,290. In December 1980 they were $45,142,752.21.'

54.  The comment by Masaji Kiyokawa and other information in the rest of the chapter about the IOC's secrecy about its finances are from an entirely reliable confidential source – and have been checked.


## 6: It's a Tough Life

56.  David Pickup's comment was made at a Reebok lunch in Hong Kong and quoted in full in *Sport Intern*, Number 3, 20 February 1992.

57.  Brundage and his two secret sons cited in *The Games Must Go On: Avery Brundage and the Olympic Movement* by Allen Guttman, page 49.

58. Flor Isava quote on difficulty of finding women accept-
    able to Samaranch to join the IOC: *Sport Intern*, Number
    19/20, 29 October 1994.
58. Reebok replaced Adidas as sponsors of the Russian
    National Olympic committee in late 1992.
62. The IOC hired New York fine arts consultants Ruder
    Finn to promote the museum. Documents filed at the
    Justice Department in Washington show the contract fee
    was $350,000 and expenses totalled a further $190,000.
    Further payments may have been made later.
62. Richard Morrison, Arts Editor of the *Times* disclosed the
    'bribes' offered to journalists writing favourably about
    the museum on 19 August 1995, Arts section.
63. The IOC briefing paper making reference to Samaranch's
    fascist record fell accidentally into the hands of a jour-
    nalist present at the museum opening who kindly sent
    it to me.

## 7: Spies, Lies and How They Nobbled a Princess

 # The majority of the information in this chapter can be
   found in the Stasi files of Karl-Heinz Wehr in Berlin.
   Waiting times after applying for files varies from six to
   twelve months.
 # Editions of *World Amateur Boxing* and *European Amateur
   Boxing*, published during the era of the GDR, provide a
   vivid picture of how news about the sport, Chowdhry
   and Wehr were sanitised by the Stasi.
66. The Adidas sports politics group no longer exists. The old
    management have gone and the company has changed
    ownership twice since.
72. Nebiolo's $20 million account in Monaco. The detailed
    sequence of events was laid out in the first edition of *The
    Lords of the Rings*, Simon & Schuster, 1992.
73. Princess Anne quoted on 'tail wagging the dog' in the
    *Times* and the *Daily Mail*, 27 April 1989.
74. Nebiolo and aftershave; *Daily Mail*, 30 June 1989.
75. Samaranch quoted that Nebiolo's election at ASOIF was
    'a great triumph for the unity of sport'; *Guardian*, 19
    October 1989.
76. Helmick quoted that he learned how not to get caught

cheating at water polo is from an article in the magazine *The Iowan* by Mary Hutchinson Tone.

76. Helmick's response to Wehr's claims are in a fax to the author dated 30 November 1995.

78. Samaranch quoted in the *Independent* of 20 July 1992 on Helmick's departure from the IOC: 'The Helmick affair is a completely isolated case of a person who did not realise he was involved in a conflict of interests. He used his office (he was a lawyer) to defend sporting causes that conflicted with the posts he was holding at the time. I personally think he paid a very high price.'

## 8: If You Know the Right People, You Can Buy a Gold Medal

\# The majority of the information in this chapter can be found in the Stasi files of Karl-Heinz Wehr in Berlin.

80. SY Kim cited on decisions at LA Games; *New York Times*, 24 September 1988.

83. Paul Konnor's appeal to Wehr and Chowdhry quoted from *Boxing USA*, December 1988.

83. Helmick quoted from *Boxing USA*, December 1988.

83. *New York Times* quoted; 24 September 1988.

85. The Park-Jones fight was reported in *Boxing News*, 7 October 1988.

86. El Arbi quoted in the USOC monthly magazine, *The Olympian*, November 1988.

86. SY Kim claiming the decision in the Park-Jones fight was fair: *New York Times*, 2 October 1988.

87. The Bowe-Lewis fight was reported in *Boxing News*, 7 October 1988.

88. *World Boxing News*, Number 18, 1989; reporting the meeting in Nairobi.

91. The article by Wehr in *The Olympian*, July 1989, had previously appeared in *European Boxing*, Number 16, 1989.

## 9: Spooky Mickey Kim, Chief Guardian-in-Waiting

\# Much of the information in this chapter comes from the following publications:

\# The KoreaGate scandal was covered extensively in the *Washington Post* and the *New York Times* from the early 1970s.

\# The scandal was examined in two sets of Congressional hearings and reports:

– Hearings before the House of Representatives Sub-committee on International Relations, 95th Congress, 1977. The sub-committee was instructed to 'conduct an investigation and study of the activities of agencies, officials, employees and agents of the government of Korea.'

– Report of the House of Representatives Investigation of Korean–American Relations, 31 October 1978.

\# *Gifts of Deceit* by Robert Boettcher with Gordon L. Freedman: this book investigates the scandal.

\# Kim Un Yong published his own book after the Seoul Games; *The Greatest Olympics*, published by Si-sa-yong-o-sa, Inc, Seoul, 1990. It contains his own version of his biographical details plus numerous interesting photographs, including Kim, Samaranch and disgraced ex-president Roh Tae Woo.

\# Also worth sampling is *The Seoul Olympics*, the inside story by Park Seh-Jik, Bellew Publishing, London, 1991.

\# The first published reference I can find relating Mickey Kim's spooky background to the Olympic movement is in 'Human rights: the shadow side of the Seoul Olympiad' by John M. Hoberman in the *Christian Science Monitor*, 20 September 1988. It appears to have been ignored by sports reporters and Olympic experts.

\# Mickey Kim's role in the Seoul games and at the IOC is also dealt with in the first edition of *The Lords of the Rings*.

94. The anonymous former Korean diplomat was recommended to me by a number of American academics and lawyers who all testified to his integrity and accuracy.

95. Kim at Buckingham Palace; *The Greatest Olympics*, page 166.

95. The decision to reduce numbers of American troops in Asia was heralded by President Nixon in Guam on 25 July 1969.

96. The reference 'A gift [$100] to an important Korean

government official, Assistant Director Un Yong Kim (Korean Secret Service) on the death of his mother': Hearings before the House of Representatives Sub-committee on International Relations, 95th Congress, Second Session, Part 4, 15, 16, 21, 22 March; 11, 20 April; and 20 June 1978, page 178.

96. The attempted shake-down by Mickey Kim on Colt Industries is reported in: Investigation of Korean–American Relations, Report of the Sub-committee on International Organizations of the Committee on International Relations, U.S. House of Representatives (95th Congress, 2nd Session), 31 October 1978, page 241.

96. The Maryville College in St Louis which awarded a doctorate to Mickey Kim has since become Maryville University. The citation which went with Kim's degree is still in their archives. Former college president Switzer has moved to Washington University, St Louis.

97. General Choi [pronounced 'Chey'] quoted that President Park wanted to use taekwondo as 'a powerful muscle for his dictatorship' is from a petition dated 29 September 1981, from Choi Hong Hi, ITF President, to the IOC executive board.

99. The suicide of election-rigging IOC member Lee Ki-Poong and his family; AP, 28 April 1960; in Brundage archive.

100. Brundage wrote to the Korean national Olympic committee on 13 May 1960, mourning the death of Lee Ki-Poong.

100. The attempted bribe from Chang Key-Young; Killanin memoirs, page 19.

100. Details of Park Chong Kyu on joining the IOC; see Olympic Review, 1984, page 738.

101. The attempted $10,000 bribe to White House special assistant John Nidecker; page 41 in Hearings before the House of Representatives Sub-committee on International Relations, 95th Congress, First Session, Part 3, 29–30 November 1977.

101. Park Chong Kyu 'Korea's Number One Thug': interview by author with former CIA analyst Phil Liechty, quoted more fully in first edition of The Lords of the Rings.

101. The air tickets given to IOC members by Seoul bid

team; *Made In America* by Peter Ueberroth, published by William Morrow, 1985, page 106.

101. 'Five Korean Air stewardesses and three Miss Koreas' see Kim's book, page 57.

102. Kim marshals his thugs in case General Choi shows up in Baden-Baden; Kim's book, page 61.

102. Kim's preferences for membership of the Seoul organising committee; his book, page 72.

102. The cleansing of Seoul for the Asian Games and two years later for the Olympics; in 'Human rights: the shadow side of the Seoul Olympiad', by John M. Hoberman in the *Christian Science Monitor*, 20 September 1988.

103. Samaranch twice urged President Chun not to hold elections; mentioned by Dick Pound in *Five Rings Over Korea*, Little Brown, 1994, page 393.

103. Pound also appears to know about Kim's spooky background. On page 348 of his Korea book is a gratuitous reference to 'Korean influence peddling scandal exposed in United States, including illegal activities of KCIA'.

103. Samaranch presents the Gold Olympic Order to President Roh Tae Woo, 3 October 1988, *Olympic Review*, 1988; and also page 229 in Kim's book.

103. Mickey Kim appointed a special envoy by President Roh; *Sport Intern*, Number 12/3, 25 June 1990.

## 10: Black Belts and Dirty Money

107. Rivalry and struggles with ITKF; from dossier circulated to media by WUKO in late 1992 – after Samaranch had withdrawn recognition.

107. Report of Louis Guirandou-N'Diaye to Berlin Session 1985, appendix 24C.

110. Letter from General Choi to Samaranch; 27 April 1988.

110. The minutes of the General Assembly of the WTF in Seoul, October 1989 demonstrate how Mickey Kim rules the federation virtually unchallenged.

112. Sang Kyu Shim in editorial in *Taekwondo Times*, January 1992.

112. Comment on up to $1 million a year flowing from America to the Kukkiwon; *Taekwondo Times*, December 1994.

113. The point that Mickey Kim is not known to have practised taekwondo is mentioned frequently by grand masters in *Taekwondo Times*.

114. The IOC executive board member's comment on Kim being 'a combination of thug and spook'; taped interview with author.

114. Kim quote that hegemony of the West over the IOC should end; in a Reuter report from Seoul, 30 December 1994.

114. Samaranch's statement on the closeness of the principles of taekwondo and Coubertin; published in *Taekwondo Journal* of the US Taekwondo Union, Vol. 4, No. 2, Fall 1985.

## 11: No Lady, No Vote: Rubbing Up and Shaking Down On the Bid Circuit

&#35; The complete Falun archive can be inspected at the municipal offices, Falun, Sweden. Much of the information for this chapter is derived from that collection of documents.

&#35; Lars Eggertz and Stig Hedlund published a book about Falun's experiences; *The Olympic Games*, 1987. It catalogues not just the hard work over several bids by the Falun team – but also how they were exploited, ripped off, and a hostess abused.

119. The IOC secret decision of 1983 to encourage as many bidders as possible for the Games of 1992; from a reliable confidential source in Lausanne.

122. Quote from Rick Nerland on the Takac family; *Anchorage Daily News*, 13 September 1988.

122. Slavkov quote; also in *Anchorage Daily News*.

127. Description of lavish bid for 1992 by Paris: *Sports Illustrated*, 'Olympic Circus Maximus' by W.O. Johnson and Anita Verschoth.

128. Staubo letter on voting procedure for the games is in Falun archive.

130. Daume, interviewed by German TV, says Barcelona and Albertville were a 'political choice'. Cited by Eggertz in his book.

131. The confidential minutes of the IOC executive board are not disclosed to the public. However, one page – page 39 – of their meeting in Stockholm in April 1988 is

available in Swedish Olympic circles, presumably leaked by a friend in Lausanne. The relevant section reads: 'Book by Mr Eggertz: The President requested the advice of the Board Members as to whether the IOC should compose a letter addressed to the Swedish NOC, expressing its surprise and dissatisfaction over the text of Mr Eggertz' book. Mr Pound was of the opinion that it would be wise to take no action. Decision: The IOC to take no action in respect of the book published by Mr Eggertz.'

131. Gafner dismissing Falun as 'bad losers' in *Anchorage Daily News*.

132. Pound claim that 'losers' make such claims quoted in *Anchorage Daily News*.

## 12: Move Over Reverend King, Billy's Had a New Dream

  \# The politics of Atlanta are more complex than the simplistic slogans about black and white harmony. One excellent guide is Clarence Stone's *Regime Politics*, University Press of Kansas, 1989.

135. Payne told the story of how he set about going for the Games at a Georgia Tech conference on 'Sports Business in Tomorrow's World' in Atlanta, October 1994.

135. Comment on Ginger Watkins; Colin Campbell, *Atlanta Constitution*, 2 September 1992.

136. San Francisco and gay representation; *Atlanta Constitution*, 9 March 1988.

136. The rival menus; *Atlanta Constitution*, 28 April 1988.

137. Samaranch on Athen's chances of winning; *Atlanta Constitution*, 30 June 1988.

137. Paul Henderson on Atlanta's 'controlled' press; *Atlanta Constitution*, 10 January 1991.

137. The public debate in Toronto was discussed by Bruce Kidd in *The Toronto Olympic Commitment: Towards a Social Contract for the Olympic Games*, Olympika, Vol. 1, 1992, pages 154–67.

138. Payne quote on legacy of facilities and housing; *Atlanta Constitution*, 12 February 1989

138. Shielding visitors from the press quote; *Atlanta Constitution*, 25 August 1989.

139. Andrew Young quoted, Atlanta as the world's human rights capital; *Atlanta Constitution*, 3 September 1989.

139. Cernusak quoted on Martin Luther King and the IOC; *Atlanta Constitution*, 27 August 1989.

139. Payne quote on empowering neighbourhoods; *Atlanta Constitution*, 21 February 1990.

139. Samaranch decision to be 'harsh' on candidate cities. From a confidential source in Lausanne.

140. Herzog quote on the need for concensus; *Atlanta Constitution*, 10 April 1990.

140. The Wehr comments on the odds on bid cities are from his Stasi files in Berlin.

141. Ueberroth quoted on integrity of IOC members; *Atlanta Constitution*, 20 April 1990.

141. Coke's outrage at suggestions they may have bought the games; *Atlanta Constitution*, 21 September 1990.

142. Spiegel article, November 1990.

142. The reference to concern about the air ticket racket; confidential source.

143. Executive board member Marc Hodler told the *Frankfurter Allgemeine Zeitung* that complaints by candidate cities about IOC members were 'minimal'. He had had 'serious words' with his colleagues but had not revealed the names 'even to Samaranch'.

144. Maynard Jackson on Georgia's swastika flag and the response from the Atlanta organising committee; AP, 23 June 1995.

145. Samaranch's response to homophobia and the Georgia flag; *Atlanta Constitution*, 11 May 1994.

145. Mbaye comment on Augusta; *Atlanta Consitution*, 9 December 1992.

146. IOC on not delving into problems at Augusta; *Atlanta Constitution*, 8 November 1992.

146. Samaranch on golf to Italian paper – and Payne wrong-footed; *Atlanta Constitution*, 29 January 1993.

146. Tightknit relationships in the organising committee; *Atlanta Constitution*, 18 January 1992.

146. Piedmont Driving Club; *Atlanta Constitution*, 19 November 1994.

147. Cramer quoted on homeless; *Atlanta Constitution*, 23 October 1994.

147. Stadium groundbreaking quote; *Atlanta Constitution*, 16 July 1993.

148. Local fears about how foreign visitors and TV crews would see dilapidated areas; *Atlanta Constitution*, July 1994.

148. Payne quoted on Olympic largesse; speaking at Georgia Tech in October 1994.

148. Reverend Timothy MacDonald quote; *Atlanta Constitution*, 7 July 1995.

149. Common Cause quoted; AP, 10 May 1995.

149. Payne quoted on private ventures; AP, 9 June 1995.

## 13: The World's Richest Man Wins Olympic Gold

# Information about the IOC members at the Hyatt hotel was offered by employees.

# I am grateful for assistance from several academics and journalists in Japan for their assistance with this chapter. Also information published by environmentalists and local protesters opposing the Nagano Olympic bid.

158. Many of the anecdotes about Tsutsumi and also his dealings with Samaranch come from *Yoshiaki Tsutsumi and the Olympics* by Gentaro Taniguchi, published by San-ichi shoho, 1992 and cited in *The Brothers*, by Lesley Downer, Chatto & Windus, 1994.

158. Other detail comes from the Nagano bid committee's published plans and budgets.

160. Samaranch asking Japanese prime minister Toshiki Kaifu for tax breaks for Japanese companies making donations to the Olympic museum: *Olympic Review*, 1989, page 495.

164. The *Sport Intern* attack on the Takac family was in edition number 9/10, 8 June 1991.

168. Helmick and *USA Today*: the stories began on 5 September 1991 and continued until Helmick's resignation from the IOC in December.

168. Helmick quote that 'an appearance of impropriety is unwarranted,' *New York Times*, 5 September 1991.

169. The USOC vice-president quoted on 'bare-knuckles discussion' was Mike Lenard, a Los Angeles attorney; *Chicago Tribune*, 6 September 1991.

169. Helmick apology quoted from *Los Angeles Times*, 8 September 1991.

169. Gosper quote on Helmick's 'elegant' solution; *The Guardian*, 5 December 1991.

Since the publication of the first edition of *The Lords of the Rings* I and Vyv Simson have been denied accreditation to Olympic meetings and events.

## 14: An Old Blueshirt Comes Home

170. Pound comment on Falun failing to win the Games is in his letter of 4 November 1986, in the Falun archive.

170. The losses met by French taxpayers for Albertville; *International Herald Tribune*, 11 July 1992.

170. Samaranch on Savoy being a winner from the Albertville games; *Olympic Review*, Number 294, April 1992.

171. Quote on Samaranch avoiding a duel with Nebiolo; confidential discussion with an IOC executive board member.

172. The cost of the IOC pavilion at Seville: all from a confidential source in Lausanne.

172. Samaranch's biography; *Olympic Revolution* by David Miller. In his postscript to the 1994 edition Miller kindly praised the first edition of *The Lords of the Rings* as 'The literary equivalent of football hooliganism.'

173. *Daily Telegraph* and *Times* quoted on Samaranch biography; 9 June 1992.

173. Samaranch on TV-AM, 8 June 1992.

173. *Time* magazine special Olympic supplement, Vol. 139, No. 27, Summer 1992.

174. *Sport Intern* comment on *Time*'s 'unjustified abuse': Number 4/5, 22 February 1993.

174. *Time*'s Richard Atkinson quoted; *Marketing*, 16 July 1992.

175. *Barcelonas* by Manuel Vázquez Montalbán: translated by Andy Robinson, published by Verso, 1992.

176. Samaranch proud of his past; quoted in the *Independent on Sunday*, 26 July 1992.

177. Maragall's opening speech and reference to Companys; *Olymic Review*, October 1992, page 473.

178. *Barcelona* by Robert Hughes, Alfred Knopf, 1992. The odour from corpses is mentioned on page 8.

179. Samaranch quoted at opening ceremony, *Olympic Review*, October 1992, page 473.
180. Tallberg quote that the athletes' village was the 'finest so far', *Olympic Review*, 1992, page 419.
180. John Stockton quoted; *Daily Telegraph*, 27 July 1992.
180. Charles Barkley quoted; *Times*, 5 August 1992.
180. NBA's Rob Levine quoted; *Daily Telegraph*, 27 July 1992.
180. Samaranch on success of basketball; *International Herald Tribune*, 10 August 1992.

## 15: Serial Freeloaders Stop Off in Berlin

183. Letter from Samaranch to all IOC members, national Olympic committees, the international sports federations and bidding cities, setting out new rules for hospitality, 3 July 1991.
184. The Berlin 2000 bid cost German taxpayers DM 86 million. Many sources including AFP, 28 January 1994.
185. Grüttke models suits. Der Spiegel, 16 September 1991.
185. Fuchs comment on being free of public scrutiny. He stated this in a taped interview with Matthew D. Rose.
186. All commercial contracts are in the archive of the Partner for Berlin City Marketing Corporation, formerly the Berlin 2000 Marketing company.
187. The incident involving a comedian pillorying Samaranch as a retired fascist was reported in Der Tagesspiegel, 31 August 1993.
187. The Daimler executive's salary eating up ten per cent of the company's contribution – see contract archive.
187. Kleinert's comment that the bid offered 'unbelievable economic opportunities'. 'Glaenzen fuer Olympia' in Die Tagaszeitung, 18 August 1993.
188. The secret strategy document on how to handle the media. All copies were subsequently shredded. However a copy is in the possession of Matthew D. Rose.
189. David Miller article praising Berlin bid. The *Times*, 21 August 1992.
190. Fuchs claim on how to win the Olympics. He stated this in a taped interview with Matthew D. Rose.
190. Fuchs' claim that Atlanta had a dossier on IOC members

that was subsequently sold to another bidding city has been denied.

192. The claim that the Berlin officials had a 'fantastic' time in Barcelona. Official transcript of Berlin state parliamentary inquiry hearings, 23 June 1995.

192. The bill from the Grand Hotel for the IOC visit. This bill was subsequently shredded. A copy is in the possession of Matthew D. Rose.

193. Scepticism about the IOC's new 'no gifts' rule. Peter Ball in the *Times*, 7 August, 1992.

193. Flor Isava's itinerary in Berlin. A specially printed programme now in the official archive of the Berlin 2000 committee.

194. Many of the hospitality bills for IOC members' visits to Berlin are in the possession of Matthew D. Rose.

195. Brigitte Schmitz comment on medical bills left unpaid by IOC members. She stated this in a taped interview with Matthew D. Rose.

196. The invitation stressing that IOC members would not need their credit cards in Stuttgart. In the possession of Matthew D. Rose.

196. Letter from Ivan Dibos to Carlos Ferrer is dated 19 July 1993.

197. Ivan Dibos's fax to Brigitte Schmitz is dated 20 July 1993.

197. Carlos Ferrer's letter to Volkswagen is dated 26 July 1993.

197. Thomas Bach was informed of Dibos's request in a fax from Berlin 2000 to him dated 11 August 1993.

197. Charles Mukora's request for $4,371 was in an invoice dated 22 August 1993. In the possession of Matthew D. Rose.

198. Walter Troger made his comment about ignoring the rules in evidence to the Berlin state parliamentary inquiry hearings, 29 June 1995.

198. Brigitte Schmitz comment on final visits to IOC members in their homes. Her evidence to the Berlin state parliamentary inquiry hearings, 9 October 1995.

198. Nawrocki's claim that the IOC never accused them of violating bidding rules. Official transcript of the Berlin state parliamentary inquiry hearings, 23 June 1995.

## 16: On Your Marks, Get Set, Lunch!

199. Chen Xitong signed the order calling troops into Tiananmen Square. Many sources, including *The Nation*, 19 June 1995, page 889.

200. Troger quote; IOC could not lose. *Guardian*, 24 September 1993.

201. Samaranch boosts Brasilia hopes; *New York Times*, 16 February 1993.

201. The IOC member in Istanbul; the sexual approach was told in great detail to a German reporter.

202. Samaranch on Manchester bid; *Times*, 14 July 1993.

 #  *The Bid*, by Rod McGeoch, Heinemann, 1994, is the story of Sydney's campaign, seen through the eyes of team leader McGeoch.

202. Scott 'coming on strong', *The Bid*, page 218.

202. Steve Bell cartoon; *Guardian*, 14 July 1993.

202. Anita DeFrantz quoted; *Sport Intern*, Number 18/19, 5 November 1991.

203. McGeoch having fun sailing; *The Bid*, page 96.

203. McGeoch and a gift request from an IOC member; *The Bid*, page 204.

203. Carrard comment in Havana; *The Bid*, page 106.

204. McGeoch and human rights; *The Bid*, page 221.

204. McGeoch on Barcelona; 'Track and field was now drug free,' *The Bid*, page 153.

204. *Sport Intern* on Sydney journalists; Number 11/12, 5 June 1993.

204. Samaranch on Sydney's hopes; *Sydney Morning Herald*, 16 May 1993.

205. McGeoch and Sir Tim Bell; *The Bid*, pages 227–8.

205. Chen Xitong's citation for his Olympic Order; *Olympic Review*, 1991, page 328. Baifa Zhang's citation is on page 329.

206. Zhang Baifa quoted on Tiananmen Square; *Sunday Telegraph*, 2 August 1992.

206. The anonymous Chinese source quoted here and in the next chapter is real and fears for their life and liberty if their identity is ever disclosed.

207. Samaranch quoted that the games can help a country; *Times*, 25 June 1993.

207. Samaranch in Shanghai; *Sunday Telegraph*, 16 May 1993.

208. Samaranch in Sydney – human rights are important; Sydney *Telegraph-Mirror*, 17 May 1993.

208. Miller on the Games as a weapon of peace; *Times*, 24 June 1993.

208. Pound on influencing China; *Daily Telegraph*, 21 September 1993.

208. Miller in *Time*, 28 June 1993. David Miller says this article was commissioned in the usual way and that he had no foreknowledge that it was to be contained within an advertising feature.

209. *New York Times* quoted on IOC visit to Beijing; 11 March 1993.

209. IOC members free shopping; *Daily Telegraph*, 19 March 1993.

209. IOC members' names on Great Wall; *Guardian*, 26 June 1993.

209. Chen Xitong on IOC as Gods; *Daily Telegraph*, 19 March 1993.

210. 'The European lobster-guzzling record' was suggested by Robert Hardman in the *Daily Telegraph*, 8 September 1993.

212. Samaranch was not backing Beijing, David Miller, *Times*, 22 September 1993.

213. Chen Xitong sacked. AP, 8 May 1995.

## 17: Knickers Off Girls, the Olympians Are Coming

# My thanks to Michelle Verroken for her paper on gender testing at the Brighton women's conference, May 1994.

# Also to Sarah Marris, producer of *Sex Games*, 11 August 1993 for BBC-TV's On The Line series, edited by Vyv Simson.

# Of great assistance were two papers by Dr Elizabeth Ferris:

– Attitudes to Women in Sport, *Medicine Sport*, 1981.

– Gender Verification Testing in Sport, *British Medical Bulletin*, 1992.

214. Mary Peters cited by Michelle Verroken.

219. Carrard quoted in minutes of meeting of scholars in Lausanne, April 1994.

220. Brighton women's conference; Sarah Springman quoted.

220. IOC press release on women in sport; 26 September 1995.

222. Anita DeFrantz quoted; AP, 26 September 1995.

## 18: Too Few Tears For the Disabled

 # Thanks to individual members of the Lillehammer Paralympics organising team and also to Tony Sainsbury who kindly commented on this chapter but cannot in any way be held responsible for the facts or the conclusions derived from them.

224. The figure of 500 million disabled people in the world is from Erling Stordahl, Director of Norway's Beitostolen Healtsport Centre.

224. Guttman quoted; *The Cord*, 24 March 1949.

226. Samaranch and Marcos share a stamp; *Olympic Review*, 1982, page 298.

226. IOC budget; some is public domain information; the rest is from confidential sources in Lausanne.

227. Meeting in Lausanne of IPC and IOC; 29 January 1991; from the IOC's minutes.

228. The IPC in Budapest in 1991; General Assembly agenda item 9.

228. Meeting in Lausanne of IPC and IOC; 4 May 1992; from the IOC's minutes.

229. Stupp letter dated 17 June 1993.

230. Andy Fleming quoted in the *Atlanta Constitution*, 1991.

230. USOC on settlement; AP, 27 April 1995.

## 19: Keep Taking the Medicine, But Don't Let Us Catch You

I am indebted to Jim Ferstle, Jonathan Jones and Brendan Pittaway who researched the Los Angeles doping cover-up for BBC TV's On the Line programme – now axed – and editor Vyv Simson, for their assistance with this chapter.

 # Other essential reading includes *Mortal Engines* by John Hoberman, The Free Press, New York, 1992.

232. Samaranch quoted, 'China is clean'; Reuter 5 October 1994.

232. OCA quoted; Reuter, 6 October 1994.

232. Bob Hasan quoted; Reuter, 6 October 1994.

232. Ashwini Kumar quoted; Reuter, 6 October 1994.

232. Nebiolo quoted; Reuter, 8 October 1994.

233. Samaranch on doping declining; Reuter 4 November 1994.

233. Yang Aihua quoted by AP, 8 September 1994.

233. Chinese Foreign Ministry spokesman denies doping; UPI, 17 November 1994.

234. He Zhenliang denies systematic doping; Reuter, 14 December 1994.

234. OCA claims individual cases of doping; UPI, 30 March 1995.

234. Samaranch in Monaco on the IOC's relentless struggle; UPI, 3 April 1995.

234. Carrard backs Chinese; AP 3 April 1995

234. Samaranch in Japan; AP 23 August 1995

235. The KGB colonel was found in retirement in Moscow by a Russian colleague in 1993. He declines any publicity.

236. Merode on Moscow being a good example for future games; speaking in Lausanne, 30 October 1980.

237. Moscow games were 'pure', *Olympic Review*, 1981, page 158.

238. Merode talking to *Sport in the USSR*, cited in *Sport Intern*, 15 February 1983.

238. Ueberroth; speaking in Lausanne, 24 November 1983.

238. US athletes practise with testing equipment before 1984 Games; Dr Robert Voy in *Drugs, Sport and Politics*, Leisure Press, 1991, page 89.

239. The dispute in Los Angeles between Nebiolo and Donike was recorded in the Stasi reports of Dr Manfred Hoppner, former East German director of sports medical services. His code name was 'Technik'.

240. Beckett, Kammerer, Yesalis and other interviews relating to testing in LA, first given to BBC TV in 1994.

243. Andrew Napier quoted on LA dope figures; AP, 22 August 1994.

243. Johnson is believed to have assumed he was taking dihydrotestosterone, then undetectable. In fact he was given Stanozolol.

243. Thanks to Ron Wall at the Paris office of AFP for help with the sequence in Seoul.

244. Samaranch quoted, winning a war against drugs; *Olympic Review*, 1988, page 692.

245. The Dubin Report quoted: Commission of Inquiry Report, published in Ottawa, 1990. 'Fallacy', page 397.

245. Pound quoted against Dubin; *Globe & Mail*, Toronto: 20 October 1990.

245. Donike's 50 positives; *Times*, 28 August 1989.

246. Kristin Otto story; AP, 5 December 1994, quoting *Swimming World*.

246. Samaranch quoted on stubborn fight; *Olympic Review*, 1992, page 143.

246. *Drugs in Sport*, Vol. 1, No. 1, February 1992.

246. Dr Voy quoted on doping in Barcelona; *Daily Telegraph*, 21 July 1992.

246. Samaranch on concrete action against doping. *Olympic Review*, 1992, page 412.

246. Merode quoted as 'optimistic'; *Independent*, 10 August 1992.

246. Samaranch quote; winning; *Independent*, 11 August 1992.

247. Nearly 1,000 dopers in Barcelona, *Belgian Olympic News*, December 1992, page 12. Also reported by AP, 11 January 1993.

248. Samaranch on cancellation of mobile testing lab; *Olympic Review*, Number 279, January 1991.

248. IOC appoints its first Medical Director, Dr Patrick Schamasch. *Olympic Review*, July / August 1993.

## 20: Gunning For the Peace Prize

# The IOC has denied campaigning for the Nobel Peace Prize. This spurred a confidential source in Lausanne to supply me with the appropriate dates and decisions taken by the executive board between 1986 and 1990, to do exactly what they now deny.

252. Grey quoted; press release issued at IOC Session in Birmingham, June 1991.

253. Samaranch speech at Albertville about the IOC helping create a wind of freedom; *Olympic Review*, 1992, page 141.

253. Samaranch quoted on IOC's leadership role in the world; *Olympic Review*, July / August 1992, page 345.

253. The *Guardian* backs Samaranch for the Nobel; 11 August 1992.

254. Miller on Samaranch's contribution to contemporary society in *Sport Intern*, Number 12, January 1993.

254. Eidsvag interviewed by author and colleagues, 1992–94.

255. Helmick quoted in *Atlanta Constitution* supplement 'The Selling of the Olympics', 12 July 1992.

256. Brandsas and Odden's story appeared in *Arbeiderbladet*, 3 February 1993.

256. Samaranch and Carrard deny Nobel campaign; AP, 4 February 1993.

256. Samaranch quoted 'I am not qualified'; *Times*, 25 June 1993.

257. Pound claiming IOC would be embarrassed at the thought of campaigning for the Nobel; *USA Today*, 4 February 1993.

257. Samaranch wrote to Mrs Brundtland in May 1993. She replied on 14 October 1993.

258. John Major in Lausanne; *Guardian*, 6 April 1993.

258. Transcript of John Major's speech in Monaco, 23 September 1993.

258. Carrard on 'close bi-lateral contacts'; Robert Hardman; *Daily Telegraph*, 22 September 1993.

259. Kidane quoted from *Continental Sports*, Number 35, January-March 1987.

259. Mickey Kim speaking in Finland; *Olympic Review*, December 1993.

259. Miller on the IOC being a worthy candidate for the peace prize; *Times*, 10 December 1993.

263. Ulvang says the IOC don't deserve the Nobel; AP, 3 February 1993.

## 21: Death In Paris

265. Samaranch and demand for Japanese taxpayers to subsidise his 1990 congress; from a confidential source in Lausanne.

265. Mandela, Mitterand and Domingo were all scheduled, in numerous IOC press releases, to appear in Paris. Their withdrawals were widely covered in the media, i.e. Reuter, 28 August 1994.

266. Carrard quoted on 'superficial approach'; AP, 21 June 1993.

267. References to Balladur and Chirac; Reuter, 30 August 1994.

267. Samaranch speech on IOC will take all decisions; 30 August 1994.

269. Samaranch justifies $16 million bill; Reuter, 3 September 1994.

270. Napier fired; AP, 15 February 1995.

270. Coubertin quoted on 'electoral uncertainty', *Olympic Message*, Number 39, page 6.

272. Carrard quoted on 'precious results'; AP, 29 August 1994.

272. Most speeches are quoted from IOC handouts.

274. Reuter comment on IOC media plans similar to totalitarian regimes; Reuter, 2 September 1994.

277. Samaranch in Lillehammer; 'The Congress in Paris may be a good way to modernise our organisation,' *Guardian*, 12 February 1994.

277. Samaranch interviewed by ABC TV's *Day One* programme in Lausanne, 24 January 1994, says the IOC is already democratic.

278. Carrard quote; 'the re-baptised "Congress of Unity" is not just a word in the air,' Reuter, 4 September 1994.

278. Nebiolo quoted; 'a good decision,' Reuter, 4 September 1994.

279. Samaranch on athletes; 'Maybe in the near future more athletes can come in,' Reuter, 5 September 1994.

280. Hasan profiled in *Financial Times*, 24 June 1994.

280. Journalists arrested; Reuter, 19 March 1995.

## 22: Keep Taking the Monkey Glands

281. Samaranch's letter to his members seeking their views on raising the retirement age; *Sport Intern*, Number 7, 22 April 1995.

282. Samaranch says he will not stand for re-election; Reuter, 5 November 1994.

284. Anita DeFrantz quoted; AP, 11 June 1995.

284. Pound quoted on laughing stock; AP, 11 June 1995.

284. Samaranch arrives in Budapest, denies he is a candidate; UPI, 12 June 1995.

284. Merode backs Samaranch; UPI, 12 June 1995.

284. Carrard; 'What the outside world may say, will be said by the outside world,' Reuter, 13 June 1995.

284. Insider quoted; 'Turkeys voting against Christmas'; Reuter, 13 June 1995.

285. 'Crushing personal defeat' for Samaranch; Reuter, 15 June 1995.

285. Pound quoted; 'It was a wonderful afternoon of democracy in action,' Reuter, 15 June 1995.

285. Carrard quoted; 'The president was quite satisfied with the outcome,' AP, 15 June 1995.

285. *Sport Intern* on thugs; Number 12/13, 15 June 1995.

286. *Sport Intern* and Samaranch's scruples; Number 12/13, 15 June 1995.

286. Anonymous quote, 'ridiculous,' UPI, 17 June 1995.

286. Hodler quoted; UPI, 17 June 1995.

287. Carrard quoted; 'He was totally out of this,' Reuter, 18 June 1995.

287. Pound quoted; 'It's not the end of the world,' Reuter, 18 June 1995.

287. Anita DeFrantz quoted; 'didn't vote against it,' AP, 19 June 1995.

288. Pound: 'Choices can be based on friendship or where your wife wants to go shopping,' *New York Times*, 12 June 1995.

## 23: Buy a Coke, Pay By Visa, Fund the Great Doping Cover-up

289. McColl of NationsBank quoted; *Atlanta Constitution*, 12 July 1992.

289. Danish cyclist Knud Jensen collapsed and died during a road race in Rome, 1960. Post mortem showed traces of nicotynal alcohol and amphetamine.

290. Predicted Atlanta profit of $160 million; *Atlanta Constitution*, 1 February 1990.

290. Samaranch in Cape Town; Reuter, 17 November 1995.

290. Samaranch in Rome; AP, 8 November 1995.

290. Puerto Rico quote; AP, 15 November 1995.

290. MacAloon quoted; Minutes of meeting of Academics in Lausanne, April 1994.

291. Michael Payne quoted; 'it really makes no difference where the games are held,' AP, 12 December 1995.

291. Diamond of NBC; at a seminar in Lausanne in 1994, *Sport Intern*, Supplement, 1 May 1994.

292. Michael Payne quoted; 'It clearly provides considerable financial security to the movement,' AP, 12 December 1995.

293. Samaranch quoted; 'The IOC is very generous,' AP, 26 September 1995.

293. Pound speech on need for taxes to subsidise the games; full version in *Sport Intern*, Number 11, 6 June 1994.

293. Coubertin quoted on need to purify Olympic movement; from 'The Olympic Renaissance,' published in *Independence Belge*, 1906, cited in *Olympic Review*, 1969, page 125.

294. Pound on Samaranch avoiding probing questions; *Five Rings Over Korea* by Richard Pound, Little Brown, 1994, page 121.

297. Pound and no conflict of interest with Adidas legal account; *Wall Street Journal*, 23 January 1986.

297. Anita DeFrantz is president of the Amateur Athletic Foundation of Los Angeles which distributes grants from the profits of the 1984 games. The Foundation's tax return for 1990 show Ms DeFrantz was paid $141,377 for a 40-hour week. In 1991 her salary rose to £150,129. Details of her salary in recent years still awaited from tax authorities at date of writing.

298. 'Puke' quote: from Australian swimming coach Don Talbot, interviewed by CBC in Rio de Janeiro, 2 December 1995.

299. Samaranch speaking in Berlin, 13 December 1995. He departed from his script to make the comment that there might be no doping in Atlanta.

299. Keller quote; *Continental Sports*, Number 25, April 1984.

## 24: We Win the Samaranch Prize for Literature

301. 'Samaranch Plays at Spies,' *El Triangle*, 18 December 1992.

302. Jean Ziegler motion in Bern parliament; 24 September 1992.

303. Prosecutor Chatelaine quoted: we had shown 'a deep contempt towards the IOC, its president and its members,' AP, 5 December 1994.

303. Samaranch claim he was only 'a high-ranking civil servant' in Franco's Spain; AP and Reuter, 7 December 1994.

304. The sentence of five days jail, suspended for three years; Reuter, 8 December 1995.

# ACKNOWLEDGEMENTS

Some of the most valuable sources in this book wouldn't thank me for thanking them publicly. But those who've risked their financial and career prospects to get Olympic truths into the public domain know who they are and how much I appreciate their help.

This book has benefited from my long working relationship with Vyv Simson, co-author of the first edition of *The Lords of the Rings*. Although he wasn't formally involved in this new book I've continued to take advantage of his insights and analysis. Vyv produced and directed our film of the last book and must take credit for the gold medal it won at the New York Television Festival as best international documentary of 1992.

I've been fortunate to enjoy the company and the ideas of Einar Odden and Frank Brandsas who took me behind the scenes at the Lillehammer Winter Games. When the work was done, their choruses of 'Always look on the bright side' livened up Storgata in the early hours. Many of their suggestions have gone into this book and one or other has always been on hand in Barcelona, Paris or Budapest when I've needed help.

I fell on my feet in America in 1994. Jay Coakley at the University of Colorado at Colorado Springs guided my research, introduced me to texts and sources and opened my eyes to why business needs to buy sport. Jay and Nancy also lent me everything from saucepans to their car, welcomed me to their Thanksgiving and cheered me up when I was homesick. Thanks also to Dennis and Danielle, Lynn and Bob, Rebecca and Don and the library staffs at the UCCS campus and the United States Olympic Committee.

John Hoberman at the University of Texas encouraged me to look more closely at why Coubertin founded the IOC, the support Hitler derived from the Olympic movement in the 1930s and its claim to be a moral organisation. One of the most original thinkers about the modern Olympic movement, Hoberman's books and academic papers are essential reading.

Matthew Rose obtained, translated and interpreted mounds of documents from the Stasi archives and later from the Berlin State Parliament probe into the Berlin 2000 bid. Matthew's advice and involvement in the project were invaluable. Special thanks also to Annette and Gwyneth Mettendorf for their support.

Clare Sambrook applied her incisive intellect to endless chapter drafts. She stripped away irrelevancies, helped establish the tone of the book and thought up most of the chapter headings.

Thanks also to Eric R. Aldin, Dick Angell, Scott Armstrong, Sebastian Balfour, Suzanne Blake, John Blystone, Celia Brackenridge, Maynard Brichford, Patrick Buckley, Pat Butcher, Pat Cheney, Richard Cléroux, Roger Cork, Ross Coulthart, Martin Daly, Nicolai M. Dolgopolov, Inge Eidsvag, Lars Eggertz, Bente Erichsen, Jock Ferguson, Jim Ferstle, Herbert Fischer, Sarasue French, Paul Greengrass, Pat Haggarty, Nick Hayes, Mike Harrigan, Peter Hildreth, Fred Holder, Mark Hollingsworth, Greg Hunter, Mary Hynes, Nikolai Ivanov, Gordon Jaks, Jonathan Jones, Bruce Kidd, Thomas Kistner,

Anne Kvadshiem, Phil Liechty, Josep Ibàñez i López, Jackie Malcolm, Sarah Marris, General George Miller, Joan Morris, Dimitry Mosienko, Phil Mushnick, Ulf Nilsson, Trygve Aas Olsen, Tom O'Sullivan, Dick Patrick, Francis Pecino, Jonas Persson, Brendan Pittaway, Dave Postman, Paul Preston, David Prouty, Niklaus Ramseyer, Jaume Reixach, Andrei G. Richter, Virginia Roaf, Cheryl Roberts, Bert Roughton, Norman Sanders, Tony Sainsbury, Frank Sambrook, Gennady Schwets, Cindy Slater, Graham Smith, Mike Spence, Rod Speidel, Doug Stewart, Clarence Stone, Tron Strand, John Sugden, Sue Taylor, Alan Tomlinson, Mike Turner, Xavier Vinyals I. Capdepon, Matti Virtanen, Eric Wattez, Mathias Werth, Paul Woolwich, Dwight H. Zakus and Jean Ziegler.

# INDEX

ABC-TV, 15, 124
Aberdare, Lord, 35–6
Acosta, Ruben, 262
Adams, Ken, 86
Adidas, 156, 269
   access to secret ballots, 70
   and Atlanta's Olympic bid, 141
   bids for the Olympics, 123, 124
   Chowdhry looks after their interests, 81
   and Chowdhry as boxing president, 66–7, 68, 71
   decline of influence, 58, 296
   increasing influence, 43–4, 46
   and the IOC leadership, 75–8
   and the Seoul Olympics, 81, 102
   sponsors centenary congress, 269
   and the swimming presidency, 76
   track and field events presidency, 74, 75
   see also Dassler, Horst
Ahmad, Sheikh, 153, 212
Air France, 269
Al–Sabah family, 57, 232
Albert, Prince of Monaco, 138, 166
Albertville, 127–30, 170
Aldin, Eric, 39–40
Alexander, Reggie, 129, 226
Ali, Syed Wajid, 124
Alliot–Marie, Michele, 275
amateur status, 50
American Express, 25
Anchorage, bid for the Olympics, 119–21, 122
Andreotti, Giulio, 63
Angell, Dick, 119–21, 122
Anne, Princess, 71–5, 151, 154, 279, 300
Antich, Salvador Puig, 178
Aosta, 157, 164
Arroyo, Augustin Carlos, 22, 282
Ashford, Evelyn, 240
Association of National Olympic Committees, 51, 182
Association of Summer Olympic International Federations, 182
'Astrid', 190–1
Athens, 136–7, 140, 141, 142

athletes:
   disabled, 223–31, 262
   gender testing, 214–19
   IOC membership, 59
   lack of power, 60
   Olympic accommodation, 180
   Olympic oath, 6
   professional, 50, 266
   use of drugs, 6–8, 60, 72, 157, 210, 232–49, 298–9
Atkinson, Richard, 174
Atlanta:
   civil rights, 138–9, 144–5, 146–7
   finances, 143–4, 145–6, 290, 292–3
   influence of games on, 289–90
   Olympic bid, 133–49
   Paralympics, 229–30
Attarbulsi, Bashir, 196

Bach, Thomas, 165, 166, 197, 273–4, 298
Baden–Baden, 50
Baillet–Latour, Henri de, 34
Bakrac, Boris, 119
Balladur, Edouard, 267
bankruptcy, 54, 290
Barcelona:
   Berlin bid leaders at, 191–2
   doping, 246–7
   1992 Games, 174–81
   Olympics bid, 127, 128
Barkley, Charles, 180
Barnes, Simon, 173
Barnier, Michel, 128, 129
basketball, 180
Battle, Charlie, 135
Baumgartl, Gustav, 87
Beamon, Bob, 40
Beckett, Arnold, 240, 241–2, 247
Beijing, 184
   hospitality, 209
   Olympic bid, 199–200, 205–13
Belgrade, 137, 141
Bell, Steve, 202
Bell, Tim, 205
Bergin, Jack, 252
Berlin:
   1936 Olympics, 35–7
   Olympic bids, 184–98, 211

Berlin 2000 Marketing Ltd, 185
Bertelsmann, 185, 186, 189
Bertil, Prince, 119, 129
bids for the Olympics, 290–1
    Albertville, 127–30
    Atlanta, 133–49
    Barcelona, 127, 128
    Beijing, 199–213
    Falun, 115–32
    Manchester, 137, 141, 184,
        201–2, 211
    millennium Games, 183–98
    Nagano, 158–62, 163–5
    Paris, 127
    Salt Lake City, 158, 162–3,
        164–5, 288
    Seoul, 98–9, 101–3
    Tokyo, 39–40
Bietz, Berthold, 197
Birmingham, Olympic committee
    meets at, 150–69
Borg, Bjorn, 129
Borzov, Valery, 59, 279
Bosnia, 26–7, 260–1
Bossard, 186
Bowe, Riddick, 87
boxing:
    medal fixing, 9–10, 79–92
    presidency, 66–8
Brandsas, Frank, 255–6
Brasilia, 183, 201
Breker, Arno, 63
bribery, 100, 101, 104, 120
    boxing, 9, 80, 89–91
Brisco–Hooks, Valerie, 240
British Olympic Association,
    154, 180
British Taekwondo Council, 113
Bromann, Jens, 224–5, 228, 231
Brundage, Avery:
    illegitimate children, 57
    as a mason, 35
    and the Mexico City Games, 41,
        42
    and the Nazis, 36, 38
    retires, 43, 287
    and Samaranch, 31–2
Brundtland, Gro, 18, 257
Budapest, 152
bureaucracy, 61
Bush, George, 138
Byun Jong–il, 83

Candler, Peter, 135
Cape Town, 290

Carl Gustaf, King of Sweden, 118,
    119, 124
Carlos, John, 41–2
Carrard, Francois, 61, 219
    on the centenary congress,
        272, 278
    doping problems, 234
    gifts, 193
    and IOC retirement age, 284,
        285, 287
    and Samaranch's bid for a peace
        prize, 256
    Sarajevo truce publicity, 26, 27
    and professional athletes, 266
    transport requirements, 203
    and Vegard Ulvang, 19–20
Carrion, Richard, 58–9, 274
Caslavska, Vera, 287
Catalans, 175–9
Catlin, Don, 240, 242
CBS, 15
Ceaucescu, Nicolae, 60
Cernusak, Vladimir, 139
Chang Key–Young, 100
Charlton, Bobby, 211
Château de Vidy, 61
Chatelaine, Roland, 301, 302, 303
Chen Xitong, 199, 205, 209, 213
Ching–Kuo Wu, 71
China:
    Beijing Olympic bid, 199–213
    doping in, 7–8, 232–4
    Ching–Kuo Wu, 81, 92
Chirac, Jacques, 267
Choi Hong Hi, 97, 102, 109–10, 113
Chowdhry, Anwar:
    and Adidas, 67, 68, 71, 75, 76, 77
    bids for the Olympics, 120, 140–1
    boxing at Seoul, 81–4, 87–92
    millennium congress, 293
    rise of, 66–78
Christie, Linford, 181, 211
Chun Doo Hwan, 99, 103, 104
Chung Eun Kim, 112
Clark, José de Jesus, 41
coats, 17–18;
Coca–Cola, 49, 58, 124, 134, 138, 141,
    211, 272
Coe, Sebastian, 240
Coles, Phil, 129, 196, 202
Colt Industries, 96, 101
Commission for the International
    Olympic Academy and Olympic
    Education, 59
commissions, 59–60

Companys, Luis, 177–8, 179
congresses, 264–80
*Continental Sports*, 123, 124
Coubertin, Baron Pierre de, 33–5, 270, 292
Coulthart, Ross, 204
Cox Enterprises, 136, 138
Cramer, Robert, 146–7
Credit Lyonnais, 269
Cross, Stuart F., 49

Daimler–Benz (Mercedes), 49, 184, 185, 187, 198, 211
Dassler, Horst:
    bids for the Olympics, 120, 123
    changes under, 296
    death, 69
    fund raising from sponsors, 48–54, 116
    influence, 44–5, 66
    and Primo Nebiolo, 71–2
    rise of, 43–6
    and Seoul's Olympic bid, 102
    and the swimming presidency, 76
    track and field events presidency, 71–2
Daume, Willi, 130, 197
De Ferrari, Vitos, 197

DeFrantz, Anita, 166, 202–3, 222, 284, 287, 297
Delcourt, Jacques, 106–9
Deng Xiaoping, 206
Dentsu, 52, 159, 161
developing countries, 297
Diamond, Peter, 291–2
Dibos, Eduardo, 57
Dibos, Ivan, 57, 124, 193, 211
    promotes his business interests, 196–7, 294
Diepgen, Eberhard, 191, 194
disabled competitors, 223–31, 262
Domingo, Placido, 265
Donike, Manfred, 234, 236, 239, 241–2, 245
drugs, 6–8, 60, 72, 157, 210, 232–49, 298–9
Dubin, Charles, 244–5
Dugal, Robert, 241–2
'Dunwoody mafia', 136
Duran, Alberto, 86, 90

East Germany:
    boxing, 9
    doping, 245–6

Stasi, 10, 65–8, 141, 245
Easton, James, 279
Edstrøm, Sigfrid, 38
Eggertz, Lars, 115–32
Eidsvag, Inge, 21, 254–5, 263
El Arbi, Hiouad, 86, 90
Elizabeth II, Queen, 154–6
Erichsen, Bente, 24
Ewald, Manfred, 61
Ezawa, Noriko, 161

Fahd, Sheik, 123, 124
Fahey, John, 212
Faisal Fahd Abdul Aziz, Prince, 57, 203
Falun, bid for the Olympics, 115–32
fascism, 15, 28–31, 175–8
Ferguson–Smith, Malcolm, 216–17
Ferrer, Carlos, 196–7, 294
Ferris, Elizabeth, 217
Filaretos, Nikos, 262
FIPO, 226
Fleming, Andy, 230
Fonseca, Flor Isava, 58
Forbes, Malcom, 139
Fowler, Cindy, 135
Franco regime, 15, 28–32, 175–8
Fuchs, Nicholas, 185–6, 190, 191

Gadir, Zein Abdel, 196
Gafner, Raymond, 117, 132
Gandhi, Indira, 60
Ganga, Jean–Claude, 212, 273, 286
Garland family, 56
Geesink, Anton, 59
gender testing, 214–19
General Assembly of International Sports
    Federations (GAISF), 104
German National Olympic
    Committee, 192
Gilady, Alex, 59, 279
golf, 145
Gosper, Kevan, 70, 131, 156, 169, 202, 274, 297
Grey International, 252, 255–6
Grimaldi family, 56
Grüttke, Lutz, 184–5
Güell family, 56
Guirandou–N'Diaye, Louis, 107–8
Guttman, Ludwig, 224
Gvadjava, Zaut, 85, 90

Hamzah, Datuk Seri, 124
Harald, King of Norway, 20

Hasan, Mohamad 'Bob', 232, 280
Havelange, João, 52, 117, 123, 212, 285
Hay, Eduardo, 219
Heiberg, Gerhard, 18, 20, 24, 229, 279, 298
Heinze, Günther, 70, 89, 90
Helmick, Robert, 70, 75–8, 83, 168–9, 255
Helsinki, 289
Hembrick, Anthony, 83
Henderson, Paul, 137, 142
Hermes, 269
Herzog, Maurice, 129, 140
Hildreth, Peter, 249
Hitler, Adolf, 35–6, 63, 289
Hodler, Marc, 118, 286
Holder, Fred, 239
Honecker, Erich, 60
Houichi, Taieb, 83, 88
Howell, Denis, 167
Hristov, Alexander, 83
Huba, Karl–Heinz, 164, 174, 204, 281, 282, 285
Hughes, Robert, 178
Hull, Don, 66
human rights, 40–1, 206–8, 280
Hunt, Shirley, 151, 164
Hunter, John, 272
Hussein, Ahmad, 57
Hussein, Uday, 57
Hynes, Mary, 247

Insanally, Samuel, 260
International Athletics Foundation, 181
International Boxing Federation, 9
International Olympic Committee (IOC), 6
    membership, 56–9, 165–7, 171, 278–80, 287, 305–16
    retirement age, 281–7
    women members, 57–8, 220–2
International Paralympic Committee (IPC), 227–9
International Sport and Leisure (ISL), 52–3, 159
International Sports federations, 182
International Taekwondo Federation, 109
International Traditional Karate Federation (ITKF), 107–8
Isava–Fonseca, Flor, 183, 193–4, 203, 282, 286
Istanbul, 184, 201, 213

Jaca, 157, 164
Jackson, Maynard, 144
Janette, Christian, 44, 45
Jean de Luxembourg, Grand–Duc, 171
Jespersen, Big Otto, 23
Jetchev, Emil, 84, 85, 87
Johnson, Ben, 233, 240, 243–5, 246
Jones, Roy, 84–5, 87, 89–90
journalists, 13–14, 150, 155–7, 187–9, 294–5
Joyner, Florence Griffith, 240
Juan Carlos, King of Spain, 60, 176, 179

Kaifu, Toshiki, 160
Kammerer, Craig, 240, 242
Karadvic, Radovan, 26
karate, 106–7
Kasule, Bob, 86, 90
KCIA, 94–8, 109–10, 114
Keita, Lamine, 195
Keller, Thomas, 299
Kempa, Heinz, 69
KGB, 235
Kidane, Fékrou, 123–4
Kidd, Bruce, 275
Killanin, Lord, 41, 45, 54, 100
Killy, Jean–Claude, 58, 287
Kim Dae Jung, 98
Kim Hae Jung, 269
Kim Taik Soo, 100
Kim Un Yong (Mickey Kim), 10–11, 156
    appointed roving ambassador, 103–4
    background, 93–4
    centenary congress, 269, 274
    joins IOC, 104
    KCIA agent, 10–11, 94–5
    Olympic values, 102
    presidency of GAISF, 104
    Seoul Peace prize, 252
    succession to Samaranch, 93, 286, 297–8
    and Sydney's millennium bid, 202
    taekwondo monopoly, 10, 105–14
    takes over taekwondo, 97–8, 102, 104
King, Martin Luther, 138–9
Kirsch, August, 191
Kiyokawa, Masaji, 54
Kleinart, Matthias, 187
Klobukowska, Ewa, 218
Konnor, Paul, 87

Korea:
  bid for the Olympics, 98–9, 101–3
  demonstrations, 103
  KCIA, 94–8, 109–10, 114
  preparations for Seoul Olympics,
    103–4
Koss, Johann Olav, 25, 275–6
Kukkiwon, 111–12
Kumar, Ashwini, 124, 211, 232
Kuts, Vladimir, 289

Lämmer, Manfred, 191, 192
Larfaoui, Mustapha, 76
Lee Hong Soo, 83
Lee Ki–Poong, 99–100
Lee Sang–Beck, 100
Levine, Rob, 180
Lewis, Carl, 240
Lewis, Lennox, 87
Lilian, Princess, 119, 129
Lillehammer:
  gets Winter Olympics, 70, 251
  IOC at, 12, 16, 17–27
  mascot, 23
  Olympic Aid, 25–6
  Paralympics, 229
  profits from, 24–5
  Samaranch and, 18–20, 25, 26–7,
    70, 254–6
Long, Lutz, 36
Lopez, Anselmo, 53
Los Angeles, 7, 237–43
Lufthansa, 185

MacAloon, John, 219, 290
McColl, Hugh, 289
McDonald, Les, 275
MacDonald, Timothy, 148
McFadden, Catriona, 151
McGeogh, Rod, 203–5
Magvan, Shagdarjav, 58, 195, 196
Major, John, 202
Manchester, Games bids, 137, 141,
    184, 201–2, 211
Mandela, Nelson, 265
Maragall, Pascal, 177–9
Marcos, Ferdinand, 226
Martin, Jean–Daniel, 303, 304
mascots, 23, 144
Mbaye, Keba, 129, 145, 157, 169, 273,
    282, 297, 303
Mecklenberg–Schwerin, Duc de, 38
medal fixing, 9–10, 73, 79–92
media, 187–9, 291–2, 294–5
Melbourne, 137, 141, 289

Mercedes *see* Daimler–Benz
Merode, Prince Alexander de, 7,
    131, 284
  doping, 236–7, 238, 241–4, 246
  gender examinations, 217
Mexico City, 40–1
Meyer, Elana, 181
Milan, 183
millennium Games, bids for, 183–93
Miller, David, 172–3, 189, 208,
    212, 253–4
Minneapolis, 136
Mitterand, François, 61, 265
*Monitor*, 190–1
Montalban, Manual Vazquez, 175
Montreal, 237
Moon, Sun Myung, 96
Moonies, 96
Moscow, 1980 Olympics, 45, 235
Moses, Ed, 275
Mukora, Charles, 58, 153, 197
museum, 61–3, 160, 209–10, 248, 252
Myrholt, Olav, 275

Nagano, 158–62, 163–5
Napier, Andrew, 19, 243, 269–70
Nardiello, Vincenzo, 85
National Basketball Association
    (NBA), 180
NationsBank, 289
Navacelle, Geoffroy de, 34
Nawrocki, Axel, 197, 198
Nazis, 35–8, 63
NBC, 15, 59, 72, 291–2
Nebiolo, Primo, 63, 181, 278
  corruption charges, 279
  and doping, 232–3, 239, 244
  and IOC retirement age, 286
  medal–fixing scandal, 73
  and the millennium Games
    bid, 212
  Samaranch and, 73–5, 155, 171
  seat on the IOC, 52, 153,
    155, 171
  succession to Samaranch, 298
  track and field event supremo,
    71–5
Nerland, Rick, 122
NHK, 161
Nidecker, John, 101
Nobel Peace Prize, 14, 200, 250–63,
    264–5
Nora, Princess of Lichtenstein, 57
Norman, Peter, 41–2

Norway:
  Lillehammer games, 12, 16, 17–27, 70, 251
  Nobel Peace Prize, 14, 200, 250–63, 264–5
Nyangweso, Francis, 81, 88, 92

oaths, 6, 9, 11–12
Odden, Einar, 255–6
Oerter, Al, 60
O'Flanagan, Kevin, 22
Olympic Charter, 12, 264
Olympic Council of Asia, 232, 234
Olympic Museum, 61–3, 160, 209–10, 248, 252
Olympic oaths, 6, 9, 11–12
Olympic Order, 60–1, 92, 101, 103, 160, 205
Olympic Solidarity, 53
Olympic Truce, 26–7, 260–1, 273
Ordez, Diaz, 41
Ostersund, 158, 163, 165, 288
Oswald, Denis, 165
Ottey, Merlene, 240
Otto, Kristin, 245, 292
Owens, Jesse, 36, 60

Pajar, Sandor, 85, 90
Paralympics, 223–31
Paris:
  centenary congress, 264–80
  Olympic bids, 127–8
Park, General, 94–9, 100
Park Chong Kyu, 100–1
Park Si–Hun, 84
Patino, Maria, 218
Payne, Billy, 9, 134–49, 276, 289–90
Payne, Michael, 291, 292
peace, 14–15, 250–63
Pescante, Mario, 279
Peters, Mary, 214–15
Pickup, David, 56
Piech, Ferdinand, 196–7
Piedmont Driving Club, 146
Poulsen, Olaf, 20, 171
Pound, Dick, 50, 156, 170, 269
  campaigns for Nobel Peace prize, 251, 253, 257, 261
  and the choice of Albertville, 170
  and disabled athletes, 228, 231
  and doping, 244, 245, 248
  and the Falun sex scandal, 131, 132
  favours Beijing, 208
  on financial resources, 24, 54

and public sector commitment, 293
Seoul Olympics, 114
and sponsorship, 25
and succession to Samaranch, 70, 284, 285, 287, 297
on winter Olympic sites, 288
press, 13–14, 150, 155–7, 187–9, 294–5
professional athletes, 50, 266
profits, 24–5, 54
prostitutes, 39–40, 98–9

Radeke, 91
Raes, André, 229
Rainier, Prince of Monaco, 211
Ramadan, Abdalla, 84
Ramsamy, Sam, 287
Raña, Mario Vazquez:
  ANOC conventions, 182
  fund-raising, 51–2
  ITKF negotiations, 108
  joins the IOC, 51, 165–7, 171
  and the millennium Games bid, 211, 212
  Olympic Solidarity, 53
  personality, 51
  receives Olympic Orders, 60
  and retirement age, 286
  succession to Samaranch, 298
Raña, Olegario, 60, 287
Rank Xerox, 211
Reebok, 58
Reedie, Craig, 279
Reixach, Jaume, 300–1
Renault, 269
Reuter, Edzard, 184, 187
Rexa, 165
Rodriguez, Antonio, 194–5
Rogge, Jacques, 165, 276–7, 298
Roh Tae Woo, 99, 103–4
Rome, 289, 290
Rosenbrock, Patricia, 196
Ruhrgas AG, 197

Salinas, Carlos, 182
Salt Lake City, 158, 162–3, 164–5, 288
Samaranch, Bibis, 31
Samaranch, Juan Antonio:
  Atlanta's bid, 136–7, 138, 140–1, 145–6
  bankruptcy rescue, 54
  Barcelona Olympics, 143, 171–81
  becomes President, 43–6

Beijing's millennium bid, 200,
    205–10, 212–13
Berlin's millennium bid, 192, 196
biography, 15, 172–5
and boxing at Seoul, 83
Brasilia's mellennium bid, 201
bureaucracy, 61
career, 28–33
Catalans and, 176–9
and Chowdhry, 68, 70, 92
creates commissions, 59
and Daimler–Benz, 49
disabled athletes, 224–5,
    227, 230–1
doping, 60, 232–4, 237, 239, 240,
    244, 246–8, 298–9
fascism, 15, 28–31, 63, 176–9,
    187, 303
and the free–loaders, 183
and Goran Takac, 121
and Horst Dassler, 43–6
illness, 69
imposes discipline, 42–3
IOC retirement age, 281–7
IOC selection, 57–8
and Kim Un Yong, 104, 106
lack of ideas, 296
lasting achievement, 296
Lillehammmer, 18–20, 25, 26–7, 70
and *Lords of the Rings*, 300–4
Manchester's millennium bid,
    201, 202
meeting in Birmingham, 151, 154,
    155, 157
millennium Games, 184, 189
Nagano's bid, 159–60, 161, 165
Nobel Peace Prize hopes, 14, 200,
    250–63, 264–5, 296
Olympian Order, 60
Olympic museum, 61–3, 160, 189,
    209–10,
    252
Olympic stamp collecting, 226
and Park Chong Kyu, 101
and Primo Nebiolo, 73–5, 155, 171
and Princess Anne, 71–5
and Raña, 165–6
the rise of taekwondo, 106, 107–9,
    110–13, 114
Sarajevo truce, 25, 26–7
Seoul games, 207
and the Seoul Olympics, 103
Sydney's millennium bid, 204,
    212–13
successor to, 297

Swedish bids for the Olympics,
    117, 119, 126–31
TOP deal, 52–3
and unity, 33, 104, 278
and women on Olympic
    committees, 221–2
San Francisco, 136
Sang Kyu Shim, 112
Sang Lee, 111
Sarajevo, 26–7
Schmitz, Brigitte, 195, 197, 198
Schmitz, Torsten, 84
Scott, Bob, 137, 142, 202, 213
seat allocation, 4, 9, 144, 148–9
Segedel, Oyvind, 18
Seoul:
    bid for Olympics, 98–9, 101–3
    boxing, 9, 79–92
    democracy and the Games, 206–7
    doping, 243–5
    East German achievements at, 65
    medal allocation, 9
    Paralympics, 227
    preparations for, 103–4
    taekwondo as a demonstration
        sport, 106
    televising athletics, 72
    world junior athletics, 181–2
Seoul Peace Prize, 251–2
Seref, Chuck, 109–10, 113
Seung–Youn Kim, 80, 81, 84, 86
Seville Exposition, 172
sex, 39–40, 98–9, 125, 130–1, 201
Sibandze, David, 125–6, 213
Sibley, Horace, 135
Siegel, Philip, 190
Silvia, Queen of Sweden, 119, 123,
    124, 129
Simson, Vyv, 174, 300
Siperco, Alexandru, 58
Slavkov, Ivan, 58, 123
Smirnoff, 181
Smirnov, Vitaly, 58, 60, 195
Smith, Tommie, 41–2
Sofia, 70
*Der Spiegel*, 142
Spitz, Mark, 292
sponsorship, 102, 123, 124, 173
    Atlanta Games, 143–4
    Barcelona, 181
    Berlin's bid, 185–7
    centenary congress, 272
    and disabled athletes, 224–5,
        228, 230
    drugs and, 237

Olympic museum, 62
Olympics embrace, 47–54
Springer, 186
Springman, Sarah, 220
stamp collecting, 226
Stanica, Tudor, 68
Stasi, 10, 65–8, 141, 245
Staubo, Jan, 128
Steadward, Robert, 228, 229
Stockton, John, 180
Stupp, Howard, 227–8, 229
Stuttgart, 195–6, 197–8
Suharto, President, 279–80
Sweden, Olympic bids, 115–32, 158, 163, 165
Switzer, Harriet, 97
Sydney, Olympic bids, 184, 200, 202–5, 212–13

taekwondo, 93, 97, 105–14
Takac, Artur, 121–2, 269
Takac, Goran, 121, 122–3, 163–4, 269
Tallberg, Peter, 180
Tarpischev, Shamil, 279
Tashkent, 183
television rights, 15, 59, 72, 291–2
ticket allocation, 4, 9, 144, 148–9
Tokyo:
    1964 Olympics, 39–40, 269
    proposed congress, 264–5
TOP, 52–3
Toronto, 137–8, 141
triathlon, 220
Tröger, Walter, 193, 198, 200
Tsukada, Tasuku, 163, 164
Tsutsumi, Yoshiaki, 61, 158–62, 165
Tulu, Derartu, 181
Tunstall, Arthur, 87
Turner, Ted, 168

Ueberroth, Peter, 101, 141, 238
Ulvang, Vegard, 19, 263, 299
United Nations, 261
United States:
    Atlanta Olympic bid, 133–49
    basketball Dream Team, 180
    boxing at Seoul, 9, 79–92
    Mickey Kim and, 94–7, 101
United States Olympic Committee, 168–9, 230, 238
Urlando, Gian Paolo, 239

Vainio, Martii, 238–9

Vazquez, Javier, 23
Vazquez, Pedro Ramirez, 23, 166
Veiteberg, Jorunn, 21
Verdier, Michele, 155–7, 255, 269
Vinyals, Xavier, 179
Visa, 24–5, 59
von Halt, Karl Ritter, 38
von Reichenau, Walter, 37
Von Schoeller, Philipp, 166
Voy, Robert, 246

Walker, Keith, 81, 83–4
Wallwork, Helena, 196
Wallwork, Paul, 81, 92, 196
Watkins, Ginger, 135
Wehr, Karl–Heinz, 9–10, 65–78
    and Atlanta's bid, 140
    boxing at Seoul, 9, 79–85, 88–92
    intelligence reports, 9–10, 64, 141
    rise to power, 65–78
    role in the Stasi, 65–8, 141
Wellumstad, Stein, 26
Wengler, Kirsten, 217
Werth, Mathias, 190
Wilson, Tay, 166
Wimbledon, 12
Windfeder, Heinz, 197
Witteman, Paul, 173–4
women, on Olympic committees, 57–8, 220–2
women athletes, gender testing, 214–19
Workers' Games, 37
World Taekwondo Federation, 98, 105, 109–10, 111
World Union of Karate Federations (WUKO), 106–9

Yang Aihua, 233
Yeltsin, Boris, 58, 60, 261, 279
Yesalis, Chuck, 247
Young, Andrew, 139
Young, Kevin, 292

Zatopek, Emil, 289
Zerguini, Mohamed, 282
Zhang Baifa, 206
Zhenliang He, 123, 156, 205, 234, 273
Zhivkov, Todor, 61
Ziegler, Jean, 302